Against the Faith is a history of the
enduri conflict
do

AGAINST THE FAITH

AGAINST THE FAITH

Essays on Deists, Skeptics and Atheists

JIM HERRICK

Prometheus Books
700 E. Amherst St. Buffalo, New York

Published 1985 by
Prometheus Books
700 E. Amherst Street, Buffalo, New York 14215
Printed in the United States of America

First published 1985
Glover & Blair Ltd., London 1985

ISBN: 0-87975-288-2
Library of Congress Catalogue Card No.: 85-43040

Contents

I should like to offer my thanks to the following:
to the ever helpful and courteous staff of the London Library; to Gordon Blair, who showed saintly patience in waiting for the manuscript, and who made many useful suggestions; to Nicolas Walter of the Rationalist Press Association and to David Berman of the Philosophy Department, Trinity College, Dublin, who took the trouble to read the manuscript and made many useful suggestions; above all to Christopher Findlay, but for whose encouragement and support this book would certainly never have been completed.

Jim Herrick

ACKNOWLEDGEMENTS

Author and publisher gratefully acknowledge permission to quote from the following sources:

Besterman: *Voltaire*. Basil Blackwell Ltd.

Büchner: *Danton's Death*, tr. Spender and Rees. Reprinted by permission of A. D. Peters & Co. Ltd.

Forster: 'What I Believe' from *Two Cheers for Democracy*. Edward Arnold Ltd.

Huxley: *The Faith of a Humanist*. Reprinted by permission of A. D. Peters & Co. Ltd.

Kristeller: *Eight Philosophers of the Italian Renaissance*. Stanford University Press.

Lucretius: *On the Nature of the Universe*, tr. Ronald Latham. (Penguin Classics 1951). Copyright ©R. E. Latham 1951. Reprinted by permission of Penguin Books Ltd.

Mossner: *Life of David Hume*. O.U.P. 1954.

Russell: *Autobiography, A Free Man's Worship, Why I am not a Christian*. George Allen & Unwin Ltd.

Sartre: *Existentialism and Humanism*, tr. P. Mairet. Methuen & Co.

Voltaire: *Philosophical Dictionary*, tr. Besterman. The Voltaire Foundation.

Wilson: *Diderot*. O.U.P. 1972.

Wing-Tsit Chan, tr.: *A Source Book in Chinese Philosophy*. Copyright ©1963, Princeton University Press.

Preface

The subject of this book is those who have placed themselves 'against the faith', in other words those who have opposed the prevailing religious faith of their time. Such opponents adopt this position for a wide variety of reasons and in many different ways. They are sometimes fiery activists hammering against leaders and leading ideas and at other times are quiet, contemplative sceptics questioning all knowledge and all orthodoxy. They can be immersed in the politics of their time, like Bradlaugh or Thomas Paine. They can be poets like Heine and Shelley, historians like Gibbon, playwrights like Büchner, or novelists like George Eliot and Mark Twain. They may be scientists like Huxley, or philosophers like J. S. Mill. They may be most at home on the public platform, like Ingersoll, or in the study like Pierre Bayle. They can be relaxed men of the world like Hume or temperamental outsiders like d'Holbach. They may lead quiet and little known lives like the freethinker Collins or the clergyman Meslier, or they may be outstanding polymaths of their age, like Voltaire or Bertrand Russell.

This book covers deists, sceptics and atheists. Without attempting to be comprehensive, I have tried to show that there is a spectrum between the three. There has often been close contact between deists, who gently criticize the Christian faith, sceptics who question all knowledge, and atheists, who detach themselves from any belief in God. Occasionally individuals have held all these positions at different periods of their lives. Furthermore the distinction sometimes made between the respectable philosophic sceptic and the disreputable agitating atheist is not clear-cut: philosophers sometimes agitate and frequently rub shoulders with activists, and reformers and campaigners often think quite deeply.

Since this book in the main covers Europe in the eighteenth and nineteenth centuries, the faith opposed is Christianity. A history of opponents to Hinduism, Islam and Buddhism would provide fascinating parallels, but that book has yet to be written. It is a mistake – and one to which opponents are particularly prone – to imagine the 'faith' as a monolithic entity, rather than an accumulation of various traditions. There can therefore be opposition to the faith from within as well as without and heresy and heterodoxy have sometimes been not far apart. (The road from Luther to humanism is a direct one.)

Between an introductory background sketch and some concluding general considerations on the twentieth century, I have chosen a number of individuals and clusters of individuals who illustrate the variety of personalities and range of ideas within the freethought, rationalist, humanist perspective. (The three adjectives have different emphases, but much in common.) I also hope that the selection provides a history of the development of this strand of thought, although neither complete nor exhaustive. My own interests have to some extent dictated the choice, but there are three ways in which I have deliberately limited myself. I omitted Darwin, Freud and Marx, about whom tomes have been written, since, while their thought indirectly undermines Christianity, they took the decline of religion for granted and the greater part of their work covered issues other than religion. I did not include the anti-clerical tradition, particularly in France and Italy, since this seems to me to be largely primed by political and economic motives rather than general philosophical considerations. I did not concentrate upon those whose anti-religious reflections led them to nihilistic and pessimistic conclusions (the most obvious omission here being Nietzsche) since the freethought-humanist tradition is essentially an optimistic one, allied to purposeful social reform.

Certain general directions in the history of freethought opposition to religion have fascinated me. I was interested in what Lecky called 'the declining sense of the miraculous', the removal of mystery from religion, which led to the abandonment of belief in miracles and supernatural events. This was accompanied by a move to a naturalistic picture of the universe, associated with the Renaissance emphasis on man and the rise of a scientific world picture. At first pantheists and deists saw the world of nature as essentially ordered and benevolent. Later such a perspective was superseded by a depiction of the cosmos as random and impersonal, and confident atheism and anguished agnosticism succeeded polite deism. Another interest was the transition from belief in a God mediated by revelation, or by the authority of priest and sacred book, to belief authenticated by individual interpretation and individual conscience. A further concern was the way in which unbelievers, contrary to the accusations made against them by the faithful, were anxious to create a morality based on truth for its own sake and the golden rule of reciprocity, rather than divine punishment and obedience to a divine code. A changing view of man's place in time led to the development of the historical perspective: history as the unfolding of God's divine plan or even as a source-book of moral fables gave way to an attempt to understand the nature of society and of change within it. This meant that the historical accuracy of religious claims came into question and the history of religion began to be looked at from the point of view of the function it served in explaining the unexplained and in giving cohesion to society or power to particular groups. Since Christianity has held a position of power in European society, opposition to its beliefs has often also involved opposition to the alliance between 'kingcraft and priestcraft' – to use Paine's famous phrase. Social reform also becomes a theme in writing about those who prefer an emphasis on the human to the transcendent. Much of the book concerns the Enlightenment of the eighteenth century and the philosophical radicalism of the nineteenth century.

I do not wish to disguise my personal sympathy for those 'against the faith', but I hope that this strand of history will be of interest to people of many persuasions. Although 'progress' is a word much used by many of the figures in this book, I have tried to avoid painting a picture of a steady progress from the dark hegemony of religious domination to the enlightened heterodoxy of the humanist reformer – to caricature a freethought view. History is more complicated, the twentieth century has given a jolt to views of progress, and the human story has (we hope) many more chapters. I recognize the limitations of the optimistic belief in the power of reason to solve all problems: I do not underestimate the fact that the emotions of love, joy, wonder and excitement are an essential part of a complete human life. Nevertheless I do believe that the idea of progress has some meaning. Most people no longer doubt that drains are better than ditches, that satellite weather forecasts are better than horoscopes, that problem solving is better than prayer, that meditation is more useful as a means of relaxation than as a route to another plane of existence. I also hope that the continuous inequality, injustice and unhappiness of the human condition can be modified, if not eliminated, by social reform. That, I will be told, is my 'faith'. Perhaps. But I doubt whether it is the prevailing orthodoxy of our time.

Jim Herrick

Introduction

'I love to consider an Infidel, whether distinguished by the title of deist, atheist, or free-thinker . . .' So wrote Sir Richard Steele in *The Tatler* (No. 111) in 1709. Steele displays the interchangeability of words describing those who criticized orthodox Christianity. He also demonstrates that the topic could by that time be one under general consideration – even if the deists, atheists and freethinkers whom he lumped together as 'Infidels' were a larger group in the fearful minds of the orthodox than in practice.

Steele elaborated by saying that he loved to consider the deist, atheist or freethinker 'by three different lights, in his solitude, his afflictions, and his last moments.' In these situations such people showed themselves in solitude 'incapable of rapture or elevation', 'in distress' with 'a halter or a pistol the only refuge [they] can fly to', and liable to conversion 'at the approach of death'. Thus Steele summarized and propagated the mythical view of the atheist or sceptic as joyless, without hope and prone to deathbed conversions – a view impossible to sustain once the lives of deists and atheists have been properly studied. Elsewhere Steele added to popular misconceptions by describing unbelievers as untrustworthy and immoral. This was a longstanding myth arising partly from the belief that, since they could not swear on the Bible with conviction, their word was of no worth and, since they did not believe in divine punishment, they would abandon themselves to unbridled lusts. As late as the nineteenth century this view survived in the words of the judge Sir John Coleridge, who attacked Shelley's poem *Queen Mab* in the sternest fashion: 'No atheist, as such, can be a true friend, an affectionate relation, or a loyal subject. . . . A disciple following his tenets would not hesitate to debauch, or, after debauching to abandon any woman. . . .'

Attacks on atheists and sceptics such as those of Steele and

Coleridge demonstrate the difficulty of writing a history of freethought and indicate the animosity which freethinkers face. The early history of freethinkers is clouded by opponents who supply much of the evidence for their existence. The hostility which critics of religion faced accounts for their tendency to be ultra-cautious or ultra-rebellious.

As with Steele, the various possible words describing those opposed to religion are frequently used very vaguely. Historically, imprecise usage has abounded. However, it is useful to have some clear definitions at the outset. 'Infidel' is one who is without faith or not of the true faith, and was at first used especially of those belonging to the wrong faith such as Islam or Judaism. Later it became a catch-all phrase of denigration. The Book of Common Prayer pleaded for 'mercy upon all Jews, Turkes, Infidels, and Hereticks' but the much more general sense was seen in the nineteenth century, as when Harriet Martineau wrote: 'The clergy complain of the enormous spread of bold books, from the infidel tract to the latest handling of the miracle question.'

'Freethinker', with its attractive associations of the mind ranging freely without taboos or limits, is a very general term. It is one to which adherents grew attached, so that *The Freethinker* became the name of a journal started in 1881 and still in existence. Opponents enjoyed using it as an all-embracing term of disapprobation, as when Swift wrote of 'the atheists, libertines, despisers of religion . . . that is to say all those who usually pass under the name of Free-thinkers' (1708).

'Theist' and 'deist' were first used almost synonymously to mean belief in a God, but not necessarily the Christian God. A theist was contrasted with a polytheist who believed in several gods and an atheist who believed in no God. A distinction between 'deist' and 'theist' developed in which 'deist' implied that knowledge of God came from use of reason together with a denial of revelation, while 'theist' was less specific. There also developed a tendency to use 'deism' in the negative sense of refutation of aspects of religion and 'theism' in the more positive sense of acceptance of a belief in God. The *Encyclopaedia Britannica* of 1878 commented: 'The later distinction between theist and deist, which stamped the latter word as excluding the belief in providence or the immanence of God, was apparently formed in the eighteenth century by those rationalists who were aggrieved at being identified with the materialists.' 'Pantheist' has been less common than 'theist' or 'deist' and refers to the belief that God is in everything and everything is in God. Such a belief is quite distinct from the belief in a personal god and has often been associated, as by Spinoza, with a belief in the divinity of nature. 'Pantheism' is in some sense a precursor of the twentieth-century belief in a 'life force'.

'Atheist' is quite clear in its meaning of 'somebody without a belief in God'. It is more complex in its usage since it has often been used to blacken anyone with the slightest doubt about the teachings of religion. 'Agnostic' is a much more recent word, coined by Thomas Huxley in 1869 (see p. 190) to mean 'without knowledge of God' and acquiring the usage of 'being doubtful about the existence of God'.

The 'sceptic' directs his doubt to all areas of knowledge. Pyrronhism is synonymous with scepticism and comes from the Greek thinker Pyrrho, who thought that, since all knowledge was acquired through our senses, nothing was certain. Sir Walter Raleigh prefaced his essay *The Skeptick* with a good definition: 'The Skeptick doth neither affirm, neither deny any Position: but doubteth of it, and opposeth his Reasons against that which is affirmed, or denied to justify his not Consenting.' Despite such accuracy the word often slithered into a general term for doubters about religion as in 'First bring in Sceptiscism [*sic*] in Doctrine and looseness of life, and afterwards all Atheism' (*Gangraena*, T. Edwards, 1646).

'Rationalist' and 'humanist' are words with rather specialized twentieth-century meanings, after earlier more general uses. 'Rationalist' meant originally 'one who values reason' and could apply equally to a Christian, deist, or atheist, provided that reason was the route by which they reached their position. In the nineteenth century it moved towards being used specifically for unbelievers and Lecky's famous *History of the Rise and Influence of the Spirit of Rationalism in Europe* (1865) covers 'the various forms of moral and intellectual development [which lead] men on all occasions to subordinate dogmatic theology to the dictates of reason and of conscience, and, as a necessary consequence, greatly to restrict its influence upon life'. The foundation at the end of the nineteenth century and publications in the twentieth century of the Rationalist Press Association gave further currency to this sense. 'Humanism' originally referred to the study of the humanities in the Renaissance and is still used by historians in this way. However, it came to be used, in the Webster's Dictionary definition, as 'a philosophy that rejects supernaturalism, regards man as a natural object, and asserts the essential dignity and worth of man and his capacity to achieve self-realization through the use of reason and the scientific method.' As early as 1876 Gladstone had used the word in something approaching this sense as a belief in humanity, when he wrote of 'Comtism or Positivism, or, as it might be called, Humanism'. 'Agnostic', 'rationalist' and 'humanist' have not generally been used as terms of abuse, partly because they achieved currency at a time when such views had become more acceptable, partly because the words have an undogmatic, humanitarian flavour less likely to affront religious believers. (I have even in recent years known the declaration 'I am an atheist' to cause a *frisson* of shock or the response 'There can be no such thing!')

Recourse to the dictionaries can help to clarify the meanings of words – 'infidel', 'freethinker', 'deist', 'theist', 'pantheist', 'sceptic', 'rationalist', 'humanist' but it cannot alter the fact that such words have often been used with vagueness, out of ignorance (an individual's personal use of words stemming from the tendency to create an individual personal religion) and wilful determination to denigrate. Disapproval of the atheist is no modern custom. The pre-Christian psalmist sang: 'The fool hath said in his heart "There is no God".' Already the coupling of atheism and immorality was to be found: 'Corrupt they are, and have done iniquity: there is none that doeth good.' A commentator such as the Rev Dr A. Cohen claims that this refers to those who 'scorn the belief that He cares how men act' rather than those who deny God's reality, but it is hard not to believe that there have always been a few complete sceptics or atheists. In view of the accusations of immorality and subversion which usually accompanied the label, the wise man did well to keep his atheistic thoughts close to his heart.

There is much evidence of deistic, sceptical and possibly occasionally atheistic thought in ancient times. All religions contain an element of rhetorical doubt – frequently seen as a necessary part of the strengthening of faith. This is true of the oldest of major world religions, Hinduism, and an example is found in the *Śvetāśvatara Upaniṣad*:

> Is Brahma the cause? Whence are we born?
> Whereby do we live, and whither do we go?
>
> Should time, or nature, or necessity, or chance,
> or the elements be considered as the cause,
> or he who is called the person?

But such general reflections should be distinguished from more thorough-going scepticism. The Cārvakā school of thought within Hinduism emerged in the sixth century B.C. and was entirely naturalistic in its view of the universe and hedonistic in its ethical outlook. Whether Cārvakā was a historical person is unknown, and the origins of the school are obscure. Its followers held that sacred literature is false and there is no deity or supernatural force, that all life is composed of material elements and there is no soul or immortality, that only direct perception gives true knowledge, and that the injunctions of priests are of no value and pleasure is the aim of life. One of the writings of the school, the *Sarva-siddhānta-samgraha*, contains statements such as:

> Only the perceived exists; the unperceivable does not exist, by reason of its never having been perceived;
>
> While life remains let a man live happily, let him feed on ghee though he runs into debts;
>
> When once the body has become ashes, how can it ever return again?

Criticism of scripture and priests could be as caustic as that of any nineteenth-century freethinker: the authors of the religious texts, the Vedas, are described as 'buffoons, knaves and demons'.

The aim of life was seen as the pursuit of pleasure. Such a pursuit has always led to the accusation of libertinism and selfishness, even though those who consciously seek pleasure are much more likely to realize that pleasure is maximized by moderation than those who seize pleasure in defiance of austere or self-denying injunctions. The *Sarva-siddhānnta-samghra* contains the words:

> The enjoyment of heaven lies in eating delicious food, keeping the company of young women, using fine clothes, perfumes, garlands, sandal paste, etc.;
>
> The pain of hell lies in the troubles that arise from enemies, weapons, diseases; while liberation is death which is the cessation of life-breath;
>
> The wise should enjoy the pleasures of the world, through the proper visible means of agriculture, keeping cattle, trade, political administration. . . .

Buddhism has always had an atheistic strand. The Buddha (*c.* 536–458) himself seems to have adopted an agnostic position about gods and paid most attention to the human problem of the eradication of suffering. As frequently happens with religious teachers, the dogmatic and superstitious elements were developed by the followers and then later by the professionals, the priests, who gained power by their claims to specialized knowledge.

A similar path is seen with the Chinese thinker Confucius (551–479), who wrote: 'To give oneself earnestly to securing righteousness and justice among the people, and while respecting the gods and demons, to keep aloof from them, that may be called wisdom'. 'Naturalistic Confucianism', which owed much to Hsun Tzu (298–238), ruled out supernatural forces. In words which were to be echoed in Pierre Bayle's *Miscellaneous Thoughts on the Comet of 1680* more than one and a half thousand years later, Hsun Tzu pointed out: 'When stars fall or a sacred tree groans the people of the whole state are afraid. We ask "Why is it?" I answer: there is no [special] reason . . . For there is no age which has not experienced eclipses of the sun and moon, unseasonable rain or wind, or strange stars seen in groups. If the prince is illustrious and the government tranquil, although these events should all come together in one age it would do no harm . . . but when human ominous signs come, then we should really be afraid. Using poor ploughs . . . spoiling a crop by inadequate hoeing and weeding . . . these are what I mean by ominous human signs.'

Although it is valuable to point out that scepticism and atheism have ancient and world-wide antecedents, the concept of opposition to the faith is quite different for religions like Hinduism, Buddhism and Confucianism, which tend to assume that a very wide range of views are acceptable, rather than those like Islam and Christianity which attempt to make converts for the correct views of the correct God.

One reason for the flowering of intellectual questioning, creative drive and a measure of rationalism in classical Greece may have been the diversity of its polytheistic religions, which included and tolerated a wide range of beliefs and practices. Criticism of the frailties and immoralities of the gods led both to scepticism and to a belief in Fate as a force underlying the rhythm and order of the universe. The anthropomorphic tendency to depict gods in man's image could be criticized as, for example, by Xenophanes: 'If oxen and horses and lions could draw and paint, they would delineate the gods in their own image.' (A criticism often made by later freethinkers, e.g. Voltaire, p.68.) The attempt to understand natural forces also complicated belief in the gods: to call the sun a 'golden clod', as did Anaxagoras, was a form of blasphemy as well as an attempt to suggest that the material of the universe had a universal basis.

The origin of such scientific speculation was amongst the Ionian philosophers, from a wealthy community in Miletus, a Greek colony on the coast of Asia Minor. Thales (630/20–546/35) believed that all matter was based on water; although this was inaccurate it was significant as an attempt to provide a naturalistic theory about the substance of the universe. *On Nature*, used as the title of a book by both Anaximander and Anaximenes, of which only the fragment of one survives, indicates an essential theme of the Ionian philosophers.

Anaxagoras moved from Asia Minor to Athens and provided a link with the great Periclean age of cultural efflorescence in the fifth century B.C. The unequalled power of Greek art and drama reveals a focus upon the human quite new in the ancient world. The myth of Prometheus bringing fire to man (which so fascinated the later freethinking poet Shelley) could be seen as a symbol of man's acquisition of new powers: in Aeschylus' version, Prometheus speaks of 'how I made men rational and capable of reflection, who till then were childish'. This did not necessarily lead to atheism, agnosticism or scepticism: the gift of reason came from the gods. The so-called 'sophists' (with whom the later *philosophes* in eighteenth-century France had affinities in the width and practicality of their inquiries) did go this far.

Protagoras (481–411) for example, began his essay *On the Gods*: 'About the gods I have no means of knowing either that they exist or that they do not exist or what they are like to look at; many things prevent my knowing – among others, the fact that they are never seen and the shortness of human life.' Another quotation from Protagoras is much favoured by humanists today: 'Man is the measure of all things, of the reality of those which are, and of the unreality of those which are not.' He became well-known and wealthy and was probably invited to write a constitution for a Greek colony but was then indicted for impiety, though, according to one source, he escaped before his trial and was drowned while trying to cross the sea to Sicily. Another philosopher who gave further evidence of criticism of religion was Critias, who provided a figure in a dialogue with the view that the gods were purely an invention of 'some wise men' as a prop to public morality.

The scepticism and debate aroused by the sophists were not necessarily popular. Aristophanes' comedy *The Clouds*, which transforms the chorus of gods into a chorus of clouds (natural forces in the universe), ridicules the 'thinking shops' and expresses a popular fear of the world being turned topsy-turvy once 'old laws and old customs are dead'. Probably, in a phrase which Burckhardt used to describe the intellectual climate in the nineteenth century, it was 'rationalism for the few and magic for the many'. The brevity of the Greek enlightenment has often been discussed: opponents say that it was only ever found amongst a few intellectuals or that criticism of accepted religion left a vacuum which all manner of superstitions rushed to fill, but its influence was long-lasting, and free inquiry may only have been checked by the social tensions arising from the Peloponnesian War. (There are parallels with the reaction to the French Enlightenment once the French Revolution faced the pressures of war.)

A series of blasphemy trials in Athens towards the end of the fifth century are often cited as an example both of how widespread irreligion had become and how strong the reaction was. Nevertheless it is difficult to draw conclusions from what may have been untypical events confined to Athens. Possibly they were prompted by personal enmities, political rivalry and the anger of those whose lucrative profession of divination was at risk, rather than a widespread clampdown on intellectual inquiry. The trial of Socrates (399 B.C.) is the most famous, but must be seen as the exceptional case of an exceptional man; there is no evidence of the impiety and immorality of which he was accused, and much about the case remains puzzling.

Plato, through whom the western world has received the thoughts of Socrates, was much exercised by the fear of disorder and a quest for universal laws. He said in the *Laws* that there are two types of atheist – those who believe that no gods exist and those who believe that the gods exist but are of no relevance to human affairs. Although far from sympathetic to atheism, he acknowledged that atheists could lead an honest life: 'For though a man should be a complete unbeliever in the being of gods; if he also has a native uprightness of temper, such persons will detest evil in men; their repugnance to wrong disinclines them to commit wrongful acts; they shun the unrighteous and are drawn to the upright.'

Aristotle, the other great philosopher of the period, was critical of Plato's attempt to create *Laws* for a perfect (and repressive) state; he preferred to observe what was pragmatically and logically possible, whether in physics or politics and sustained the Greek emphasis upon a study of ethics and the natural world in which the divine cannot be found to play any dynamic role.

By the time of Aristotle's death in 322 B.C. the empire of Alexander the Great had transformed the Greek city states into the monarchies and bureaucracies of the Hellenistic world. In this period two schools of thought developed of enduring relevance to the history of unbelief and scepticism: Epicureanism and Pyrrhonism.

Epicurus (341–271) was a teacher who attracted a community of followers which was a cross between an academy and a sect. The garden on the outskirts of Athens in which he conversed with his followers is legendary for providing food for thought as well as the table. His main concern was the achievement of peace of mind and a life of contentment. He was not proposing a pursuit of pleasure. Indeed he knew that pleasure was to be measured by the 'limits of reason', as much as the removal of those fears and ills which obstructed a pleasant life. He thought terror of the gods was one of man's chief fears. But he taught that, although the gods existed, they lived apart from mankind and were not interested in humanity. He also sought to obviate the fear of death. For him life was the supreme good and it was not difficult to achieve good and endure ill. Among the principal means of procuring contentment he counted self-sufficiency, fearlessness, a measured enjoyment of the appetites and friendship.

Epicurus was vilified as a rogue by his opponents and praised as 'a man of unsurpassed goodwill to all men' by his admirers: somewhere in between was a human being who believed in being human. The ideas of Epicurus grew into one of the most extensively propagated of all Greek schools of thought. His belief that it was expedient to follow the religious customs of one's own society for the sake of an untroubled life meant that Epicureanism could survive happily side by side with other religions.

The existence of the gods was also doubted by the Sceptics, of whom Pyrrho (365–275) and Carneades (213–129) were important representatives. Pyrrho is the earliest avowed complete sceptic. He took part in the campaigns of Alexander the Great, and the variety of customs and religions which he encountered presumably influenced his opinions. He thought that our senses, being our only sources of knowledge, could tell us nothing with certainty, and sought peace of mind in the somewhat despairing attitude that it is best to follow the customs of one's own society and avoid change.

Carneades, who became head of the Platonic Academy during the second century B.C., used his scepticism to compile a very thorough critique of theism. He dismissed reports of appearances of the gods as old wives' tales. He queried the *argumentum e consensu gentium*, the often used argument from the supposed general consent to religion, on the grounds that the need for an argument showed that religion could be questioned. He also added that a plebiscite was not regarded as a satisfactory test of truth in other spheres. After examining the possible attributes of a deity he concluded that no consistent picture could be given; if God was personal this limited His supposed omniscience; if God was perfect He could not also be virtuous, since virtue consisted in overcoming imperfections. His criticism of the argument from design anticipates Hume's *Dialogues on Natural Religion*.

Roman times produced less profound sceptical and atheistic thought than the high-point of Greek civilization. Cicero (106–43) Lucretius (*d.* 55 B.C.) and Sextus Empiricus (*fl.* A.D. 200) deserve brief mention. Cicero's book *De Deorum Natura* (*On the Nature of the Gods*) is a rich source of arguments about belief in the Roman world. He himself was probably an agnostic. His importance has been stressed by modern humanists because of his emphasis on human responsibilities and civic virtues.

Lucretius turned the philosophy of Epicurus into a great philosophical poem, *De Rerum Natura* (*On the Nature of Things*) which was the medium by which Epicureanism reached the Roman world and was subsequently revived in the seventeenth century. A sample quotation indicates the tenor of his writing: 'Poor humanity, to saddle the gods with such a responsibility and throw in a vindictive temper. What griefs they hatch for themselves, what festering sores for us, what tears for our prosperity! This is not piety, this oft-repeated show of bowing a veiled head before a graven image; this bustling to every altar; this kow-towing and prostration on the ground with palms outspread before the shrines of the gods; this deluging of vow on vow. True piety lies rather in the power to contemplate the universe with a quiet mind.'

Sextus Empiricus, who wrote around A.D. 200, was a sceptic. He recorded many anti-theistic arguments in *Concerning the Gods*, a section of one of his works, but refused to reach a decision himself. His influence encouraged a consistent agnosticism and scepticism, and he was enthusiastically quoted in the Renaissance by Montaigne and Raleigh and later admired by Hume.

The development of Christianity into a predominant cultural influence coincided with the so-called 'Dark Ages'. Christianity developed as an amalgam of ideas from Eastern cults, Jewish religion, the classical world and pagan practices. It is hard to believe that scepticism did not survive at a popular folk level, but in the absence of written evidence this must be speculation. During the Middle Ages sceptical inquiry and unbelief were expressed only as a form of heresy – and, while it is an exaggeration to say that Christian rulers stifled all free inquiry, absence of striking speculative thought is notable until the late Middle Ages, when the rediscovery of Aristotle through Arabian thinkers led to a measure of non-religious and rationalist thought.

Three movements influencing the re-emergence of criticism of religion were the Renaissance, the Reformation and subsequent wars of religion, and the rise of science. The revival of classical learning and the non-religious emphasis on human behaviour led to a much wider range of inquiry on matters such as immortality or divine intervention, but freethought did not become widespread. Humanism was the *studia humanitatis*, the study of the arts of rhetoric, grammar, literature and philosophy, and there were no particularly irreligious implications in the humanism of the Italian universities. However, there was a civic, worldly emphasis which contrasted with much of medieval Christian teaching. This mood was well expressed by Vittorino da Feltre (1378–1446), an Italian tutor and educationalist who taught for many years at the University of Padua: 'Not everyone is called to be a lawyer, a physician, a philosopher, to live in the public eye, nor has everyone outstanding gifts of natural capacity, but all of us are created for the life of social duty, all are responsible for the personal influence which goes forth from us.' The Italian universities had a strong tradition of secular training for the legal and medical professions rather than theological disputation.

Two Italian Renaissance philosophers who contributed to the eventual development of unbelief are Pompanazzi and Bruno. Pompanazzi (1462–1525) studied and then taught philosophy at Padua University. His most controversial work, *De Immortalite Animae* (1516) (*On the Immortality of the Soul*), weighed the arguments for and against the immortality of the soul: the view that the intellect has no action that is independent of the body and its implication that nothing could survive the body's decay was strongly put, but, since the matter must be doubtful, Pompanazzi fell back upon the view that the question should be decided by faith and the scriptures rather than reasoned argument. However, he firmly queried the Christian belief in posthumous rewards and punishments by arguing that virtuous actions without reward are superior to those with reward.

Pompanazzi's work was very controversial, but he escaped inquisition or dismissal perhaps because of his concept of the double truth, which proposed that reason could lead to one conclusion while faith required another. The idea of the 'double truth' was very useful for those who wished to think radically without offending orthodoxy and later freethinkers charged its espousers with hypocrisy and cowardice. Nevertheless, there is no reason to doubt the sincerity with which Pompanazzi adhered to it.

Two other treatises published posthumously and sometimes republished clandestinely in the sixteenth century were even more congenial to freethinkers. *De Fato* (*Of Fate*) propounded a classical, stoical concept of fate and *De Incantationibus (Of Incantations)* offered a natural explanation of events attributed to spirits and demons and of the astrological interpretation of the stars. Pompanazzi, though not himself altogether a sceptic or unbeliever, clearly examined ideas which foreshadowed the development of free thought.

Giordano Bruno (1548–1600) was a true Renaissance man in the breadth of his interests – science, mathematics, philosophy, literature – and the *mélange* of occult and rational in his outlook. His impetuous and combative temperament and his martyrdom at the hands of the Inquisition made him a hero of later freethinkers. He was seen as a symbol of freedom of thought versus the Catholic Church by members of the Italian Risorgimento and the international freethought movement, which honoured the quatercentenary of his death by a memorial celebration in the Campo di Fiori in Rome, where he had been burned.

Bruno was a Dominican monk who narrowly escaped from a heresy indictment for his doubts about theology as a young man. He roamed Switzerland, France, England, Germany – an argumentative and restless figure. In Geneva he became a Calvinist, but quickly ended the experiment when he found the Reformed Church as unenthusiastic about freedom of thought as the Roman Church. In England between 1583 and 1585 he made friends with Sir Philip Sydney and others at Queen Elizabeth's court and enemies at the University of Oxford. His public disputation at Oxford on astronomical and philosophical matters led to a violent exchange and provoked him to write the six dialogues which contain much of his most controversial writing. He defended the Copernican theory that the sun was the centre of the solar system, but more original was his development of the philosophical implications of an infinite universe with an infinity of solar systems. *De la causa, principio e uno* (1584) (*Concerning the Cause, Principle and One*) put forward the idea that all substance is a manifestation of God and *De l'infinito, universo e mondi* (1584) (*On the Infinite, Universe and Worlds*) presents an infinite universe as the image of an infinite God. This pantheism contains echoes of Lucretius and foreshadows the monism of Spinoza or Haeckel. He was a less original scientist than Galileo, who successfully competed with him for a post at Padua University; but he was bolder in spelling out the philosophical implications of displacing the earth from the centre of the universe.

Equally important was Bruno's criticism of Christian ethics, as for example in his satirical work *Spacci de la bestia trionfante* (1584) (*The Expulsion of the Triumphant Beast*), and enthusiasm for the peaceful coexistence of diverse religious views and their free discussion put forward in the *Articuli centum et sexaginta* (*160 Articles*) written while travelling in Germany. At that time he stayed in a Carmelite convent in Frankfurt-am-Main and the Prior said that 'he did not possess a trace of religion'. (All historians of atheism become wary of such accusations which often mean 'his religion is different from mine'.)

The case for religious toleration could not have been more firmly demonstrated to Bruno than by the experience of his last eight years. While staying in the Venetian household of Giovanni Moncenigo, he was denounced to the Inquisition by his host, probably out of personal spite rather than doctrinal disapproval. He spent seven years in prison in Rome, claiming in his defence that his philosophy was not an attack on Christianity, but ultimately (unlike Galileo) refusing to recant and going to the stake as a heretic and a martyr to freedom of thought.

Not all criticism of the autocratic and immoral behaviour of the clergy or of points of Catholic dogma was anti-religious, and criticism within the Christian framework culminated in the Reformation. Luther's famous break with Rome and foundation of a reformed church was in some ways a renewal of religious belief, but in other ways his ideas led towards scepticism and humanism. The emphasis on studying the Bible in the vernacular was likely eventually to produce a critical readership. The bypassing of the Pope and church hierarchy as mediators between man and God and the importance placed upon the individual conscience were likely to lead to personal, unorthodox interpretations of religious ideas and an individualistic morality separated from belief in a divinity. Diversity of belief is inimical to theocratic hegemony. A century of devastating wars of religion caused many people to question all religious belief: where some were vigorously attached to the Protestant or Catholic party, others quietly declared to themselves 'A plague on both your houses'.

Montaigne (1533–1592), one of the greatest of all sceptics, saw the implications of religious divisions: 'for the vulgar . . . once they are emboldened to criticize and condemn the opinions they have previously held sacred (like matters of salvation), and once they see that some articles of their religion have been called into question, will soon come to regard their own beliefs as equally uncertain and to accept nothing at all on authority' (*Apologia for Raymond Sebond*). He was able to observe how religion created rifts in his own family and, towards the end of his life, had the opportunity to negotiate between warring factions in France. After a public life as a magistrate in the Bordeaux Parlement, he retired to his tower and wrote the many *Essays* upon which his reputation rests. It was no ivory tower in which he isolated himself from the world, and a return to public life as mayor of Bordeaux gave him ample material to write about his principal fascination – human behaviour. One of the maxims inscribed on the wall of his study was 'Homo sum, humani a me nihil alienum puto.' (I am a man, I consider nothing human to be alien to me[Terence].) Another quotation dear to him was 'Que sais-je?' (What do I know?), which he had struck on one side of a medal; on the other side were the words 'All that is certain is that nothing is certain' and a pair of scales suspended in balance. His scepticism was influenced by Sextus Empiricus who, together with Lucretius, was one of the many classical authors whom he admired. He was a sceptic on the grounds that our senses provide unreliable knowledge and from his observation of the variety of human custom and behaviour. The long essay *Apologia for Raymond Sebond* is one source of his views on religion: his irony and scepticism make it difficult to be sure of his position, though he was certainly not an atheist but saw nature as a book which reveals God's existence – an anticipation of naturalistic religion. His essays show him preoccupied with human behaviour, rather than theological matters, but he did not have an exalted view of man's capacities, being sarcastic about Protagoras, who 'told us a tall story, making man the measure of all things, when he had never taken his own'. He also cautioned against an overestimate of the power of reason, criticizing Luther for using

'Lady Reason' to judge 'divine things by human measure'. While on the brink of humanism in many ways, Montaigne also provided two of the major criticisms of humanist optimism: he was cautious about the extent of human powers and the use of reason. Montaigne brought psychology and anthropology as tools to analyse religion: he doubted miracles and gave psychological explanations of the stigmata of St Francis and the holy cures. He compared religious practices and while on his travels in Rome observed a circumcision, an exorcism and a procession of flagellants: 'Everyone calls barbarous what is not the custom with him.' Comparative religion was extended to the Scriptures in a comment that the idea of the Flood, the Incarnation and the Virgin Birth all existed outside the Christian tradition. Above all, he warned against man's tendency to see himself at the centre of all things: 'Man creates his image of divinity according to its relations to himself . . . man can only imagine according to his capacity.'

A friend and disciple of Montaigne, Pierre Charron (1541–1603), was one of the targets of an increasing attempt by clergy to identify and eliminate atheists. His best work, *De la Sagesse*, pursues Montaigne's idea of self-knowledge, but his exhortation to study oneself as a way of understanding God has risky implications: the student might look into himself and find only himself and no other. Charron attacked superstition, but probably remained Christian, though he presented a God closer to the First Cause of the deists than the traditional Christian God. He recommended meditation upon 'the goodness, perfection and infiniteness of the all-comprehensible and unknowable, as the Pythagoreans and the most worthy philosophers teach'.

By this time a torrent of abuse of atheists, far stronger than sceptical or atheist thought itself, pursued those thought dangerous to religious orthodoxy. One victim was Vanini (1585?–1619) born in Naples and burned in the town square of Toulouse. A roving, witty priest, his attack on unbelievers *Amphiteatrum aeternae providentiae divino-magicum, christiano-physicum, nec non astrologo-catholicum, adversus veteres philosophos, atheos, Epicurios, Peripateticos et Stoicos* printed a year before his death, perhaps as a cover-up for his own atheism, contained enough questioning and irony to substantiate his reputation – which went down the ages as that of 'le martyr de l'athéisme'; Voltaire compared him to Socrates.

The extent of atheism and doubt by the beginning of the seventeenth century remains a matter of controversy; the atheist-hunters detected a lot of smoke, so that there must have been some fire.* Discretion was the better part of self-preservation. In England there was the accusation (by a Jesuit anxious to vilify members of the English court) against 'Sir Walter Rawley's [*sic*] schoole of Atheism . . .' and the report (from a government spy) that the dramatist Christopher Marlowe 'persuades men to Atheism willing them not to be afeard of bugbears and hobgoblins'. It is difficult to disentangle Marlowe's alleged atheism from the accusation and counter-accusation relating to his probable spying activities and the mystery of his death in a tavern brawl. A report accused him of a scoffing, mocking attitude to religion: he was supposed to believe that 'Christ was a bastard and his mother dishonest' and 'that St John the Evangelist was bedfellow to Christ and leaned alwaies to his bosome, that he used him as the sinners of Sodoma'. There is no doubt that his plays contain lines critical of religion, but dramatists cannot be assumed to share the views of their most outspoken characters. In *The Jew of Malta*, Barabas declares, with an echo of Machiavelli:

> I count religion but a childish toy,
> And hold there is no sin but ignorance.

In *The Massacre of Paris*, the Duke of Guise comments upon the misuse of religion as a source of power:

> Religion! O Diabole!
> Fie, I am asham'd, however that I seem,
> To think a word of such a simple sound,
> Of such great matter should be made the ground.

Sir Walter Raleigh's reputation as an atheist was never substantiated, but never disappeared. His writings contain some conventional pious platitudes, but his essay *The Skeptick*, which summarises the views of Sextus Empiricus, suggests that at least the explorer's mind ranged into the territory of doubt. The cry at his trial for complicity in a plot against the throne – 'O damnable atheist' – was presumably an attempt to prejudice his defence. So strong were the rumours of the spread of atheism at this time that 'Her Heighness Commission for causes Ecclesiastical' [*sic*] was appointed in Dorset to investigate the matter. The highlight of its findings was the report

* David Berman has argued, convincingly, that the first avowedly atheistic work in English is the *Answer to Dr Priestley's Letters to a Philosophical Unbeliever* (London 1782) usually attributed to Dr Mathew Turner. *Question* 11. Rationalist Press Association. 1978.

of a Mr Fraunces Scarlett, minister at Sherborne, that a local shoemaker had said that a sect of people believed that Hell was only poverty and suffering and that there was no life after death.

A famous comment on atheism in this period was Bacon's essay *Of Atheism*. Bacon, who was influenced by Montaigne, was not preoccupied with unbelief, but *Of Atheism* was much quoted, especially by opponents of irreligion. He distinguished between contemplative atheists, whom he thought to be rare, and scoffing atheists, who, he thought, diminished man's nobility 'for certainly man is of kin to the beasts by his body; and if he be not of kin to God by his spirit, he is a base and ignoble creature'. Despite his dislike of atheism, his view of its causes is perceptive: he speculated that atheism arose from 'divisions in religion' and from 'scandal of priests'. His view that 'a little philosophy inclineth man's mind to atheism; but depth in philosophy bringeth man's mind about to religion' has often been quoted against atheists. But for all his detestation of atheism as 'in all respects hateful', his views of knowledge and especially science have been adduced as promoting that new learning which eventually 'cast all in doubt'. Bacon was not an original scientist but his theory that understanding of nature came from experiment and observation rather than reading and analysing the received views, contains the kernel of the scientific attitude. He was exaggeratedly praised as a theorist of science, but Dryden's couplet contains an element of truth:

> The world to Bacon does not only owe
> Its present knowledge, but its future too.

When eighteenth-century *philosophes* attempted to categorize and make available to everyone the entirety of human knowledge in the *Encyclopédie*, they acknowledged Bacon's *Novum Organum* as an influence.

Descartes (1596–1650), in the field of science and mathematics, Hobbes (1588–1679), in the sphere of political thought, and Spinoza (1632–77), in philosophy and religion, all ushered in a 'new age'. Science was not at first seen as the enemy of religion; for was not the scientist exploring God's great gift of the world? But the thought of these three men contains the germs of European rationalism. Descartes intended his studies to support religious truth, but the dictum 'Cogito ergo sum' ('I think, therefore I am') could be misinterpreted by others as a licence to base all human thought on reason, and the Cartesians were accused of being atheistic because of their mechanistic conception of the universe. Even if God wound up the watch, the divinity kept apart from the laws of matter and motion which kept it ticking. Spinoza outlined a pantheistic view of God and nature as identical and rigorously studied the Bible in a way that led to textual criticism. Hobbes' *Leviathan* provoked a Parliamentary committee to look into atheism; he never professed atheism himself, but his naturalistic explanation of religion suggests an unavowed unbeliever.

Science and the 'new philosophy' are part of the indirect cultural influence upon deistic and atheistic thought, but not to be equated with it. The climate changed from the atheist-hunting of the late sixteenth century to the most reasonable discussion of atheism in the entry 'Atheism and Atheists' in Pierre Bayle's *Historical and Critical Dictionary* (1697), which answered Steele's complaint against atheists, deists *et al* twelve years before he made it:

> It has been asserted, that a moral Atheist would be a monster beyond the power of nature to create: I reply, that it is not more strange for an Atheist to live virtuously, than for a Christian to abandon himself to crime! If we believe the last kind of monster, why dispute the existence of the first?

I

Pierre Bayle and Jean Meslier: Open scepticism and covert atheism

Pierre Bayle (1647–1706) was about as pure a sceptic as it is possible to be. A substantial article, in his celebrated *Dictionary*, on the Greek philosopher Pyrrho indicated his interest in 'Sceptics, Zetetics, Ephetics, Aporetics, that is to say examiners, inquirers, suspending and doubting men'. Although he did not follow Pyrrhonism to its nihilistic conclusion that nothing can be shown with any certainty, he emulated it in that he also 'sought truth as long as he lived' and followed Pyrrho in 'the art of disputing about everything' while being fully aware that 'Pyrrhonism (or Skepticism) . . . is justly detested in the schools of Divinity'. His life was quiet, studious and uneventful, but his works, which Voltaire declared to be 'the library of nations', were widely influential in the eighteenth century.

Bayle was born in the small French village of Larla near the Pyrenees. It was an area with independent traditions at the centre of the Albigensian region. As a Huguenot district it had been a battle-ground between Catholics and Protestants in the 1620s: memories of such religious strife must have been part of the conversations which surrounded Bayle as a child and may have lingered in the mind of a man who was to abhor religious persecution.

His father was a Protestant minister who taught him Greek and Latin. He had an insatiable curiosity and a remarkable memory and read with such intensity that his parents worried about the effect of excessive study upon his frail health. At the age of nineteen he attended a Protestant Academy in a nearby town, but grew ill through overwork. According to a friend, Desmaizeux, who wrote *A Life of Bayle* after his death, his favourite authors were Plutarch and Montaigne; he knew parts of the latter by heart.

When he was twenty he was sent to Toulouse to study at a Jesuit college. It was not uncommon for Protestants to send their sons to Jesuits to take advantage of their admired powers of education and scholarship, in the confidence that early Huguenot training would prevent apostasy. In Bayle's case such confidence was misplaced. He was led to examine the Catholic faith seriously and he was sufficiently impressed with its logic and universality to be converted; but he soon doubted the wisdom of his conversion and he 'recovered the light he had lost'. Since a decree of 1635 there had been penalties in 'Catholic' France against converts who lapsed, and Bayle, after secretly abjuring his Catholicism before his brother and Huguenot ministers, fled to Geneva. Gibbon followed a similar pattern of conversion and relapse in the next century and was fond of drawing parallels between himself and Bayle 'who afterwards emerged from superstition to scepticism'. Gibbon found that the experience of two versions of Christianity led to scepticism, not a return to devotion, but Bayle, unlike Gibbon, was ostensibly a committed Christian for the remainder of his life.

Bayle expanded his reading at the University of Geneva. He studied theology, biblical criticism and philosophy and must have been influenced by the current interest of reformed ministers in the ideas of Descartes.

Bayle set aside any family hopes that he would follow his father and brother into the ministry. He took up various posts as a private tutor in Geneva, Rouen and then Paris, but in 1675 he obtained a position in the chair of philosophy at the Protestant Academy in Sedan. A friend from Geneva, Basnage, who taught at Sedan, pointed out the vacancy as suitable for his talents and he successfully competed with other candidates in a public disputation on the subject of time. He embarked on an uncontroversial teaching career at a centre of Protestant intellectual thought, and the professor of theology at Sedan, Jurieu, saw no reason to suspect that his record would lead him to write works which upset the Protestant orthodoxy: 'As I believed, he was sincere in his return to us, we resolved to keep the matter (of his conversion at Toulouse) secret and to proceed. He was several years in the Academy . . . neither doing or saying anything that gave offence.' However in his last year at the Academy Bayle was busy writing *Miscellaneous Thoughts on the Comet of 1680*, which was to give deep offence and to set Jurieu and himself on a course of two decades of bitter enmity.

By the time this was published in 1682, Bayle had left the Sedan Academy. It was forced to close in 1681 as part of Louis XIV's campaign against the Huguenots, and as a result of contact with an admiring Dutch student Bayle was offered the professorship of philosophy and history at a recently established Protestant Academy in Rotterdam. Its title of École Illustre, which was somewhat optimistic at the time Bayle moved there, became quite accurate, as a result of his renown and the increased number of distinguished Huguenots forced into exile. Bayle remained in Rotterdam until his death in 1706.

Thoughts on the Comet of 1680 was published anonymously. Although anonymity was sought by many sceptics and freethinkers for sensible reasons of caution and prudence, in Bayle's case genuine modesty also may have been a motive. The comet of 1680 led to much public discussion of the extent to which such events were to be seen as divine portents or presages of disaster. Fontenelle (1657–1757), the witty French sceptic, whose hundred years spanned the period of Cartesian influence and the Enlightenment *philosophes*, wrote a play satirising superstitious reactions to the comet. On balance thinkers no longer took a superstitious attitude towards comets. Indeed the astronomer Edmund Halley observed one so carefully that he was able to calculate its trajectory. Bayle also saw the movement of comets as part of 'the ordinary works of nature which, without regard to the happiness or misery of mankind, are transported from one part of the heavens to another by virtue of the general laws of motion'. But the major part of the *Thoughts* is devoted to philosophical and theological, not scientific, discussion.

His ridicule of belief in signs and portents included a side-swipe at astrology, which illustrates the sharpness of his scepticism (and his continuing relevance today):

> Consider, I pray, whether you are not renouncing all shame and sincerity to advance such principles. Because a comet appears in a group of stars which the ancients thought fit to call the Virgin, therefore, shall our women be barren, or have frequent miscarriages, or die old maids. I know of nothing which hangs so ill together! To offer such things in seriousness, shows the greatest contempt of mankind, and the most scandalous lying impunity.

Bayle suggested that comets and other portents were far too numerous to presage anything in particular and pointed to many occasions where they could be interpreted equally as good or bad omens.

His discussion of Christianity, paganism and atheism arose from the question, which other writers as far back as Plutarch had raised, of why God allowed comets to appear as signs to non-Christians and pagans: would not this reinforce the beliefs of unbelievers and idolaters?

> So that, were it the purpose of God to produce comets as signs of his wrath it would be true to say that he is quickening a false devotion almost all over the world, increasing the number of pilgrims to Mecca, multiplying the offerings to the most famous impostors, inducing men to build mosques for Mohammedan worship, causing the invention of new superstitions among the dervishes – in a word, stimulating many abominable things which otherwise might not have been.

Some had argued that God preferred idolaters to atheists. (Similarly some Christians today argue that though Christianity is the one true religion, other world faiths are a second-best path to God that is much preferable to atheistic humanism.) Bayle doubted whether atheism would ever become widespread, because of people's tendency towards credulity and the desire of rulers to use religion for political purposes and the need of priests to preserve their dignity:

> Do you doubt that the least effects of nature were not used as marks of the wrath of heaven? It was to the interest of pontiffs, priests, and augurs, as much as it is to the interest of lawyers and doctors that there should be lawsuits and sickness. No wonder they took care that the people should not grow slack in their religion.

Bayle also considered that atheists would be no worse than idolaters, since they were often less wicked than pagans, like Nero or Heliogabalus, who were thoroughly religious and thoroughly immoral: 'It is only common prejudice that induces us to believe that atheism is a fearful state.' He considered human behaviour to be the result of temperament and custom rather than belief and pointed out that Christians did not always follow their principles, and instanced Epicurus as a man who had questioned immortality and the existence of the gods but who had lived a moral life.

There was a famous passage in which Bayle asked what a society of atheists would be like. It was a question that was frequently referred to by eighteenth-century deists and sceptics. Bayle saw no reason why a society of atheists should not be possible or should be worse than any other, as long as it was provided with the laws and justice necessary for the ordering of any society; but he made no suggestions that it would be any better, and did not anticipate the Enlightenment belief that the removal of superstition would go hand in hand with the progress of man; nor did he have any utopian belief in the primitive innocence of man freed from the bonds of religion and government. In the *Dictionary*, he wrote of the anarchistic atheism of Kruzen, the German, who founded a sect of *Conscientianes* in about 1673, because 'there was no other God, religion, or lawful magistracy, than conscience, which teaches all men the precepts of Justice, to do no injury, to live honestly, and give everyone his due'. Bayle thought 'one must be stark mad, to believe that mankind can subsist without magistrates'.

Despite its anonymous publication Bayle was soon well-known to be the author of *Thoughts on the Comet of 1680* and it was widely read with two editions in France in 1699 and 1704, and an English translation in 1708. His post at Rotterdam was not arduous and he had sufficient time to pursue his own studies and writings. He spoke with pleasure of his quiet life: 'I get up and retire when I wish. I go out if I wish and I do not go out if I do not desire to do so, except for the two days on which I give lectures.'

The Revocation of the Edict of Nantes by Louis XIV in France in 1685 led to persecution and the exodus of Huguenots from France. The Revocation was justified by its supporters with the dishonest argument that tolerance was no longer necessary, since conversion of all Huguenots was now complete. Bayle attacked the draconian methods of conversion used by the French Jesuits and Dragonnades and criticized Catholic apologists, such as M. Maimberg, on the grounds that 'angry' historians could not be relied upon.

At the same period as the Revocation Bayle received bad news of his family. His younger brother died in Paris while studying in the spring of 1684; his father died a year later, illness being accelerated by the loss of a son and the sufferings of his church. Bayle's elder brother, a minister, went into hiding after the Revocation, but surfaced and carried on his work as a minister: he was imprisoned and died of ill treatment. Pierre Bayle's grief was heightened by his belief that his brother had been maltreated because of his own writings.

This sequence of events led to Bayle's most emotional work: *Ce que c'est que la France toute Catholique* was a passionate plea for tolerance of belief and a forceful denunciation of the French treatment of the Huguenots. Among the arguments advanced for toleration was the suggestion that persecutory and intolerant forms of religion would encourage deism and abandonment of religion. A similar argument was put forward when Bayle expanded his pleas for religious toleration in the *Philosophical Commentary* on the words of Jesus Christ, 'Compel them to come in', where it is argued that there is nothing more abominable than to make conversions by force.

He attributed irreligion to the practices of Christians: 'The age we live in . . . is full of freethinkers and deists. People are amazed at their number, but for my part I am amazed that we have not more of this sort among us considering the havoc religion has made in the world, and the extraction of all virtue which inevitably appears when it, the church, authorizes all imaginable crimes.'

Bayle thought there was ground for tolerance because of the limited knowledge we have of the minds of others, because forcible conversion breeds hypocrisy, and because of the right of the individual 'erring conscience' for error could be sincere. This influential book is comparable to Locke's *Letter on Toleration* of 1689; but Locke does not go as far in extending tolerance to all beliefs: Locke would have withheld freedom of speech and worship from sects thought to be a danger to the state (including Roman Catholics) and from atheists who, he thought, could not be relied upon to stand by oaths and covenants which were necessary bonds of society. Bayle included atheists, Socinians, Catholics and Mohammedans in his defence of toleration. He was a pioneer in working out general grounds for tolerance and unusual as someone within the reformed church, most of whose leaders did not learn the lesson of toleration from the experience of persecution.

In 1684 Bayle started a journal of news, book reviews and correspondence called the *New Republic of Letters*. It was a significant venture in the history of journalism and was genuinely cosmopolitan in its contact with European men of letters. He was forced to abandon the editorship when his health broke down through overwork in 1687. When he resumed work after many months of rest, he became embroiled in controversy and became the victim of intolerance. Jurieu, a leading Calvinist theologian and a pastor in Rotterdam, attacked the *Philosophical Commentary* because he wished 'to destroy the dogma of indifference [impartiality] of religious and of universal tolerance'. Bayle defended himself vigorously, but Jurieu was able to persuade the Dutch Reformed Church that his views were dangerous and he was deprived of his professorship in 1693.

Bayle settled down to a frugal, studious life free from 'the disputes, cabals and professional snarlings that reign in our academies'. He was unconcerned with 'diversions, parties, games, banquets, days in the country, visits, and such other recreations necessary to a great many other studious men' and was thankful for 'the greatest and most charming leisure that a man of letters could desire'. He never married and his writings show strong prejudice against women. Among the few light pleasures of his life were travelling puppet shows and bookshops.

The *Historical and Critical Dictionary* appeared in two large folios in 1697 and was *prima facie* a biographical dictionary. Despite some items on towns and rivers and pieces such as that on Helen of Troy and female courtesans to provide lighter touches, the preponderance of articles covered sixteenth- and seventeenth-century figures. There was some biblical criticism, and the article on King David broached a topic that was to vex many eighteenth-century deists: how could the 'man after God's own heart' be responsible for such bloodthirstiness, cunning and polygamy? 'Have not even the Turks and Tartars a little more humanity?' Another topic which was much to exercise eighteenth-century deists was the decline of miracles since the early days of Christianity: Bayle thought that 'miracles ought to be kept as much as possible for a great necessity'. He was impressed by psychological explanations: 'The bones of a dog would as effectively produce a cure, if the sick person who relies on relics, formed the same imagination concerning those bones as concerning the bones and ashes of martyrs'.

The *Dictionary* shows that Bayle believed in a natural morality and tended towards the Manichean view that good and evil were separate forces which could not stem from one omniscient god. He defended the character of doubters and sceptics, such as La Mothe le Vayer and Averroes.

Another unorthodox thinker admired (though not entirely agreed with) was Spinoza, who, he rather inaccurately said, was 'the first to reduce Atheism to a system, and formed it into a body of doctrine, ordered and connected according to the manner of Geometricians'. Spinoza's (1632–77) deep ethical concern with 'the good', his honest and lovable personality, and his steadfast endurance of opposition have made him much admired by freethinkers. The *Tractatus Theologico-Politicus* presents God and nature as one infinite whole. He was a monist seeing all substance as a unity which contains the inexhaustible attributes of God. His philosophic pantheism was combined with early biblical criticism and his reputation was such that by the time of Bayle the adjective *misérable* would accompany his name when mentioned by theologians. Philosophers consider the

Ethics to be his masterpiece, but although it appeared in the Latin edition of his *Opera Posthuma* in 1677, it was not reprinted elsewhere until 1802. The geometric, Euclidian terms in which the *Ethics* is presented make it difficult reading for the non-specialist, but it is one of the profoundest and most attractive attempts to work out an ethical system which does not derive directly from religion. Bayle's article on Spinoza is understandably one of the more substantial items in the *Dictionary*.

Bayle was brought before the ecclesiastical consistory of Rotterdam as a result of Jurieu's continuing antagonism towards him and admonished for indecency and tending to 'weaken the need of believing in God and Providence'. Bayle agreed to rewrite some articles in the *Dictionary* and to publish a letter disavowing other parts – but his revisions were minor (and in the case of the article on David printed side by side with the original) and his letter of retraction was not widely distributed.

The *Dictionary* was a great success and went through many editions in the eighteenth century. It influenced English deists, historians such as Gibbon and Voltaire, writers of the German Aufklärung such as Lessing, and the Encyclopedists, whose debt to Bayle's *Dictionary* is obvious.

Bayle became more retiring and accepted his weakness of lungs as an incurable hereditary disease which 'does not permit me to plan for a long stay in this world'. According to his friend Desmaizeaux, he 'died in tranquillity, and without anyone near him' on 28 December 1706. Since he had never overtly abandoned his religion he was buried in a French church in Rotterdam.

Bayle's careful, scholarly scepticism and his renown as a writer contrast sharply with a little-known contemporary priest who produced a devastating attack on Christianity which was not printed in full until the nineteenth century. Jean Meslier (1664–1729) was a country *curé* who wrote one of the most vehement and thoroughgoing attacks on religious institutions and religious faith in general and Christianity in particular that has ever been written. His *Testament* was a handwritten manuscript of five to six hundred closely written pages in which he bequeathed his contempt for Christianity and despair that ordinary people should be kept in bondage by the imposture of clergy and rulers.

Meslier was born in the Ardennes in 1664. His father entered him for a seminary at Rheims, presumably after some instruction by the local *curé*. He allowed himself to be directed towards a career in the church because, as he regretfully admits in the *Avant-Propos* to the *Testament*, his parents hoped to secure for him a life which was 'more gentle, more peaceful, and more honourable in the world than that of ordinary people'. He was nominated to a curacy near his birthplace in 1689, resided in Étrépigny and served the few hundred inhabitants of this and the neighbouring village of Balaives until his death in the summer of 1729.

Little else is known about his life, except that he came to the notice of the archbishopric of Rheims in 1716 for speaking in the pulpit against 'the seigneurs and great of the world'. He was reprimanded and taken to Rheims for one month's confinement. An anonymous *Summary of the Life of Jean Meslier* which circulated underground in the eighteenth century, refers to an occasion when he refused to recommend the local *seigneur* in his prayers. Apart from this there is no evidence that he was not in all respects an efficient and effective local priest, with a strong sense of duty and an unusually large library. There was a suggestion in the *Summary* that weariness with life and disgust with his task led him to commit suicide by refusing food and drink. His almost schizoid channelling of all his detestation of Christianity on to paper while steadily undertaking his function as a priest has led to accusations of his being a 'psychological monstrosity'. But the dangers of publication were such that only a foolhardy wish for punishment could have tempted the author of so ferocious a manuscript. He may well have felt that he could genuinely best serve the community by counselling and helping the ordinary folk around him with as little reference to religion as he could get away with.

His manuscript quickly went into circulation as one of the most widely known of clandestine publications and came to the attention of Voltaire, d'Holbach and other *philosophes* who must have been startled by its forthrightness and the completeness of its materialism and atheism. Voltaire published an edited extract in 1762; it gave sections critical of Christianity acceptable to deists and left out the arguments against the existence of God and the sections on the tyrannies and injustices of the great. The first edition to be published was that of the Dutch nineteenth-century rationalist Rudolf Charles d'Ablaing van Gienerburg in 1864. Not until 1970 was a complete and thoroughly edited French edition begun. Meslier, like Thomas Paine, whose plainness and fire he shared, almost slipped out of the conventional history books. Nevertheless, his voice still comes through to us as the cry of anguish, fury and despair at the injustices and deception of Christianity.

The *Testament* is divided into eight sections, each of which presents a different 'proof'. In the first and second it is argued that religions are 'inventions and purely human institutions' and faith, especially the Christian faith, is founded on uncertainties, contradictions and absurdities. In the third and fourth parts Meslier examines the Old Testament and proposes that the claims of revelation are false and that the prophecies are contradicted by history and cannot be interpreted symbolically without becoming ridiculous. In the fifth and sixth parts Christianity is accused of propounding false doctrines and morality and perpetuating the misery of the people by favouring oppression and injustice. Christian morality is attacked for the idea that pleasure is wrong, the belief that poverty and renunciation are virtues, and the instruction to love your enemies, which is impractical and leads to injustice.

The seventh and longest section constitutes half of the book and argues against belief in a God. Meslier says that the natural order did not require a sovereign creator since it could be seen as purely matter and motion in so far as we could comprehend it. He also thought that the disorder and evil on earth destroyed the idea of an all-powerful and all-good God. The final section suggests that the soul is not spiritual and immortal, but simply a modification of matter (in animals as well as humans) which is perishable. He concludes with an appeal for the oppressed to unite against their oppressors and for those readers who had been convinced by his arguments to use their influence to persuade others of them.

In comparison with the cautious scholarly work of Bayle, Meslier is direct and comes to clear-cut conclusions. Although his writing shows evidence of wide reading, it has the flavour of a deeply-convinced man speaking straight to another individual:

> You will think, perhaps, my dear friends, that among the great number of false religions there are in the world, my intention will be to except from their number at least Christianity, apostolic and Roman, which we profess and which we say is the only one to teach genuine truth, the only one which recognises and adores, as is required, the true God, and the only one which leads men on the path to salvation and eternal happiness. But disabuse yourself, my dear friends, disabuse yourself of that, and generally of all that your pious ignoramuses, or your mocking and self-interested priests and doctors, press you to say and to believe, under the false pretext of the infallible

> certitude of their supposedly sacred and divine religion. . . . Your religion is no less vain, no less superstitious than any other; it is not less false in its principles, not less ridiculous and absurd in its dogmas and maxims; you are no less idolaters than those you blame and condemn for idolatry; the idols of the pagans and of your religion are only different in names and figures. In a word, all that your priests and doctors preach to you with such eloquence touching the grandeur, excellence and sanctity of the mysteries that they make you adore, all that which they recount to you with such gravity, with the certainty of their claimed miracles and all that which is given out to you with such zeal and such assurance concerning the grandeur of the rewards of heaven, and concerning the terrifying punishments of hell, are no more at bottom than illusions, errors, dreams, fictions and impostures, invented firstly for political ends and ruses, continued by deceivers and imposters; finally received and believed blindly by the ignorant and rude common people, and then eventually maintained by the authority of the great, and the sovereigns of the earth, who have favoured the abuses, the errors, the superstition and the imposture which are upheld by their laws in order to hold the mass of men in yoke and make them do all that their rulers want.

Bayle and Meslier represent opposite ends of the spectrum of free-thinkers: Bayle was scholarly and cautious, tolerant and questioning without coming to firm conclusions, while Meslier was angry and disillusioned, and bold and decisive in his rejection of all religious faith. This is not to say that Bayle was without passion or animus – he detested persecution; nor that Meslier was without learning – his knowledge of classical writing and Montaigne and Descartes was considerable.

Lord Shaftesbury, an English moralist and deist, who met Bayle in Rotterdam, paid tribute to the value of Bayle's scepticism:

> I think the world, and in particular the learned world, much beholden to such proving spirits as these. . . . What injury such a one could do the world by such a search for truth with so much moderation, dis-interestedness, integrity, and innocency of life, I know not. But what good he did I in particular know and feel, and must never cease to speak and own.

2

The English deists: Removing the mystery from God

The third Earl of Shaftesbury was a moralist and deist whose writings were admired and disdained in the early eighteenth century. He was one of a group of English deists, whose ideas and styles varied considerably and who were in no sense linked as a propagandist clique, yet whose writings are a significant step in the history of freethought. Any discussion of them is complicated by their frequent denial of unorthodoxy, for they often professed to be true Christians and agreed with their critics in deploring atheism. The greatest historian of freethought, J. M. Robertson, has referred to the confusion of the period which arose from the 'distribution of heretical views among the nominally orthodox, and of orthodox views among the heretics'. The deists opened the door upon atheism, materialism and rejection of Christianity, but sternly proclaimed they had no intention of crossing the threshold.

Attacks from their opponents created an impression of a much stronger, more cohesive atheistic group than can possibly have been the case. The most famous outburst against them came from Bishop Berkeley, in *The Minute Philosopher*, where he lashed out at the unorthodox with a virulence unworthy of so lucid a philosopher. He also wrote in his *Discourse to Magistrates* of an 'execrable fraternity of blasphemers' in Dublin, who formed 'a distinct society, whereof the proper and avowed business shall be to shock all serious Christians by the most impious and horrid blasphemies, uttered in the most public manner'. Swift proposed in *A Project for the Advancement of Religion* (1709) to 'prevent the publishing of such pernicious works as under the pretence of freethinking endeavour to overthrow those tenets in religion which have been held inviolable in almost all ages'. At Cambridge University in 1739 proceedings were taken against an 'atheistical society' and a certain Tinkler Ducket, a fellow of Caius College in holy orders, was prosecuted in the Vice-Chancellor's

Court and expelled for spreading atheism and for an attempted seduction. Here, as often since the relaxation of puritanism after the Restoration, the enemies of atheism were able to adduce the further danger of libertinage. As with the 'reds under the beds' attitude to 'immoral' communists in the twentieth century, the atheists were certainly far less numerous, dangerous or 'immoral' than their opponents feared. However, deism was a potent force which bridged the age of heresy and persecution and the age of enlightenment.

Deism is belief in a deity which works through nature and underpins a benevolent universe without active participation; it is a much more impersonal force than the paternal figure of Christianity. Theism, which was not always clearly distinguished from deism, gave somewhat more personal attributes to the deity but did not equate it with the god of any specific religion. The term 'natural religion' was often used, since deists thought that God was a natural part of the universe and would almost never contradict its natural laws by miracles; 'natural religion' was thought to be a characteristic of all mankind and all ages, regardless of the particular religious institutions of any one period. Biblical chronology and biblical accounts of supernatural events were analysed critically by deists, and there was examination of apparent biblical contradictions such as God's love for David, whose actions were a poor example for Christians. Reason was thought to be a God-given faculty and it was presumed that God intended it to be used for an understanding of the world; reason was a surer route to the understanding of God than revelation or miracles which depended upon the unreliable accuracy of a reporter, and which appeared to have died out since the early age of Christianity. Protestants had long criticized the more superstitious elements of Catholicism, and criticism of superstition and the miraculous were found in varying degrees among quite conventional Anglican clerics.

Anthony Ashley Cooper, the third Earl of Shaftesbury was born in London on 26 February 1671. He was the grandson of the first Earl, who was Lord High Chancellor during the reign of Charles II. The first Earl was a friend of the philosopher John Locke and a 'founder' of the Whig party, but during a period of Tory, royalist reaction he was arrested for high treason. He was acquitted and fled to Holland where he later died 'disappointed but smiling'. His son, the third Earl's father, was infirm and weak and his wife was chosen with the aid of Locke. Shaftesbury, the deist and moralist, was indebted to Locke as an intellectual and personal influence, since he was placed under his grandfather's guardianship and Locke was given charge of his education. His daily instructress, Mrs Elizabeth Birch, used Locke's and Montaigne's method of teaching classics conversationally so that he could read Greek and Latin fluently by the time he was eleven. A brief period at Winchester College was most unhappy: he was delicate and had to endure taunts because of the downfall of his grandfather. When he was eighteen, his education was completed by a private tutor, who was also a travelling-companion on a long European tour, where his contact with artistic and classical influences imbued him with a permanent love of painting, sculpture and music. On return to England, this quiet and good-humoured man devoted himself to study.

After a career in the House of Commons, brought to a close through ill health after only three years, Shaftesbury travelled to Holland in 1698. It may have been on this occasion that he first met Pierre Bayle. A story, perhaps apocryphal, is recorded in which Shaftesbury pretended to be a medical student and met Bayle *incognito*; Bayle had to leave in haste to meet a more distinguished guest – 'my Lord Ashley' (i.e. Shaftesbury). The amusement that resulted when they immediately re-met was said to have cemented their friendship.

While he was in Holland an unauthorized publication of his work the *Inquiry Concerning Virtue* (1699) took place (probably instigated by John Toland, whose actions were especially ungrateful since he was receiving a stipend from Shaftesbury). Shaftesbury bought up copies of the unauthorized impression, completed the treatise and had it published himself. The *Inquiry* contains much of his reflections upon morality and religion.

In 1700 he took his seat in the House of Lords, but poor health and Queen Anne's dislike of Whigs caused him to resume a quiet, studious life. He revisited Holland, where he polished his writings. In 1708 he published *Essays on Tolerance & Freedom & Wit & Humour* and in 1711 his major *opus*, the *Characteristics of Men, Manners, Opinions, Times*. The *Characteristics* was in three volumes and included miscellaneous essays and a reprint of the *Inquiry*. In 1711 he moved to Italy seeking a warmer climate for his health. He was weak with consumption, and only the warmth of Naples and the care of his wife preserved him for another two years. He died in 1713 in his forty-second year. It was said that he bore 'his pain and agonies with patience, but also with perfect cheerfulness and the same sweetness of temper he always enjoyed in the most perfect health'.

Shaftesbury's amiable and benevolent nature was attested to by all who knew him. The poet James Thomson wrote of his wish:

> To teach the finer movements of the mind
> And with the moral beauty charm the heart.

It has been said that where Spinoza was intoxicated by God, Shaftesbury was intoxicated by virtue. Warburton, an opponent of the deists, said he was 'temperate, chaste, honest, and a lover of his country'.

His personality must partly account for his cheerful view of God and generous view of man. He wrote to a student at Oxford, whom he was maintaining: 'For never do we more need a just cheerfulness, good humour, or alacrity of mind, than when we are contemplating God or Virtue.' Although assigning an important role to the 'Universal Mind' as the originator and observer of the world, Shaftesbury contemplated virtue with much more enthusiasm than the deity. He described the Supreme Being as 'a witness and spectator of life' and thought that this Being was to be perceived by reason rather than revelation as a part of nature rather than the supernatural.

He defended freethinking, but thought that atheists had a 'sour', 'morose' view of the deity which they rejected, and misunderstood the natural harmony of the universe. He disliked the picture of the universe which he thought resulted from atheism, a world which in his view was 'mere Accident' and contained only the 'Chaos and Atoms of the Atheists'. He did not attack atheists but thought that they lacked a prime aid to the contemplation of virtue: ''tis very apparent how conducting a perfect Theism must be to virtue; and how great deficiency there is in atheism.'

Virtue he saw as a moral sense, almost a kind of taste, which was an innate human faculty. The 'Sense of Right and Wrong' he described as 'as natural to us as natural affection itself, and a first principle in our constitution and make.' He quarrelled with the Christian views of rewards and punishments, which he thought discouraged the 'Love towards Equity and Right, for its own sake, and on account of its own natural Beauty and Worth'. A sense of virtue is not best developed by rewards and punishments: 'There is no more Rectitude, Piety, or Sanctity in a creature thus reformed, than there is Meekness or Gentleness in a Tiger strongly chained, or Innocence and Sobriety in a monkey under the discipline of the whip.' His high view of human nature was criticized by Bernard de Mandeville, who wrote in his *Fable of the Bees* (1723) that Shaftesbury 'seems to require and expect goodness in his species, as we do a sweet taste of grapes and China oranges, of which, if any of them are sour, we boldly pronounce that they are not come to that perfection nature is capable of'. Perhaps the ease of his life and gentleness of his temperament blinded him to the harsher aspects of human nature. Yet, this 'virtuoso of humanity', as Herder later called him, experienced a considerable vogue in the first half of the eighteenth century and is one of the most attractive of the deists.

Not even the most intense critics of freethinking could find any evidence to discredit Shaftesbury's ideas by calumny against his character. This was far from the case with the somewhat vain John Toland, who incurred the wrath of Shaftesbury by taking advantage of his acquaintanceship to produce pirated editions of his *Inquiry* and some of his letters. The title of Toland's first major work, *Christianity Not Mysterious* (1697), provides a most apposite phrase for the route by which some moved via deism towards agnosticism. Although perfectly orthodox Christians might approve the emphasis on human reason, there can be no doubt, as the history of religion in the last two hundred years demonstrates, that Christianity without mystery is rather like life without oxygen.

Toland was born in Co. Donegal in 1670. His parents were probably Catholic and he said that he was 'educated from his cradle in the grossest Superstition and Idolatry'. As a youth he rejected Catholicism and became as 'zealous against Popery, as he hath ever since continued', for 'God was pleas'd to make his own Reason, and such as made use of theirs, the happy instruments of his conversion'. (The emphasis on reason and the anti-Catholic flavour are typical of both Anglican and deist writings.) His education took place at Redcastle, near Londonderry, at a college in Glasgow, and at Edinburgh University where he obtained the degree of Master of Arts in 1690. He travelled to England and Holland, where he studied for two years at the University of Leyden, being supported by a group of English Dissenters who hoped he would become a Minister. He then returned to England and at Oxford took advantage of 'the Conversation of learned men' and 'the publick Library'.

Christianity Not Mysterious was his first substantial work and immediately gained him much notoriety. The two central arguments of his treatise rely upon an examination of the meaning of mysteries in the New Testament and early Christianity and a comparison between the mysteries of nature and the mysteries of religion. 'Mystery' in the New Testament, he claimed, meant exclusion from the gentiles, or as yet unrevealed secrets, or 'anything veil'd under parables, or enigmatical forms of speech'. He was attracted to the idea that a more rational, if esoteric, truth in Christianity was hidden from the vulgar and uncomprehending. (The history of such an attitude is long-standing and ranges from Bruno, some of whose dialogues Toland translated, to modern views of Gnostic contributions to Christianity.) Toland saw no reason to believe that the mysteries of religion were different from the mysteries of nature; just as the mysteries of nature were 'those things imperfectly known to us' so the revealed truths of the Christian religion 'can be made as clear and intelligible as natural things which come within our knowledge and comprehension'.

Toland's treatise alarmed the public and replies were quickly published. There was outrage in Dublin, where he took his book in 1697. He was harangued from the pulpit; his book was declared heretical and ordered to be publicly burned by the hangman; but he returned to England before prosecution could proceed. The strength of reaction may have been exacerbated by his indiscreet behaviour.

A tendency towards self-justification and to disclaim the more trenchant implications of his writings suggest that he was motivated by the quest for esteem as well as truth. However, his writings are consistently interesting and denigration by his opponents has given his writings an undeserved neglect. A strongly anti-clerical view of priests is seen in a poem which is probably correctly attributed to Toland (even if written by another hand it indicates a more popular level of suspicion of religious leaders). *Clito, a Poem on the Force of Eloquence*, contains a figure, Adeisdaemon (without superstition), who asks whether Eloquence can speak the truth in religious topics and proclaims:

> Nor will I here desist: all holy Cheats
> Of all Religions shall partake my Threats,
> Whether with sable Gowns they show their Pride,
> Or under Cloakes their Knavery hide,
> Or whatsoe'er disguise they chuse to wear,
> To gull the People, while their Spoils they share.

For the remaining twenty years of his life Toland was a vigorous controversialist and traveller. Among his better-known works was *Letters to Serena* which resulted from visits to Prussia and his correspondence with the learned Princess Sophie and the Queen of Prussia. They contain a study of the origin of prejudice, and details of his criticism of Spinoza's views on the motion of matter. Three further works merit mention. *Nazarenus* (1718) suggests that the original idea of Christianity was to combine Gentiles and Jews in 'one body of fellowship' and concentrate upon 'the renovation of the inward man'. A form of universal religion is hinted at – 'wherein alone the Jew and the Gentile, the Civiliz'd and the Barbarian, the Freeman and the Bondslave, are all one in Christ, however otherwise differing in their circumstances'. The *Pantheisticon* (1720) is a dialogue between the President and members of a philosophical society in which members are encouraged to love Truth, Liberty, and Health and be 'cheerful, sober, temperate and free from Superstition'. The singing of 'suitable verses from the antients' suggests an Epicurean influence. The *Tetradymus* (1720) contained further rational interpretation of Biblical events, such as a speculation that the Pillar of Cloud and Fire which guided the Israelites out of the wilderness referred to a common nomadic practice of lighting fires as a guide across the desert rather than to divine guidance. One section of *Tetradymus* shows how early freethinkers used the example of the martyrdom of Hypatia to discredit the Christian tradition. Toland writes of Hypatia as 'a most beautiful, most virtuous, most learned, and every way accomplish'd Lady; who was torn to pieces by the Clergy of Alexandria, to gratify the pride, emulation, and cruelty of their Archbishop CYRIL, commonly but undeservedly styled Saint Cyril'.

During the final four years of his life Toland lived in Putney, frequently visiting London. Illness was apparently worsened by excessive purging, though he retained sufficient energy to write a diatribe against doctors, *Physic without Physicians*, joining the long line of sceptics from Moliere to Shaw whose critical minds were turned towards the priests of the body as well as the spirit. His sympathetic biographer, Des Maizeaux, gently suggested that 'he might have employed his talents much better than he has done. But he had the misfortune to fall into an idle, indiscreet way of living, which he indulged to his death.' This rebuke is somewhat vague: charming letters written to a mistress indicate a man of sensitivity as well as sensuousness, and whatever other direction he may have indulged himself in it does not appear to have affected his clarity of mind. An anonymous *Elegy on Mr Toland* lamented the loss of a true, if erratic, original:

O hadst thou liv'd to banish all the Dreams
Of fab'lous Ages and the Monkish Themes
Of Miracles, of Mysteries, and Tales,
(Where fancy over common sense prevails)
Then might we mourn thy fate with less concern,
With less regret behold thy sacred Urn.

Toland's writings contain one of the clearest indications of the extent to which deists wished to distance themselves from atheists and to which 'atheism' was seen as a term of abuse. He wrote in his *Vindicius Liberius, or Mr. Tolands's Defense of Himself, Against the late Lower House of Convocation and Others:*

> People ought to be very tender and reserv'd in accusing a Man of any Thing that manifestly turns to his Disadvantage: but making one pass for a Traitor, a Parricide, or Murderer, are nothing, even in the Eys of the World, to charging him with *Atheism*: for such a Person is not only justly lookt upon as one that has no Reason or Reflection, but likewise as under no Tyes of Conscience, of Obligations or Oaths, when he has an Opportunity of doing Mischief; and so not to be trusted in any private or public Capacity. . . .
>
> I could produce many Instances to this purpose from the antient Philosophers; the Heathen Priests represented the primitive Christians as Atheists both in Doctrine and Practice, and the People at their Instigation treated 'em as such; the first Reformers, with their followers, met with the same unjust Measures from the Papists; and, at this present Time, when the Inquisitors can make no other accusation good against their Prisoner, they take Care to Charge him with Atheistical Notions and the most enormous crimes, whereby he's straight condemn'd by the public Voice, and all Men's Ears are stops against any Thing that can be said for one they conceive to be such a wicked Wretch. . . .

Despite this kind of declaration and the difficulty of finding any explicit atheism, some deists may have been speculating in atheistic directions. A plausible case has been made to suggest that Anthony Collins (1676–1729) was a 'speculative atheist'.* Collins was educated at Cambridge and became a student at the Temple. He was a friend of John Locke, who exchanged affectionate letters with him

*David Berman also argues that it is 'highly probable that Collins 'was, in fact, a strong-minded atheist, with a proof for the non-existence of God.' *Anthony Collins and the Question of Atheism in the Early Part of the Eighteenth Century*. Proceedings of the Royal Irish Academy, 1975.

and left him a small legacy. In common with many other free-thinking men, he visited Holland. Collins was respected as a man of kindness and integrity and in 1715 he became a Justice of Peace in Essex (a good reason for not stating clearly his boldest reflections upon religion). Whether atheistic or deistic, he was a genuine lover of free inquiry as is indicated in a letter to him from Locke: 'Believe it, my good friend, to love truth for truth's sake is the principal part of human perfection in the world, and the seed-plot of all other virtues; and if I mistake not, you have as much of it as I ever met with in anybody' (1703). His most famous book the *Discourse of Free-thinking* (1713) created an uproar and Collins temporarily fled to Holland. Collins' later works examined Biblical prophecies, concluding that they were not to be relied upon: *A Discourse of the Grounds and Reasons of the Christian Religion* (1723), which contained attacks on prophecy, attracted sufficient criticism for Collins to publish a reply, the *Scheme of Liberal Prophecy Considered* (1727).

Other deists also questioned the authenticity of Bible tales. Thomas Woolston (1670–1733) had a reputation as a studious and charitable man, and was attracted to an allegorical interpretation of the Bible. He took orders but later left the Church and declared his intention of starting a new sect called the 'enigmatists', presumably to be composed of followers of the allegorical interpretation of the scriptures. Although the period did contain ribald mockery* most deists were sober and earnest questioners. Woolston took his allegorical approach to the stage of speculating upon the literal truth of the resurrection and virgin birth in *A Moderator between an Infidel and an Apostate* (1752). His *Six Discourses on the Miracles of our Saviour* (1727–9) anticipated the theories of Christianity as a myth which Strauss put forward in the nineteenth century and caused Woolston to be tried for blasphemy in 1729. He was sentenced to a year's imprisonment and given a fine; his inability to pay the fine meant that he remained in prison until his death in 1733.

Another much discussed book, at the high point of deist controversies, was Matthew Tindal's *Christianity as Old as Creation* (1730), which presents a straightforward theistic view and is accompanied by strong doses of anti-clericalism. The book provoked numerous replies, one of which, by Dr Waterland, was in its turn anonymously opposed in Conyers Middleton's *Letter to Dr.*

*See *Reason, Ridicule and Religion* (1660–1750) by John Redwood, Thames and Hudson, 1976.

Waterland. Conyers Middleton pointed out that Christian apologists placed themselves in an impossible position by maintaining the historical accuracy of every Biblical statement.

Conyers Middleton (1683–1750) remained within the church and academic world while working upon books demonstrating the truth of natural religion. He was a fellow of Trinity College, Cambridge, and accepted various curacies. The sceptical tendencies of his *Letter to Dr. Waterland* caused him to be threatened with loss of his Cambridge degree and for many years he diverted his energies into a life of Cicero, much admired at the time for its style. In his last few years he launched another sceptical work: *A Free Inquiry Into the Miraculous Powers* (1748) created an enormous stir and somewhat overshadowed Hume's much more philosophically profound essay on miracles.

Bolingbroke (1678–1751), in retirement, read and admired Middleton's writings, saying of his 'very accurate search into ecclesiastical antiquity' that it was the 'sole principle upon which the consistency of the Gospels and their authority can be supported'. Bolingbroke's spectacular political rise and fall is well-known. He was erratic, brilliant, hedonistic. His father was a Restoration rake who left his son in the charge of his grandmother, Joanna. She forced him to spend many hours with volumes of the Presbyterian divine, Dr Manton, 'who taught my youth to yawn, and prepared me to be a High-Churchman, that I might never hear him read nor read him more'. Dr Manton's writings gave him a permanent distaste for all religion.

His political career came to an end when he was exiled in France after falling into disgrace after the accession of George I. At his estate in Orleans he was visited by Voltaire, who found him to have 'all the learning of his country and all the politeness of ours'. When he returned to England, Bolingbroke was barred from politics, but he attracted a circle of poets, politicians and pamphleteers who opposed Walpole's Whig ascendancy. Alexander Pope, the poet, was a neighbour and Bolingbroke's greatest legacy is often said to be the influence which his discussions with Pope had upon the deistic philosophy of the *Essay on Man*. His theological doubts were not printed until after his death, presumably because, as he wrote in his *Letter to Mr. Pope*: 'I have been a martyr of faction in politics, and have no vocation to be so in philosophy.' Bolingbroke believed in a Supreme Being limited by reason, whose attributes and wisdom are seen in his work and his world. This was accurately reflected in Pope's picture of 'The great directing Mind' of a world in which

> All are but parts of one stupendous whole,
> Whose body nature is, and God the soul. . . .

The posthumous publication of Bolingbroke's works caused Dr Johnson's indignant accusation that he charged the blunderbuss against religion and morality, but 'had no resolution to fire it off himself'. The accusation is unfair, but Bolingbroke's shot was somewhat tardy, since by 1751 much of the force of deistic controversies was spent. Some commentators claim that deism declined because of a diversion into industrialism and imperial expansion. The poet Gray wrote that 'the mode of freethinking has given way to the mode of not thinking at all'. The deist dislike of enthusiasm and taste for reasoned contemplation of nature was challenged by the zeal and emotionalism of evangelists like Whitefield and Wesley in the 1730s. The controversies about deism, however, may have become less heated, not because their force was spent but because of the wide currency of aspects of natural religion and because the arguments were entering a new phase in which more thoroughgoing atheism and materialism were being considered. Later in the century a Prime Minister such as the younger Pitt apparently 'never went to church in his life . . . never even talked about religion' (*Memoirs of Lady Hester Stanhope*), and a poet like Robert Burns could include a generous smattering of natural religion in his verse. Edmund Burke asked, in his *Reflections on the Revolution in France*: 'Who now reads Bolingbroke and the older deists?' But after Gibbon, Hume and encounters with French *philosophes*, who needed to?

Most deists earlier in the century had seen themselves as part of a respectable debate about the nature of religion and the universe. They were not part of a radical political tradition attacking a whole range of society's values and institutions. A man with claims to be described as the first British freethought lecturer and journalist, and who was in a more fiery radical mould, was the schoolmaster, Peter Annet (1693–1769). He lost his job as a schoolmaster in the 1740s after he published a bitter attack on the apologetics of Bishop Sherlock. He was probably the author of *A History of the Man After God's Own Heart* (1761), which considered the problem of God's favour for the immoral King David.

In 1761 he published nine numbers of the *Free Enquirer*, which impugned the authenticity of Old Testament history. In 1763 he was tried for blasphemy on the grounds that the *Free Enquirer* had ridiculed the Scriptures and tried to show 'that the prophet Moses was an impostor, and that the sacred truths and miracles recorded and set forth in the Pentateuch were impositions and false inventions, and thereby to infuse and propagate irreligious and diabolical opinions in the minds of his majesty's subjects and to shake the foundation of the civil and ecclesiastical government established in this kingdom'. Annet was convicted and, although in his seventies, was sentenced to one month's imprisonment in Newgate, to stand twice in the pillory and to endure one year's hard labour. He was described as 'withered with age', but retained sufficient self-respect and respect from others to keep a small school at Lambeth upon his release.

Peter Annet provides a link between the respectable, sometimes even clerical, deists and the later iconoclastic deists like Thomas Paine and atheist agitators like Richard Carlile. The influence of the British deists does much to explain the slow course of British free-thought before the nineteenth century. On the one hand the small advance was a crucial step on the road away from faith and the mysteries of religion, on the other hand the powerful presentation of a natural religion and 'directing Mind' delayed the move towards a complete disavowal of religious belief. The deists provide a crucial link with the Enlightenment, for Voltaire was impressed with the deists on his visit to England, Diderot was deeply affected by the moral concern of Shaftesbury, whose writings he translated, and d'Holbach relied heavily upon deistic texts in his campaign of pamphleteering against religion.

3

Voltaire: Écrasez l'Infâme

Voltaire (1694–1778) advanced no startlingly original ideas which challenged religious belief. He was a deist rather than a fully-fledged atheist. He was not a philosopher in the common usage of the word and had little patience with metaphysics or system-building – the 'metaphysico-theologico-cosmolonigology' of Pangloss in *Candide*. He was primarily a man of letters and ideas, immersed in the arguments and public affairs of his time and would most have wished to have been remembered as the author of successful tragedies and epic poems. He approved the social usefulness of religion and believed passionately in justice and tolerance; above all he is remembered as the flail of superstition in general and of the Catholic Church in particular.

'Voltaire' was the assumed name of François-Marie Arouet, born in 1694, the son of François Arouet, a notary and town official, and Marie Marguerite Daumoart from a family of the petty provincial nobility. He said that at his birth it was not expected that he could live. In his energetic eighty-four years' life, he was almost never free from the feeling of ill-health and frequently thought death was imminent. His skeletal frame and burning eyes suggest a tubercular constitution, but hypochondria certainly contributed to his incessant concern with his own health. Little of his childhood is known, and the few autobiographical accounts he left show no self-introspection and recount events, not intimate experiences or feelings. He was educated at a Jesuit school in Paris, Louis-le-Grand, which produced a number of freethinkers and brought him 'under the influence of teachers whose beliefs were at least masked by their classical humanism'.* Before leaving school he was experimenting with the writing of verse tragedy.

*Theodore Besterman. Voltaire's most thorough and admiring biographer. All translations in this chapter are by him unless otherwise indicated.

His father's ambition that he follow a sensible legal career came into conflict with his literary aspirations. Two early odes contain major themes of his life's work: 'Le Vrai Dieu' considers the contradiction of the Christian notion of a god who immolates himself by 'the sacrifice of God to God's own wrath', and 'La Chambre' bristles with indignation at social injustice: 'Hasten, destroy injustice, seize longed-for liberty at the end of the combat.'

Querying religion and the uneven justice of the *ancien régime* were common pastimes for the freethinking group at the Temple to which Voltaire gravitated in preference to law school. The group, known as the *libertins*, were led by Chaulieu, a hedonist dubbed the 'Anacreon of the Temple'. Voltaire's father thought he was sinking into a life of dissipation and packed him off to The Hague, where he had his first serious love affair and met refugees escaping religious persecution, who provided him with a vivid example of the consequences of intolerance. Returning in disguise after an unsuccessful attempt at elopement, he briefly pacified his father's furious threats to imprison him by *lettre de cachet* or exile him to the West Indies by resuming legal training. The lure of literature, a new lover and the Temple circle were irresistible. Voltaire overstepped even the liberal mood of the regency of Philippe d'Orléans in a rhyme insinuating an incestuous relationship between the Regent and his daughter.

Although always anxious to avoid direct conflict with the authorities, Voltaire was never prudent in choosing what to publish. His sense of defiance and mockery always overcame his consciousness of risks. When he was famous, caution over publications was argued by his friends, but it was frustrated by pirated editions and circulated manuscripts as well as his own reluctance to hide his wit under a bushel. There was a flourishing trade in the clandestine circulation of forbidden texts; censorship, which could be very severe, was also arbitrary and inefficient. Evasion of censorship gave to much of the writing of Voltaire and other *philosophes* a prevailing irony, which added to its appeal, but also (as intended) made it difficult to pin down the author's own views with any exactness. The arbitrariness and uncertainty of the censorship system must have especially infuriated Voltaire – and all his life he was concerned with justice and penal reform, which is not surprising from a man who spent much of his life in flight or exile or under threat of imprisonment.

His first exile, from Paris to Sully-sur-Loire, caused him little hardship, for he became the guest of the Duc de Sully, a fellow disciple of the Temple. A flattering letter disclaiming responsibility for the offending verses about Philippe d'Orléans enabled him to return to Paris. Thus began a life-long practice of disowning his own writing, a factor which complicated the accurate editing of his numerous works. He soon placed himself in danger again by a satirical piece about the boy king which led to his arrest without trial by *lettre de cachet*, and his first period in the Bastille. The Bastille became a symbol of a harsh and unjust system, but Voltaire does not seem to have suffered severely during his stay of almost a year in 1717 and 1718. He was able to write and began his epic poem about Henri IV. He changed his name from Arouet to Voltaire, and 'learned to harden myself against adversity, and I found in myself a courage I had not expected from the flightiness and the errors of my youth'.

A few months after release from the Bastille, Voltaire achieved his first resounding stage success with the production of *Oedipe* by the Comédie Française. It was an immediate success and contains deeply felt expressions of disgust with absolute authority and priests.

During the next half-dozen years Voltaire acquired a reputation as a poet and tragedian and moved in literary and aristocratic circles. He was also gaining notoriety for his deistic views and his criticism of Christianity. A long poem *Épître à Uranie*, written in 1722 but only published surreptitiously ten years later, contains a thoroughgoing condemnation of Christianity: 'So, lovely Uranie, you want me to become by your command a new Lucretius, to tear away with a bold hand, before you, the blindfold of superstition; to display before your eyes the dangerous image of the sacred lies with which the world is filled; and to learn from my philosophy to despise the horrors of the tomb and the terrors of the other life.' The writer asks to be shown the God who is hidden from us, not a monster that must be hated; a monster who created men in his own image so that he could abuse them, and gave them evil hearts in order to punish them. The deist complaint, to be reiterated by Thomas Paine and others, was that the Christian God was a travesty of the natural God of the universe.

Voltaire made diverse remarks about God in his numerous works and letters, preferred wit and irony to metaphysics, and often fitted his remarks to particular occasions. This has left much room for arguments about his deism and the nature of the God he believed in. The conclusion of *Épître à Uranie* written quite early in his life perhaps gives a fair picture of the impersonal but vaguely benign force he believed to underpin the universe:

> Consider that the eternal wisdom of the most high has with his hand engraved natural religion in the bottom of your heart; believe that the simple candour of your mind will not be the object of his immortal hatred; believe that before his throne, always, everywhere, the heart of just man is precious; believe that a modest bonze, a charitable dervish, find grace in his eyes rather than a merciless Jansenist or an ambitious pontiff. Ah! but what matter indeed by what name he be implored? Every homage is received, but none does him honour. A god has no need of our assiduous attentions: if he can be offended, it is only by injustice; he judges by our virtues, and not by our sacrifices.

The idea that all religions can contain a germ of deist truth was characteristic of a writer who was fascinated by information from all quarters of the globe and impressed by the relativity of customs. Fanaticism was what Voltaire thought so unworthy of any deity. The appeal of Henri IV as the subject matter for his epic poem *La Henriade* lay in that French king's ending of the sixteenth-century wars of religion. *La Henriade* was started during his first spell in the Bastille and published unofficially in 1723. Many regarded it as a masterpiece rivalling Virgil's epic. The description of the massacre of St Bartholomew could only appal a conventional French Catholic; so keenly did Voltaire feel the horror of massacre and religious persecution that he claimed he was invariably ill with a high temperature on St Bartholomew's Day.

In 1726 he quarrelled with the Chevalier Rohan and once again was thrown into the Bastille. Quarrelsomeness and over-reaction to criticism were a constant feature of his life and it cannot be said that the bitter feuds and quarrels upon which he wasted much nervous energy were all the responsibility of his enemies. Like all mortals he was infected with the weakness of his virtues: he detested injustice and unfairness, but he misinterpreted and was oversensitive to some criticism, and the vigour and animus which he showed in the demolition of superstition and restoring the wronged Calas or Sirven families were sprayed indiscriminately on all opponents. After a month in prison he gained release by offering voluntary self-exile and prepared to set sail for England.

His two years in England profoundly influenced his thinking. He was impressed with the religious tolerance, and thought deeply about the ideas of Locke and Newton. He was always torn between shining at the centre of society or seeking peace and quiet to pursue his addiction to work. For much of his stay he was a guest of Sir Everard Fawkener in the village of Wandsworth, but he met some English notables, re-established contact with Bolingbroke and corresponded with Pope and Swift. The fruits of a relatively quiet period in his life were gathered in his *Letters concerning the English Nation*, first published in 1733, and republished in France as *Lettres Philosophiques*; they were taken, rightly, as an implicit criticism of French society. The letters range over English government, trade, theatre, science and philosophy and praise English tolerance of different religious sects.

Voltaire's comments on the *Pensées* of Pascal were not published in the original version of the *Lettres* but appeared in the French 1734 edition. The contrast between Pascal and Voltaire finely illustrated the antithetical outlook of two quite distinct minds. Voltaire quotes Pascal: 'Let me therefore be no longer reproached for lack of clarity, since I make a point of it; but let the truth of religion be recognized in its very obscurity, in the little understanding we have of it and in our indifference about knowing it.' Voltaire replied: 'What strange marks of truth Pascal advances! What other marks does falsehood possess? What! in order to be believed it would be enough to say: *I am obscure, I am unintelligible!* It would be much more sensible to offer our eyes only the light of faith instead of these learned twilights.'

The *Lettres Philosophiques* caused an order to be sent out for Voltaire's arrest and for the book to be burnt by the public executioner, because it was 'the greatest danger for religion and public order'.

By this time Voltaire had been back in France for five years, during which his flow of plays, poems and letters never ceased and his interest in historical writing and research developed. In 1729, on his return from England, he devoted much effort to ensuring his financial security: he focused his intellect and knowledge of public affairs upon exploiting a loophole in a public lottery and acquired a fortune. Many writers will envy the single-mindedness with which he applied his abilities to ensuring sufficient finances for a lifetime's comfort. In 1731 he published a life of Charles XII of Sweden: part of the edition was seized by the police, its attitude to monarchy being less than adulatory. The following year he began work upon *Le Siècle de Louis XIV*, not to be published until 1751. He was among those eighteenth-century historians, of whom Bayle had been the precursor, who wrested history from the hands of the theologians.

Gibbon owed more to him than he cared to admit. A preface to *Charles XII* opens in a typically epigrammatic fashion: 'Incredulity . . . is the basis of all wisdom.' Voltaire had an ambivalent attitude to monarchy; he loathed arbitrary rule, but always hoped for an enlightened despot, a philosopher king. His relationship with Frederick II of Prussia and correspondence with Catherine the Great of Russia are evidence of this attitude. The nineteenth-century radicals who enjoyed his vitriolic condemnation of priestcraft, found in him no scourge of kingcraft.

Voltaire continued to write plays and *Zaïre* was performed in 1732. It opens with a declaration of the relativity of morals and religious customs. An increasing knowledge of different religions is a major aspect of the move away from belief in the absolute truth of any one religion in the eighteenth century. Zaïre says in the first scene of the play:

> Custom, law bent my first years to the religion of the happy Muslims. I see it too clearly: the care taken of our childhood forms our feelings, our habits, our belief. By the Ganges I would have been a slave of the false gods, a Christian in Paris, a Muslim here.

Mahomet, written and performed ten years later, contains similar implications. In demonstrating that the Mahommedan religion was based upon false miracles, personal ambition, and ruthless fanaticism, Voltaire, as his audience knew, was making a comment with relevance to Jesus Christ and Christianity. A dedication of the play to Pope Benedict XIV was written tongue in cheek.

In 1733 Voltaire fell in love with Madame du Châtelet. They were lovers and then close friends until her death during the birth of her child by Saint-Lambert in 1749. She was a woman of formidable intellect who had displayed a precocious knowledge of languages and possessed a remarkable aptitude for mathematics and philosophy: her partnership with Voltaire was intellectual as well as amorous. Voltaire spent much of their seventeen years' friendship at her château at Cirey in Champaigne. A correspondent's portrait of the pair catches a characteristic mood of this phase of his life: 'The two of them are there alone, plunged in gaiety. One writes verse in his corner. The other triangles in hers.'

Voltaire's interest in Newton was reinforced by Mme du Châtelet. He wrote the *Éléments de la Philosophie de Newton*, first published in 1738 in Amsterdam because refused a licence in France, which was extremely influential in popularizing the physics of Newton. 'God said "Let Newton be" and there was light', but the light was spread across Europe by Voltaire. From a viewpoint of alarm and antagonism, a Jesuit publication commented upon the efficacy of Voltaire's use of the printed word: 'Newton, the great Newton, was, it is said, buried in the abyss, in the shop of the first publisher who dared to print him. . . . M. Voltaire finally appeared, and at once Newton is understood or in the process of being understood; all Paris resounds with Newton, all Paris stammers Newton, all Paris studies and learns Newton.' Study of Newton made Voltaire realize that the metaphysics of Descartes was untenable. It was no longer possible to believe that God had endowed men with knowledge of basic principles and that logical arguments would give an understanding of scientific laws: 'The only way in which man can reason about objects is by his analysis. To begin straight from first principles belongs to God alone.' Newton left plenty of room for an active deity, whose intervention was necessary to keep the laws of nature functioning. Voltaire thought that atheists had been misled by Cartesian ideas, while 'almost all the Newtonians I have seen, accepting the vacuum and the finite nature of matter, accept as a result the existence of God'.

Court society had its appeal for Voltaire, though he was never at ease among courtiers. He was ambitious for fame and financial support, flattered by the thought that he could influence diplomats and rulers, and above all sought the favour which would give him protection to publish freely. He wrote an entertainment for the marriage of Louis XV's heir, wrote a popular poem praising a French victory at Fontenoy, was appointed official historiographer to the king, and finally elected to the Académie Française. But he complained of being the king's buffoon, and at fifty abandoned the life of a courtier with some relief after his predictable failure to be discreet.

Voltaire never quite abandoned his vain dream of a philosopher-king, whose tolerant and benevolent rule would benefit all his subjects. His relationship with Frederick II of Prussia shows all the characteristics of an intense love-hate relationship. Voltaire received his first letter of admiration from Frederick in 1736, while he was crown prince. The correspondence, which reached nearly a thousand letters, continued until Voltaire's death. Disenchantment with Voltaire's hopes for enlightened rule from Frederick II must have quickly arrived when, on his accession in 1740, Frederick embarked on military conquests ill-befitting a king devoted to benevolence and reason. They discussed philosophy seriously, they were a mutual admiration society, but their motives and interests were quite antithetical. Frederick wanted Voltaire, the most renowned man of letters in all Europe, as a jewel in his court; how far Voltaire was deceived by this autocratic egomaniac and how far he was in his own way attempting to use the situation to his own advantage is not easy to ascertain.

After the death of Mme du Châtelet and more than usually weary of the pursuit of his publications by the French authorities, he acceded to Frederick's wooing and departed for Berlin. He had every comfort and found time for study, writing and a love affair, in between correcting Frederick's execrable verse. Other *philosophes* at the court included the materialist La Mettrie; and he it was who reported Frederick's overheard comments about Voltaire: 'I shall need him another year at most; you squeeze the orange and you throw away the peel.' Voltaire was not to depart without a retaliatory squeeze, but meanwhile completed and saw through publication *Le Siècle de Louis XIV*.

The parting quarrel between Frederick and Voltaire was provoked by a scientific argument between König and Maupertuis in which each took sides: it really concerned who was to serve the interest of whom, and spiralled into a furious clash in which Frederick called Voltaire 'the greatest rascal in Europe' and Voltaire deserted the court. Voltaire converted the whole business into a biting and witty satire, *Diatribe du docteur Akakia*, and Frederick was the laughing-stock of Europe when he ordered it to be burnt in a public square in Berlin. Voltaire fled to Frankfurt, but he and his niece, Mme Denis, suffered the indignity of arrest at bayonet point before achieving freedom. Some years later Voltaire resumed correspondence with Frederick, and there can be no doubting the fascination for him of the man he described as 'Mon Patron, mon disciple, mon persécuteur'.

After an unsettled year, Voltaire, perhaps influenced by a printer who offered to publish his work with care, bought a country house outside the city of Geneva in 1755. He named the house Les Délices: 'It is a palace for a philosopher with the gardens of Epicurus: it is a delicious retreat.' His niece, who had been his mistress since 1744, was to be his permanent companion for his remaining years. He sought peace and took an increased interest in gardening and his estate. The Calvinist Genevan authorities at first relaxed their dispensation sufficiently to allow this deist, officially a Catholic, to settle in their republic.

Voltaire's hopes of calm collapsed within a few months as strains developed between himself and the Genevan Calvinists. At first he was compelled to repudiate a pirated edition of parts of his long poem about Joan of Arc, *La Pucelle*. Then a poem in which he praised the pleasures of his Swiss haven was publicly burnt because of a tactless reference to a former Duke of Savoy. Irritation increased when the public were forbidden to attend theatrical performances at the theatre which he built at Les Délices. A more serious cause of friction was a reference to Calvin in a public letter in which he praised the tolerance of the Genevans: he overestimated this, for he was formally condemned by the civil and religious authorities in Geneva for his phrase, 'Calvin had an atrocious soul as well as an enlightened mind'. The incident which most outraged the Genevan authorities was the publication of the article on Geneva in *L'Encyclopédie*. D'Alembert had written the piece, but, since he had stayed with Voltaire while working upon it, Voltaire was implicated. The article was extremely complimentary to Geneva, but the inaccurate and over-optimistic view that the Genevan church was essentially Socinian (a European sect which foreshadowed Unitarianism) and had turned Christianity into an ethical doctrine caused a furious assertion of Calvinist dogmatism. Voltaire sought another home and in 1759 bought an estate at Ferney, just within the French border but distant from the French authorities.

Voltaire's period at Les Délices was extremely productive. The pirated edition of *La Pucelle* appeared. He had begun the poem as early as 1730, but it was only given an authorized publication in 1762. A burlesque epic of twenty-one books, it revolves round the idea that the virginity of Joan of Arc had been an essential ingredient in her role as saviour of France – an idea which Voltaire thought a huge joke and presented with great ribaldry. A depiction of Hell wherein resided many worthies such as Marcus Aurelius, 'the good Trajan', 'eloquent Cicero' and 'Socrates, child of wisdom', as well as preachers, prelates, monks and nuns, would have offended believers. (In a later letter Voltaire suggested, as a piece of hilarity, that Joan of Arc might one day be canonized.)

Experience was contributing to a darker strand in Voltaire's work; the quarrels in Berlin and friction with the Genevan authorities were bitter experiences and the Seven Years' War and the Lisbon earthquake horrified Europeans. Voltaire was deeply affected by the earthquake, which had caused massive destruction and loss of life, and wrote a poem in response to the event. A letter written while preparing the poem shows his state of mind:

> My dear sir, nature is very cruel. One would find it hard to imagine how the laws of movement cause such frightful disasters in the *best of possible worlds*. A hundred thousand ants, our fellows, crushed all at once in our ant-hill, and half of them perishing, no doubt in unspeakable agony, beneath the wreckage from which they cannot be drawn. Families ruined all over Europe, the fortune of a hundred businessmen, your compatriots, swallowed up in the ruins of Lisbon. What a wretched gamble is the game of human life! What will the preachers say, especially if the palace of the Inquisition is still standing? I flatter myself that at least the reverend father inquisitors have been crushed like others. That ought to teach men not to persecute each other, for while a few holy scoundrels burn a few fanatics, the earth swallows up one and all.

He attacks Leibniz, the great German philosopher and deist, whose view of God's creation of the universe as 'the best of all possible worlds' was caricatured: 'Leibniz does not tell me by what invisible twists an eternal disorder, a chaos of misfortunes, mingles real sorrow with our vain pleasures in the best arranged of possible universes, nor why the guilty suffer alike this inevitable evil. . . .' But he did not offer his own solution to the problem of evil.

His best-known treatment of this theme came in his most popular work, *Candide*. Its wit, sharpness and topicality caused six thousand copies to be sold within weeks of publication in 1759. The sly irony enraged and delighted Europe and *Candide* and his other *contes*, especially *L'Ingénu*, are the most enduring examples of attack on religion by ridicule rather than analysis.

Candide, a naive and innocent young man, is an ideal vehicle for exposing some of the absurdities of philosophy and religion. In South America he escapes death because he is not a Jesuit: 'But after all, there is some good in the pure state of nature, since these people instead of eating me, offered me a thousand civilities as soon as they knew I was not a Jesuit.' Voltaire's belief in the universality of religion and the irrelevance of priests is seen when Candide finds himself in El Dorado:

> Candide was curious to see the priests; and asked where they were. The good old man smiled. 'My friends,' said he, 'we are all priests; the King and all the heads of families solemnly sing praises every morning, accompanied by five or six thousand musicians.' 'What! Have you no monks to teach, to dispute, to govern, to intrigue and to burn people who do not agree with them?' 'For that, we should have

> to become fools,' said the old man; 'here we are of the same opinion and do not understand what you mean with your monks.'

The idea that a deity takes a personal interest in each individual is queried in the words of a Dervish: 'When his highness sends a ship to Egypt, does he worry about the comfort or discomfort of the rats in the ship?' Apart from the excuse for gibes in all directions, *Candide* counters the fatalism of Panglossian belief in 'the best of all possible worlds'. Voltaire wrote in the margin of his copy of Pope's *Essay on Man*: 'What can I hope when all is right?' The famous conclusion to *Candide*, 'Il faut cultiver notre jardin', does not endorse a selfish isolated existence, but implies the need for cultivation, action and work. Voltaire was a meliorist and reformist, not a utopian or fatalist.

In his last nineteen years at Ferney, Voltaire lived out a far from serene old age. His writing was more *engagé* than ever, and his role as a reformer and campaigner developed. Three cases of injustice absorbed much of his energies in the 1760s: the Calas case, the plight of the Sirven family, and the execution of La Barre. All three cases involved religious bigotry. The Calas case was made a *cause célèbre* by Voltaire's involvement. The son of the Protestant Jean Calas was found dead (probably by suicide), and his family were accused of murdering him to prevent him becoming a Catholic. Religious hysteria in Toulouse led to the torture and execution of Jean Calas. Voltaire, suspicious of the charge that a whole family would combine to murder one of its members, investigated and became convinced of injustice. His campaign to restore the reputation of the family took several years and it has been claimed that he was the first man of letters to marshal public opinion in defence of a cause. His essay *Traité sur la tolérance* emerged from his involvement with the case; its publication was delayed in order not to prejudice the outcome.

A similar case, that of the Sirven family, took nine years to resolve. The family were accused of causing the death of their daughter to prevent Catholic conversion. The case of La Barre, tortured and executed for blasphemy in 1766, shocked Voltaire deeply. This youth of nineteen refused to doff his hat to a religious procession and mutilated a wooden crucifix. Voltaire was the more haunted by 'this sentence so execrable, and at the same time so absurd, which is an eternal disgrace to France', because possession of his *Dictionnaire Philosophique* may have contributed to La Barre's punishment.

The *Dictionnaire Philosophique* was one of the most important of his later works and contained a convenient summation of his ideas in a style which is still extremely readable. The first edition, published in 1764, was immediately condemned by the government and church as an 'alphabetical abomination'. Voltaire, who had written some articles for the *Encyclopédie* edited by Diderot, was critical of that compendium's caution in the face of the authorities. He also thought a more concise book would have a wider impact: 'Twenty folio volumes will never make a revolution. It is the little portable volumes of thirty *sous* that are to be feared. Had the gospel cost twelve hundred sesterces the Christian religion would never have been established.'

The *Dictionnaire*'s references to religion and the Bible are lucid and full of irony (biblical knowledge was discouraged by the Catholic church). He described his approach:

> I think the best way to fall on the infamous [*l'infâme* meant the Church for Voltaire] is to seem to have no wish to attack it; to disentangle a little chaos of antiquity; to try to make these things rather interesting: to make ancient history as agreeable as possible; to show how much we have been misled in all things; to demonstrate how much is modern in all things thought to be ancient, and how ridiculous are many things alleged to be respectable; to let the reader draw his own conclusions.

The essence of the *Dictionnaire Philosophique* lay in exact examination of biblical 'events', satire of selective use of the Bible and comparison of Christianity with an independent ethical code. His humour is seen in an entry on Councils:

> It is reported in the supplement of the council of Nicaea that the fathers, being very perplexed to know which were the cryphal or apocryphal books of the Old and New Testaments, put them all pell-mell on an altar, and the books to be rejected fell to the ground. It is a pity that this eloquent procedure has not survived.

A dialogue about a priest's catechism shows the non-theological simple priest whom Voltaire could admire:

> I shall always speak of morality and never of controversy. God forbid that I should elaborate on concomitant grace, the efficacious grace we resist, the sufficient grace which does not suffice; or examine whether the angels who ate with Abraham and Lot had bodies or whether they pretended to eat. There are a thousand things my audience would not

understand, nor I either. I shall try to make good men and to be good myself, but I shall not create theologians, and I shall be one as little as I can.

This brings the retort:

Oh! what a good priest! I'd like to buy a country house in your parish.

The entry under 'God' concludes with a delightful anecdote warning against preaching any clear anthropomorphic view of God:

Before receiving your instruction, I must tell you what happened to me one day. I had just had a closet built at the end of my garden. I heard a mole arguing with a cockchafer; 'Here's a fine structure,' said the mole, 'it must have been a very powerful mole who did this work.' 'You're joking,' said the cockchafer; 'it's a cockchafer full of genius who is the architect of this building.' From that moment I resolved never to argue.

The substantial entry under Atheism condemns that outlook as did his critical reply to d'Holbach's materialistic *Système de la nature* in 1770. In the *Dictionnaire* he refers to Bayle's question whether a society of atheists was possible, and in answering in the affirmative points to the Roman senate at the time of Cicero. He thought fanaticism was infinitely more dangerous than atheism and that the ambitious and voluptuous had better things to do than 'compare Lucretius with Socrates'. Nevertheless he said atheists were misguided and if they existed did so in reaction to the monstrous representatives of religion:

If there are atheists, who is to be blamed if not the mercenary tyrants of souls who, in revolting us against their swindles, compel some feeble spirits to deny the God whom these monsters dishonour?

The Atheist article contains the frequently implied view that religion is a useful tool for maintaining public order: 'It is absolutely necessary for princes to have deeply engraved in their minds the notion of a supreme being, creator, ruler, remunerator, and avenger'. This is a view not entirely consistent with his suffering at the hands of avenging rulers.

At Ferney he was the ruler of his own tiny kingdom. His benevolence caused the growth of a prosperous community, his tolerance drew watchmakers from Switzerland, he fought excessive government taxes and church tithes. He came to loathe his role as a 'sight' for visiting tourists. His building of a church surprised contemporaries, and his attendance at two Easter communion services, on one occasion preaching against drinking and theft, was seen as controversial and provocative. The reasons for his presence are unclear: maybe he genuinely wanted to be an 'ethical priest' and '*encourager les autres*' in good behaviour; perhaps, as death approached, he feared denial of a respectable burial; did he enjoy the idea that his actions were provocative and would enrage more orthodox priests? Presumably his motives were mixed.

A stroke at the age of seventy-three did not diminish his powers. In the last decade he continued to pour forth a stream of pamphlets, letters, corrected editions, and articles. Disagreement with atheism and adherence to deism did not cause his assault on *l'infâme* to diminish. *Homélies prononcées à Londres* dealt with atheism, superstition and the Old and New Testaments. The conclusion is forceful:

> Let us therefore reject all superstition in order to become more human; but in speaking against fanaticism, let us not imitate the fanatics: they are sick men in delirium who want to chastise their doctors. Let us assuage their ills, and never embitter them, and let us pour drop by drop into their souls the divine balm of toleration, which they would reject with horror if it were offered to them all at once.

His enthusiasm for dramatic writing, which had successfully launched his literary career, did not decline. He wrote two plays, *Irène* and *Agathode*, in his eighty-fourth year. Mme Denis, with whom his relationship was now less easy, spent time in Paris and persuaded Voltaire, who had long contemplated, feared and dreamed of returning to the capital, to travel there to supervise a production of one of his last plays. He embarked in March 1778 and returned to Paris in triumph. He was met by representatives of the Académie Française and Comédie Française and received hundreds of callers, including Benjamin Franklin. His apotheosis, as it has become known, was to be crowned and cheered at a performance of one of his plays. The whirl of activity was too much for him; his health broke and within three months he died.

Priests eager for a death-bed conversion bombarded him with letters and visits to which he responded with a contradiction of evasive and conciliatory reactions. A declaration in the presence of his loyal secretary, Wagnière, enunciated his position: 'I died worshipping God, loving my friends, not hating my enemies, detesting superstition.' His biographer, Besterman, has commented that it 'only remained for the church to besmirch his deathbed and to poison his memory'. A plan to prevent a decent burial was foiled, but collected editions of his work were suppressed, and the Archbishop of Vienne told his parishioners that it was a mortal sin to subscribe to a complete edition of his writings. But, though much of his writing was polemical and of his time, he is still read for his wit and perspicuity, and admired for his energy and passionate efforts on behalf of tolerance and justice. He complained that Pascal taught men to hate and proclaimed his own preference: 'I would sooner teach them to love one another.'

> Il [Pascal] enseigne aux humains à se haïr eux-mêmes,
> Je voudrais malgré lui leur apprendre à s'aimer.

4
Diderot and the encyclopedists: The mastery of knowledge

The *Encyclopédie*, published between 1751 and 1765, is a key work of the Enlightenment. Its seventeen volumes were the product of twenty years' toil and the aim was both a summary of all human knowledge and a programme to revolutionize man's thinking. Diderot edited the *Encyclopédie* and wrote much of it himself, but many of the *philosophes* contributed. The *philosophes* – propagandists, journalists, and men of public affairs as much as philosophers – came to be seen as a dangerous cabal by their opponents in the middle of the eighteenth century. They were more overtly atheistic than any other prominent literary group (except perhaps the Bloomsbury Group) and their confidence in progress through reason, science, knowledge and social reform was seen as a direct threat to the Church. The alarm with which the orthodox reacted to the *philosophes* was demonstrated by the 'Due Warning' of a minor publicist, Jacob-Nicolas Moreau, who invented the word 'Cacouac' to ridicule them as a species of 'savage, fiercer and more redoubtable than the Caribs. Their weapons consist solely of a poison hidden under their tongues . . . Their whole substance is nothing but venom and corruption' (*Mercure de France*, October 1757). The view of the *philosophes* themselves was expressed by d'Alembert in his *Éléments de Philosophie* (1759):

> If one examines carefully the mid-point of the century in which we live, the events which excite us or at any rate occupy our minds, our customs, our achievements, and even our diversions, it is difficult not to see that in some respects a very remarkable change in our ideas is taking place, a change whose rapidity seems to promise an even greater transformation to come. Time alone will tell what will be the goal, the nature, and the limits of this revolution, whose shortcomings and merits will be better known to posterity than to us . . . Our century is called, accordingly, the century of philosophy *par excellence*.

Diderot (1713–1784) was born in Langres and his family were noted for their church connections. At a local Jesuit college Diderot won prizes and later wrote of the impact which the classics had made upon him: 'At an early age I sucked up the milk of Homer, Virgil, Horace, Terence, Anacreon, Plato and Euripides, diluted with that of Moses and the prophets.' A quotation from an adult work displays his attitude to religious feelings as psychological experiences and may be a memory of his adolescence:* 'There comes a moment during which almost every girl or boy falls into melancholy; they are tormented by a vague inquietude which rests on everything and finds nothing to calm it. They seek solitude; they weep; the silence to be found in cloister attracts them: the image of peace that seems to reign in religious houses seduces them. They mistake the first manifestations of a developing sexual nature for the voice of God calling them to Himself; and it is precisely when nature is inciting them that they embrace a fashion of life contrary to nature's wish' (*James the Fatalist*).

Whether in quest of religion or the excitement of the capital city, the youthful Diderot was discovered by his father about to run away to Paris. The father turned an escapade into a new start in life by taking his son to Paris. Information about Diderot's life in Paris from the ages of sixteen to twenty-nine is scarce. He continued his education, probably at the Jesuit college, Louis-le-Grand, and then gained a Master of Arts degree at the University of Paris. At first his father sent money, but as he failed to settle down to a profession relations became strained and he suffered considerable poverty. He studied, tutored, became a regular theatre-goer, wrote sermons and did translation work.

In 1741 he met Anne-Toinette Champion, the pious, upright, domestic, hard-working woman who was to become his wife. This was a most unsuitable match; he was extravagant and disorganized, she sensible and prudent.

He scratched an income from free-lance journalism and translation during the early years of his marriage. He had taught himself English and in 1745 his translation of Lord Shaftesbury's *An Inquiry Concerning Virtue and Merit* was published. Shaftesbury's deism and interest in morality influenced Diderot profoundly. A dedicatory epistle he wrote contains a reproof of religious conflict: 'But if you will recall the history of our civil troubles, you will see half the nation bathe itself, out of piety, in the blood of the other half, and

*A point made by Diderot's most thorough biographer, Arthur Wilson.

violate the fundamental feelings of humanity in order to sustain the cause of God: as though it were necessary to cease to be a man in order to prove oneself religious!' In addition to religious disputes, the corrupt state of the church enmeshed in the *ancien régime* fuelled the *philosophes*' contempt for institutional religion.

Diderot's first two original works show his interest in the question of religion, though at this stage he was deistic rather than atheistic. The *Pensées Philosophiques* (1746) is a collection of aphorisms, such as 'Superstition is more injurious to God than atheism'. Christianity no longer seemed tenable to him: 'If there were a reason for preferring the Christian religion to natural religion, it would be because the former offers us, on the nature of God and man, enlightenment that the latter lacks. Now, this is not at all the case; for Christianity, instead of clarifying, gives rise to an infinite multitude of obscurities and difficulties.'

The Sceptic's Walk (1747) was a 'conversation concerning religion, philosophy and the world'. It presents an allegory which describes the path of thorns (Christianity), of chestnut trees (philosophical deism), and of flowers (libertinism). Most favourably portrayed is the 'tranquil abode' of the chestnut path of philosophical deism: 'Gentleness and peacefulness regulate our proceedings; theirs are dictated by fury. We employ reason, they accumulate faggots. They preach nothing but love, and breathe nothing but blood. Their words are humane, but their hearts are cruel.'

The Paris Parlement condemned the *Pensées Philosophiques* and ordered it to be burned, declaring that it 'presents to restless and reckless spirits the venom of the most criminal and absurd opinions that the depravity of human reason is capable of; and by an affected uncertainty places all religions on almost the same level, in order to finish up by not accepting any'. Such pronouncements were a useful advertisement to those who sought sceptical works, but they also indicated the dangerous areas into which Diderot was advancing. *The Sceptic's Walk* must have been read clandestinely, for it was not published until long after his death.

Diderot translated a medical dictionary in three volumes by Robert James, assisted by Toussaint, whose *Les Moeurs* (1748) was one of the first books in France to set out the arguments for natural morality without religious belief. This gave Diderot an abiding interest in physiology, but more important it gave him experience of encyclopedia work. He was approached by a publisher with the idea of translating Ephraim Chambers' *Cyclopaedia, or Universal*

Dictionary of the Arts and Sciences. The details of individual publishers and translators are complex, but by 1746 Diderot was on the payroll and the project had changed into a plan to produce a substantial, original French *Encyclopédie*. Diderot may have initiated the nationalistic and commercial venture of a monumental French encyclopedia, certainly by 1747 he was its driving force, having become chief editor with d'Alembert as his assistant.

His reputation as a writer was established by the publication of his *Letter on the Blind* – an essay occasioned by public interest in the public removal of blindfolds after an operation on cataracts on a girl cured of congenital blindness. It created a considerable stir and there were two editions in 1749. He discussed the psychology of blindness with great understanding and also raised matters of perception and the nature of knowledge, including knowledge of God. He deduced the relativity of ethics and moved towards a position of implicit atheistic materialism. He thought deprivation of sensory information would produce variations in moral sense, and suggested that the habit of dressing for appearance would mean nothing to a blind person. The argument parallels that by which Montesquieu and others had sought to demonstrate the relativity of morals by description of the variation of customs between different countries. It told strongly against a universal Christian morality donated by God to man.

Diderot also used the perspective of a blind person to query natural religion and the idea that a deity was evident in the marvels of nature. He invented a dying speech for the famous English mathematician, Nicholas Saunderson, in which he protested that the marvels of nature were no argument for God to someone 'condemned to pass my life in darkness': 'Let us not talk of that great and beautiful spectacle which was never made for me!' Saunderson proceeds to demolish the idea that God explained all that was inexplicable:

> We encounter some phenomenon that is, in our opinion, beyond the powers of man, and immediately we say, 'Is it the work of God'. Our vanity will admit no lesser explanation. Can we not reason with a little less pride and a little more philosophy? If nature presents us with a knot that is difficult to untie, then let us leave it as it is; let us not insist on cutting it there and then and on employing for the task the hand of a being who thereupon becomes a knot even more difficult to untie than the first. Ask an Indian why the globe remains suspended in the air and he will reply that it is borne on the back of an elephant. And on what

> does the elephant rest? On a tortoise. And the tortoise, who supports that?*

Unfortunately Saunderson had made no such speech and the Royal Society was indignant: this kind of inaccuracy gave an advantage to Diderot's opponents, but was characteristic of his prodigious and effervescent talent. Voltaire wrote to Diderot to comment upon *Letter on the Blind* and they began a correspondence that was never very enthusiastic. Voltaire defended the concept of God, and Diderot conceded: 'I believe in God, although I live very happily with atheists. . . . It is very important not to mistake hemlock for parsley; but not at all so to believe or not in God.' Despite this concession none of his later writings indicate a clear belief in God.

Diderot continued his preparation of the *Encyclopédie*, but in July 1749 his rooms were searched for manuscripts 'contrary to Religion, the State, or Morals' and he was arrested and imprisoned at Vincennes. Threats of disorder had led to a panic by the authorities and many suspect writers were rounded up. (A personal dislike of Diderot on the part of the Secretary of State for War and Director of Publications, the Count d'Argenson, may have contributed to his arrest.)

In the first few weeks in prison, he was so desperately frustrated at his inability to put his irrepressible flow of ideas on paper that he used a toothpick for a pen and a mixture of wine and pulverized slate for ink and covered the margins of the few books in his possession with script. His conditions soon improved, perhaps as a result of representations from Voltaire to the prison governor, the Marquis du Châtelet, who was a relative of Voltaire's lover. He was able to set up an editorial office and receive visits from his wife and friends.

The pleadings of his publisher pointing out that the *Encyclopédie* was 'undertaken for the glory of France and the shame of England' may have effected his release, which occurred after three months. Under interrogation he had denied authorship of his works and then confessed and promised not to offend again: he was not martyr material and, unlike Voltaire, would have found exile from Parisian *salons* and friendships unendurable. He did not want to lose the prospect of a long-term salary as editor of a work of potential international fame, and knew he must learn to steer a path between the permissible and the forbidden in the arbitrary and erratic censor-

*Diderot's *Selected Writings*. Edited by Lester G. Crocker, translated by Derek Coltman.

ship of eighteenth-century France. Imprisonment left an indelible mark and caused a certain caution and indirectness in the *Encyclopédie* (of which Voltaire complained) and his failure to publish his more challenging works in later life.

By 1750 the first volume of the *Encyclopédie* was heralded by publication of a *Prospectus*. This indicated the range of the work and aimed to attract subscribers. It referred to a systematic organization of knowledge that relied heavily upon Bacon's *Novum Organum* and Jesuits immediately levelled an accusation of plagiarism. This initial joust between Jesuits and encyclopedists was to develop into a bitter feud, but at first served to whet the public appetite. The philosophy and aims of the *Encyclopédie* were set out in the *Preliminary Discourse* by d'Alembert which appeared with the first volume in 1751. D'Alembert was at pains to counter the accusation of plagiarism, by full acknowledgement of the debt to Bacon's classification of knowledge. The debt to Bacon's attitude to science and to Bayle's thoroughgoing scepticism was greater. D'Alembert's *Discourse* is often quoted as a lucid and complete summary of the ideas of the *philosophes*.

The *Discourse* suggested that empirical gathering of knowledge would give mankind the power of changing his destiny and wanted it to extend to an 'experimental physics of the soul'. The *Encyclopédie* therefore became much more than a work of reference: it became a programme for change and transferred knowledge and authority from the clerical to the secular domain. The *Discourse* makes reference to the Omnipotent Being and Supreme Intelligence – distinctly more abstract concepts than most Christians would have used – and leaves little room for revealed religion: 'A few truths to be believed, a small number of precepts to be practised: such are the essentials to which revealed religion is reduced.' D'Alembert publicly denied that the method of the *Encyclopédie* refuted divine knowledge; but many readers deduced that it left little room for a divine role.

The first volume of the *Encyclopédie* was typical of what was to follow in a further seventeen volumes. Part of its popularity was due to its practical use as a book of reference covering towns and countries, words, synonyms and grammar. Thorough attention to trade and technology enhanced this aspect of the work – two of Diderot's most substantial articles in the first volume were on steel and on agriculture. A long article by Diderot on 'Encyclopédie' in Volume V justified the venture and demonstrated his belief that increased knowledge was favourable to human betterment: his aim was that 'our descendants being better instructed, may become at the same time more virtuous and happy; and that we may not die without having deserved well of the human race'.

Diderot had written in his *Pensées Philosophiques* that 'scepticism is the first step towards truth' – and this, rather than direct assault upon religion, was the approach of the *Encyclopédie*. The use of cross-references as signposts to sceptical items placed in unlikely places became famous. An article on the obscure Roman god of speech, Aius Locutus, was the occasion for a defence of freedom of speech, though even here criticism of censorship was tempered by a suggestion that writings critical of religion or government should only appear in a learned language.

Two favourite techniques for casting doubt on the teachings of Christianity were a description of sects, heresies and other religions which demonstrated the astonishing variety of religious practice, and the lambasting of pagan religions which turned out to contain practices suspiciously similar to those of Christianity. The article on Christianity made many comparisons with Mohammedanism and treated religion as a social phenomenon. The article on Damnation contained a straight-faced description of Christian doctrine which managed to query its whole rationale while remaining ostensibly respectful towards Christian ideas.

There was much querying of biblical facts, without direct challenge to the truth of the Bible. An article on Noah's ark looked at the problems of building it in such meticulous detail as to leave in doubt the possibility of it ever having been successfully constructed, let alone launched upon the seas filled with its comprehensive quota of animals. The contrast between fundamentalist interpretations of the Bible and empirical observation was starkly illustrated in a contemporary anecdote: 'One day in the eighteenth century some Swedish scientists discovered a certain alteration in the shores of the Baltic. Immediately the theologians of Stockholm made representations to the government that "this remark of the Swedish scientists, not being consistent with Genesis, must be condemned." To whom reply was made that God had made both the Baltic and Genesis, and that, if there was any contradiction between the two works, the error must lie in the copies that we have of the book, rather than in the Baltic Sea, of which we have the original' (Duclos, *Les Encyclopédistes*).

The *philosophes*' belief in their own capacities is seen in the article on the Chaldeans: 'One must be oneself very little of a philosopher not to feel that the finest privilege of our reason consists in not believing in anything by the impulsion of a blind and mechanical instinct, and that it is to dishonour reason to put it in bonds as the Chaldeans did. Man is born to think for himself.' The political aspects of the *Encyclopédie* in areas such as justice, government, natural right and authority, were quite as alarming to the orthodox and the rulers as the religious aspect. The frontispiece to the 1751 edition of the first volume of the *Encyclopédie* contains an illustration of Truth 'wrapped in a veil, radiant with light which parts the clouds and disperses them'; lifting the veil from Truth are Reason and Philosophy, and at her feet are Theology and all the branches of knowledge.

Religious leaders did not like being placed at the feet of Truth and below Reason and Philosophy and Diderot had to face furious opposition. Despite commercial success and increasing demand, a satirical verse indicated the dangers which opponents saw in the *Encyclopédie*:

Je suis bien encyclopédiste,
Je connais le mal et le bien.
Je suis Diderot à la piste;
Je connais tout, je ne crois rien.

(I am a good Encyclopaedist
I know both good and evil.
I follow hot on Diderot's trail;
I know everything and believe nothing.)

The events surrounding the thesis of the Abbé de Prades crystallized early opposition. The Abbé de Prades was acquainted with the *philosophes* and contributed to the *Encyclopédie*. He submitted his thesis to the theology faculty of the University of Sorbonne and it was accepted, but it had been approved on the nod by a theologian preoccupied with his own work. His thesis was thought to defend natural religion and to contain parallels with the *Preliminary Discourse*. It was condemned by the Sorbonne, the Archbishop of Paris and the Pope. Not all eighteenth-century clerics were totally opposed to natural religion, but with the publication of the *Encyclopédie* religion and irreligion were polarized and the various shades of deism and natural religion began to disappear. The Bishop of Montaubon, to whom the Abbé de Prades was responsible, said:

> Up till now Hell has vomited its venom, so to speak, drop by drop. Today there are torrents of errors and impieties which tend toward nothing less than the submerging of Faith, Religion, Virtues, the Church, Subordination, the Laws, and Reason. Past centuries have witnessed the birth of sects that, while attacking some Dogmas, have respected a great number of them; it was reserved to ours to see impiety forming a system that overturns all of them at one and the same time.

Pamphlets from either side focused upon the case of Prades, who prudently slipped away to the court of Frederick the Great. There were accusations that Diderot and d'Alembert had written parts of the Abbé's thesis and their project was clouded in odium by association. At the same time Jesuit factions attempted, unsuccessfully, to seize editorial control of what promised to be a popular venture.*

An *arrêt* from the Conseil du Roy suppressed further publication, sale and distribution of the *Encyclopédie* in 1752. This prohibition was rendered ineffective by the assistance of the director of publications, Malesherbes, who arranged for tacit permission provided that articles were submitted to nominated theologians. Malesherbes was a man with such devotion to genuine free speech for all views that he annoyed even the *philosophes* by permitting publication of rabid criticism of them. It was said that 'the Encyclopedists were mistaken in not believing in Providence, for it was manifestly for their sake that Providence gave to Malesherbes the direction of the book trade'.

The position of the *Encyclopédie* became even less secure in 1757. An attempt to assassinate Louis XV led to an attack on freedom of ideas and a royal proclamation threatening death to all writing or publishing material 'tending to attack religion, to rouse opinions, to impair Our authority, and to trouble the order and tranquillity of Our States'. French failure in the Seven Years' War accentuated opposition to the *philosophes*, who were associated in the public eye with the enemy, Frederick the Great. Jesuit criticisms were getting bolder and one Jesuit preached a sermon against the *Encyclopédie* in the presence of the king. The article on Geneva, by d'Alembert, which caused Voltaire difficulty with the Genevan authorities, created public controversy. D'Alembert showed reluctance to continue in the face of continual hostility, writing to Voltaire in 1758:

* So bitterly hostile to the *Encyclopédie* were the Jesuits that two hundreds years later a Jesuit periodical referred to it as 'the most formidable machine that was ever set up against religion' ('Deuxieme centenaire de *L'Encyclopédie*', *Études*, CCLXXII [1952]).

'I am worn out by the insults and vexations that this work brings down on us.'

The publication of *De l'Esprit* by Helvétius in 1758 shocked orthodox readers. Though he was not a contributor to the *Encyclopédie*, the materialism and utilitarian ethics of Helvétius were thought to demonstrate the excesses to which the ideas of the *philosophes* could lead. The Attorney General expressed what seemed to be a widespread fear in 1759, when he warned the Parlement of Paris that 'there is a project formed, a Society organized, to propagate materialism, to destroy Religion, to inspire a spirit of independence, and to nourish the corruption of morals'. The Parlement decreed that the sale and publication of the *Encyclopédie* be suspended. A couple of months later a royal decree completely suppressed it because of 'the irreparable damage that results from it in regard to morality and religion'.

The extensive range of Diderot's interests is seen in his vivid and intimate letters to his friend Sophie Volland. He also wrote plays and art criticism and published, anonymously, *Thoughts on the Interpretation of Nature*, an essay on the scientific method with an epigraph from Lucretius: 'Those things that are in the light we behold from darkness.' But his life was dominated by his work on the *Encyclopédie*: coping with proofs, contributors and printers as well as writing his own substantial articles.

Undaunted by the ban in 1759, Diderot decided to continue the work underground and publish and sell it abroad if necessary. He did this in the face of the real danger of arrest, and friends urged flight. To add to his woes his father died at this time. Although he suffered some months of nervous exhaustion, he was resilient and able to force himself to return to work on the *Encyclopédie*. The experience of adversity and depression matured him: his two masterpieces, *Le Neveu de Rameau* and *Le Rêve d'Alembert* were yet to be written. If he displayed compromise and inconsistency in his life, he also possessed outstanding tenacity in completing the *Encyclopédie*.

Many of Diderot's contributors deserted him. D'Alembert could only be persuaded to write uncontroversial, mathematical pieces, but de Jaucourt continued to undertake enormous quantities of routine work. De Jaucourt was an aristocrat of great integrity from a Calvinist background. He believed in political liberty and tolerance of all religious beliefs and himself retained an unbigoted belief in God. Between 1759 and 1765 Diderot toiled, first in the production of plates, which were less controversial and then in the production of the final ten volumes. He had to endure what amounted to character assassination on the stage in a play *Les Philosophes* (1760) by Palissot. He was prevented from direct counter-attack by the secrecy with which he had to pursue the project. In 1762 he was infuriated to discover that he had been taken in by a police spy – an especially disturbing experience for someone so open in his conversation with strangers.

As the opus was nearing its completion he experienced a further blow, which appears to have hurt him more deeply than any other set-back. Le Breton, one of his publishers, made cuts in many articles without Diderot's knowledge, and after he had dealt with the proofs. Diderot wrote of the material being 'surreptitiously mutilated, garbled, made hash of, dishonoured', but it is difficult to ascertain how destructive the cuts were. He claimed, 'I shall bear the wound until the day I die', and his friend, Grimm, said: 'The discovery put him into a state of frenzy and despair that I shall never forget.' It is alleged that he never again spoke of the *Encyclopédie* with enthusiasm or pride. The temptation to renounce the project must have been great, but he had obligations to other publishers than Le Breton and also to the subscribers; the secrecy of the operation made public complaint impossible. Le Breton's betrayal soured his triumph, but in September 1765 he was able to write: 'The great and cursed work is finished.' He had devoted the best part of his life to the most influential encyclopaedia in history.

During those years in which he was labouring secretly on the *Encyclopédie*, he remained as sociable as ever and was a frequent visitor to d'Holbach's house at Grandval, where many *philosophes* entertained each other. The writings which he completed during this period were a novel *La Religieuse* (*The Nun*), *Le Neveu de Rameau* (*Rameau's Nephew*) and *Addition aux Pensées Philosophiques* (*Addition to the Philosophical Thoughts*). *The Nun*, which became a favourite of French anti-clericals in the nineteenth century, is a psychological study of a cloistered life and was not published until 1796.

Rameau's Nephew is a glitteringly entertaining fictional dialogue between Moi (Diderot) and Lui (Rameau's nephew). Many old debts were settled in the excoriations of contemporaries – but with lightness as well as venom. *Rameau's Nephew* is essentially a dialogue between a pure selfish hedonist and a conventional follower of the moral codes. It was rewritten many times and not published in his lifetime.

Addition to the Philosophical Thoughts is sharper than the original *Pensées*, while avoiding overt atheism. It was not published in his lifetime, apart from the semi-private circulation of the *Correspondance Littéraire* of Grimm, where it first appeared in 1763. Some disillusion and pessimism is seen in these aphorisms, and a famous caustic account of the origin of religion is included:

> A man had been betrayed by his children, by his wife, and by his friends; some disloyal partners had ruined his fortune, and had plunged him into poverty. Pervaded with a profound hatred and contempt for the human race, he left society and took refuge alone in a cave. There, pressing his fists into his eyes, and contemplating a revenge proportional to his grievances, he said: 'Evil people! What shall I do to punish them for their injustice and to make them all as unhappy as they deserve? Ah! if it were possible to imagine it – to intoxicate them with a great fantasy to which they would attach more importance than to their lives, and about which they would never be able to agree!' Instantly he rushed out of the cave, shouting, 'God! God!' Echoes without number repeated around him, 'God! God!' This fearful name was carried from pole to pole, and heard everywhere with astonishment. At first men prostrated themselves, then they got up again, asked each other, argued with each other, became bitter, cursed each other, hated each other, cut each other's throats, and the fatal wish of the misanthropist was fulfilled. For such has been in the past, such will be in the future, the story of a being at all times equally important and incomprehensible.

Diderot's financial problems were resolved in an unexpected manner. He attempted to sell his library and, failing to receive a satisfactory price in Paris, wrote to Catherine II, Empress of Russia, offering to sell it to her. She had courted his attention and that of other French *philosophes* since she came to power in 1762. She wrote back agreeing to buy the library and asking Diderot to remain its keeper until his death, also offering an honorarium as fee. When she forgot to send the honorarium she sent him the equivalent of fifty years' fees, thus ensuring financial security, if not longevity.

In 1769 Diderot wrote another masterpiece not published in his lifetime – *D'Alembert's Dream*. In the unusual form of conversations and a dream, it combines scientific speculation, literary dexterity and delightful touches of humour and eroticism. He examined the puzzling difference between organic and inorganic matter and speculated upon units of a rather cell-like nature, which could divide in a continuous process. It prefigures Darwinism in its view of nature as a transforming process and even foreshadows ideas comparable to genetics. The sweeping attempt to look at the material of the entire cosmos implicitly leaves no room for a deity and suggests complete scientific materialism.

Angélique, Diderot's daughter, married in 1772; the event left him lonely and conscious that a phase of his life was over. However, he finally felt free to accept Catherine II's persistent invitation to visit Russia. In Moscow he had conversations with her about government, manufacture, justice, tolerance and other such topics. There is no evidence that she took the slightest notice of his ideas, even if impressed with his flow of words. He must have realized Catherine's motive in surrounding herself with famous men of letters and artists. The Duchess of Choiseul, who had criticized the *philosophes* for allowing themselves to be used by Catherine, aptly described the situation: 'She flatters herself that their base eulogies will impenetrably conceal from the eyes of her contemporaries and from posterity the heinous crimes by which she has astonished the universe and revolted humanity.' Diderot found the trip stimulating but frustrating, and suffered some ill-health in the Russian winter.

After the Russian visit, Diderot's final ten years were less vigorous. Nevertheless the instinct to explore his ideas on paper never waned. The problem of Christianity was again considered in *Entretien d'un Philosophe avec la maréchale de xxx*: religion was seen as irrelevant to morals and to human mortality, but the gentle non-polemical essay was not totally contemptuous of Christianity. He also worked on a criticism of Helvétius's *De l'Esprit*, where he found the pure utilitarian hedonism an over-simplification. The novel *Jacques, the Fatalist* was very experimental in form and explored the nature of morality and free will.

Diderot was influenced by the shift in the 1780s in French thinking from philosophy to politics, seen in the intense interest in the reforms of Necker, initiated by Louis XVI, and the intense disappointment at their rapid discontinuation. Criticism of despotism was a consistent theme of the *Encyclopédie* and of Diderot's thinking. More than most of the *philosophes*, he favoured demands for greater democracy and condemned even 'enlightened' despotism. A preoccupation with Seneca and the reigns of Claudius and Nero arose from his fascination with philosophers' attitudes to unenlightened rulers. An essay on Seneca was expanded into a work on those two emperors, which became a rather ineffective and unfortunate *apologia pro vita sua*. (He was, like many, influenced by Rousseau's powerful but untruthful soul-bearing *Confessions*.) He justified the extent to which he had criticized religion:

> It seems to me that if one had kept silence up to now regarding religion, people would still be submerged in the most grotesque and dangerous superstition . . . regarding government, we would still be groaning under the bonds of feudal government . . . regarding morals, we would still be having to learn what is virtue and what is vice. To forbid all these discussions, the only ones worthy of occupying a good mind, is to perpetuate the reign of ignorance and barbarism.

He was prone to resurrect old quarrels and display too much self-righteousness, and a bitter attack on Rousseau went beyond reasonable bounds in justifying his earlier conflicts with the brilliant paranoid who had at one stage been a warm friend and contributed articles on music to the *Encyclopédie*.

During the ill-health of his last few years he bore discomfort stoically and held to his convictions steadfastly. He worked intermittently upon a complete edition of his writings and on notes for *Elements of Physiology*, probably in preparation for a larger work on the nature of man. It concludes with a characteristic sentence: 'There is only one virtue, justice; only one duty, to be happy; only one corollary, not to overvalue life and not to fear death.'

Diderot died suddenly on 31 July 1784. Although there were doubts about whether he would obtain a respectable burial, since the clergy often refused to bury unbelievers, he was interred at the Paris church of Saint-Roch. It was renamed the Temple of Genius during the revolution. But Diderot was not a revolutionary, though his writings did much to shift public opinion during the eighteenth century. His last words are alleged by his daughter to have been 'The first step towards philosophy is incredulity'. They may be apocryphal, but it was this step towards incredulity in all spheres which was the great achievement of Diderot and the *Encyclopédie*.

5
D'Holbach: 'Raining bombs on the house of the Lord'

'It is raining bombs on the house of the Lord. I go in fear and trembling lest one of these terrible bombers gets into difficulties.' When Diderot wrote these words in 1768, his close friend d'Holbach was secretly leading the bombing raid. Between 1760 and 1770 d'Holbach masterminded the publication of some twenty or thirty pamphlets, edited, translated and partly written by himself. Their theme was clearly stated in the title of the first of the batch, *Christianity Unveiled*, attributed posthumously to Nicolas Boulanger. D'Holbach wrote in *Christianity Unveiled*:

> Many men without morals have attacked religion because it was contrary to their inclinations. Many wise men have despised it because it seemed to them ridiculous. Many persons have regarded it with indifference, because they have never felt its true disadvantages. But it is as a citizen that I attack it, because it seems to me harmful to the happiness of the state, hostile to the march of the mind of man, and contrary to sound morality, from which the interests of state policy can never be separated.

D'Holbach was probably the first avowedly atheist writer. His emphasis on attack, his vigorous pamphleteering efforts, his hammering of the record of Christianity, and the most thorough-going materialism of his position, gave him a unique and under-estimated place in the history of the Enlightenment. He was also a key figure in binding together the *philosophes* and ensuring, as host at Grandval and in Paris, that their ideas were constantly shared and their writings at times almost a communal effort.

Paul Thiry d'Holbach was born in Edesheim, near Landau in the German Palatinate, in 1723. D'Holbach's uncle, Francis Adam Holbach, lived in Paris, where he had made a fortune during the latter years of Louis XIV's reign and became naturalized, ennobled and possessed of a 'd' before his name during the Regency of Louis XV's childhood. D'Holbach's mother died while he was young and he was living with his uncle in Paris by the time he was twelve.

Paul d'Holbach's uncle owned property in the Low Countries, near Maastricht, and Paul moved there during the War of the Austrian Succession. He spent the term-time at Leyden University and the holidays at his uncle's estate. Leyden was one of the freest and liveliest universities in Europe, and amongst his friends were two Englishmen, Mark Akenside and John Wilkes. He later translated Akenside's poem 'Pleasures of the Imagination' and remained in touch with Wilkes for many years. When Wilkes left Leyden in 1746, d'Holbach wrote of the sorrow of parting, which ended 'those delightful evening walks at Leyden'. But there were compensations: 'I act pretty well the part of a country squire – i.e. hunting, shooting, fishing, walking everyday – without to lay aside [*sic*] the ever charming conversation of Horace, Virgil, Homer and all our noble friends in the Elysian fields.'

He returned to Paris at the end of the war in 1748 and was naturalized in the following year. A cousin of his, who had also been brought up by his uncle, married a wealthy gentleman from Flanders, Nicolas d'Aine. Their two daughters, d'Holbach's second cousins, were both to become his wife. The eldest married him in 1750, and linked the fortunes of his uncle and the d'Aine family. Wealth and a court sinecure thus saved him from some of the constant financial worries which bedevilled other *philosophes*. But the fear of losing his money and position may have led to the cautious anonymity of his future publishing programme.

His mother-in-law's château at Grandval became an open house for the *philosophes*. His first wife died in 1754 and his friends encouraged him to travel. Two years later he married his deceased wife's sister, Charlotte Suzanne, and many of the *philosophe* guests testified to her charm, devotion to her children, and sharp humour.

After he was established in Paris, d'Holbach quickly became friendly with Diderot and other *philosophes*. Abbé Morellet, writing in what must have seemed a different age, after the French Revolution and the rise and fall of Napoleon, gave a vivid picture of d'Holbach's *salon*:

> The Baron d'Holbach held two dinner-parties regularly each week, on Sundays and Thursdays, where – without prejudice to the other days of the week – ten, twelve, or even fifteen or twenty, men of letters, men of the world, or foreigners, who loved and cultivated the things

of the mind were wont to meet together. There was plenty of food, and good food too; excellent wine, excellent coffee; plenty of discussion and never a quarrell; the simple manners that are suited to intelligent and educated men, yet do not degenerate into ill-breeding; gaiety without folly; and so much charm in the company there that although we arrived at two o'clock, as was then the custom, we were often nearly all still there at seven or eight in the evening. . . .

And it was there too – one must admit it – that Diderot, Dr Roux, and the good Baron himself, used dogmatically to argue the cause of absolute atheism – as in the *System of Nature* – with persuasiveness, a good faith, and a probity that was edifying even for those who, like myself, did not share their beliefs. For it must not be thought that these ultra-liberal opinions were held by all the members of this society – *philosophique* though it was, in the unfavourable sense sometimes given to that word. A goodly number of us were theists – and not ashamed of it – and we defended ourselves vigorously against atheists, though we loved them for being such good company.

D'Holbach's social occasions were noticeable for the liveliness and intellectual daring of the participants and also for their cosmopolitan company. Morellet cites a list which included 'Hume, Wilkes, Sterne, Galiani, Beccaria, Caraccioli, Lord Shelburne, Count Creutze, Veri, Frizi, Garrick, the Crown Prince of Brunswick, Franklin, Priestley, Colonel Barré. . . .' D'Holbach was not himself much of a traveller – the world came to his doorstep – but he stayed with the actor Garrick on a visit to England in 1765. His English contacts were to be a useful source of pamphlets and a useful route for the devious publication and distribution of his own writings.

Amongst the salon *philosophes* Diderot was d'Holbach's closest friend and collaborator. Their relationship was enduring, but uneasy. Diderot found d'Holbach's moodiness difficult and vividly depicted d'Holbach's temperament in a letter to Sophie Volland:

Can you imagine, my friend, how someone who has an excellent heart, good spirit, whom one could not with justice deny any of the essential human qualities and whose goodness and generosity on important occasions are notable, can contrive deliberately to make disagreeable the lives of his mother-in-law, wife, friends, domestics, and all who surround him? How can he so alternate between the delicate and the churlish? . . .

The Baron would destroy himself by reading history which only serves to injure his spirit and incense his heart. He only looks at the atrocities of man and his nature. More and more he comes to hate his fellows. Will an encounter with some black pages make him tremble?

> He takes secret delight in regaling me with the details. He is sure that if life resembles what he has shown me, he cannot go on.
>
> On such days he seems touched: first with pleasure, then with pain. It is impossible to be on good terms with this wretched man. You can only care for him and pity him. He is the first victim of his faults.

The peevish side of his personality was revealed mainly to his close friends: the cosmopolitan visitors saw only a man of charm and generosity. His friends were loyal however, and Diderot, despite some disagreements and periods of distance, remained close to him until his death. D'Holbach's bitterness and anger certainly showed itself in the harshness of his attacks on Christianity.

One of the fruits of Diderot and d'Holbach's friendship was d'Holbach's articles for the *Encyclopédie*. D'Holbach's translation from German of treatises on mining, the formation of metals, stratification, and other aspects of mineralogy and physics brought him membership of academies in Berlin, Petersburg and Mannheim and were a useful contribution to the dissemination of scientific knowledge. Although not a practising scientist, his interest in science was enduring and he kept a cabinet of scientific specimens at Grandval. He contributed some four hundred articles to the *Encyclopédie* between 1751 and 1765. Many were very short factual items, but there were long essays on fossils, glaciers, the sea, volcanoes and mines and also pieces on the constitution of the Holy Roman Empire.

D'Holbach may well have been influenced by the thorough-going materialism and lurid description of man's religious history to be found in *De l'Esprit* by Helvétius; but the condemnation of the book and Helvétius's narrow escape from imprisonment may have been a further reason for his decision to publish clandestinely when he embarked upon his own attack on Christianity.

Although Helvétius's name was not on the title page of *De l'Esprit*, his authorship could hardly be secret since he had been publicly discussing its ideas for years. He conversed with Montesquieu and disagreed with the thesis put forward in *De l'Esprit des Lois* that differences of behaviour were related to a person's country and environment. Helvétius preferred to believe that all differences were due to education. Either view is part of the shift away from the religious concept of differences arising from the variety of God-given endowments. Helvétius developed to its utmost the idea that human faculties are due entirely to sense impressions. It followed, he thought, that control of the input would change the nature of people: education and legislation could therefore create geniuses and ethically trained citizens. He thought moral behaviour was limited to attraction and repulsion of each individual's self-interested experience of pleasure or pain. People were especially shocked that he separated religion and morality. *De l'Esprit*'s most lasting influence was in presenting education as an instrument of social change. The English Utilitarians admired Helvétius and James Mill inflicted the proposed attempt to create a genius by education upon his son, John Stuart. The more general view that education should be concerned with producing satisfied individuals and good citizens rather than selfless worshippers or martyrs and saints has been an enduring aspect of the move away from religious faith.

D'Holbach began his programme to educate the public about atheism with the publication of *Christianity Unveiled* in 1761. At what point his anti-clericalism turned into atheism is unclear. An anecdote* recounts d'Holbach's conversion from deism to atheism by Diderot, but the evidence is of a steady progress from science to scepticism, from the ardent pantheism of Akenside's poem 'Pleasures of the Imagination' to anti-clerical distaste for Christianity, and finally to avowed atheism.

Christianity Unveiled was attributed to Nicolas Boulanger who had died two years before its publication. Boulanger was a civil engineer engaged in the construction of main roads; he developed an interest in geology, the early history of man, and the history of religion and folklore as a response to disturbances of nature. His frequent appearance at d'Holbach's house gave it the soubriquet 'la grande boulangerie'. D'Holbach appointed himself Boulanger's literary executor and posthumously published his *Oriental Despotism* (1761), the indirect message of which did not escape contemporary Western despots. D'Holbach's position as literary executor gave plausibility to Boulanger's alleged authorship of *Christianity Unveiled*, and he was carrying out Boulanger's suggested programme of presenting a picture of the errors of history. The sub-title of *Christianity Unveiled* was 'An Examination of the principles and effects of the Christian religion'. D'Holbach depicted Christianity as a combination of Judaism and Eastern mythologies which dominated by playing upon the fears and passions of humanity and by blinding reason with a

*Gorat: Memoirs historiques sur la vie de Monsieur Suard, sur ses écrits, et sur le 18e siècle [1820].

series of fantastic dogmas and rites. This *mélange* produced conflict within states and wars between nations. He thought that freedom of thought would cause superstition to 'fall away by itself'. 'Tolerance and freedom of thought are the veritable antidotes to religious fanaticism.'

He was not prepared to risk imprisonment, but he doubtless thought that superstition would fall away if enough people read enough of the right pamphlets. After 1765, an avalanche of polemical works poured from d'Holbach's house. They were translations, collaborations and original works: he continued his policy of attributing them to dead or imaginary authors. This has created a nightmare for bibliographers, for it was not until after his death in 1789 that d'Holbach's authorship was openly divulged, although it was certainly already known to friends.

D'Holbach was assisted in his campaign by the brothers Naigeon. Jacques-André Naigeon lived with d'Holbach as his secretary from about 1765 onwards and, in his own words, enjoyed 'his full confidence and his most intimate, most tender, and most constant friendship'. He was a pedant with an interest solely in classics without the usual range of interests of the Enlightenment. He did much to edit, 'correct' and tidy up d'Holbach's careless writing. According to Diderot, with Naigeon anti-clericalism became a kind of nervous *tic*. Naigeon had a high opinion of his own contribution to d'Holbach's writings, and in his obituary article and later writings about him provided the primary source for knowledge of his life. Naigeon's brother assisted by copying manuscripts and transporting them to Amsterdam for printing. There were indirect routes by which they then circulated back to France: on one occasion d'Holbach received copies with a batch of new English novels.

The book and pamphlet trade was dangerous. Hawking forbidden books might bring profit or the galleys. Diderot wrote of an incident in which a pedlar sold copies of *Christianity Unveiled* to a grocer's apprentice, who sold one to his master. After an argument the grocer reported the apprentice to the police for dealing in forbidden books. The pedlar, his wife and the apprentice were condemned to three days in the pillory; then the boy was branded and sent for nine years in the galleys, the pedlar similarly was branded and given five years' galley service, while his wife was imprisoned for five years.

D'Holbach's pamphlets are repetitive and authorship is very uncertain some cases. They fall roughly into three groups: existing manuscripts, reprinted with amendments and additions by d'Holbach and Naigeon; translations; original works by Naigeon and d'Holbach, with the division of work not being easy to distinguish.

Works known to have been in existence in manuscript for some time were *Letter from Thrasybulus to Leucippus*, which claimed to be translated from the Greek or written by a philosopher to dissuade his sister from taking the veil, *Critical Examination of the Apologists of the Christian Religion*, known to have been already in existence and *The Military Philosopher, or Difficulties of Religion*, written during the final years of Louis XIV's reign and subsequently reprinted with additions by d'Holbach. Straightforward translations were principally from the English deists. Among the best-known works are Peter Annet's piece about David, *History of the Man after God's own Heart,* Anthony Collins' *Examination of the Prophets who founded the Christian Religion*, John Toland's *Letters to Serena*, and Thomas Woolston's *Discourse on Miracles*. A curiosity was a translation of the seventeenth-century English pamphlet *Of the Torments of Hell: the foundations and pillars thereof discovered, searched, shaken, removed* (London, 1658). Such works were important in the move towards a critical approach to the Bible.

Original works by d'Holbach, with the collaboration of Naigeon, include *Sacred Contagion, or the natural History of Superstition*, *Essay on the prejudices and the Influence of opinions on customs and the happiness of mankind*, *Letters to Eugénie or Preservative against prejudice*. *The Critical History of Jesus Christ, or reasoned Analysis of the Gospels* was the first (rather primitive) attempt to write a life of Jesus from a purely human viewpoint. D'Holbach's pamphleteering has been criticized as weak in scholarship and limited in understanding of the psychological appeal of religion, but he was indefatigable and strongly influenced subsequent criticism of religion and the clergy.

Eventually d'Holbach inflated all his ideas into a long two-volume work entitled *System of Nature*. It was published in 1770 and attributed to J. B. Mirabaud, a long-deceased secretary of the French Academy. In *System of Nature* the materialist basis of all life is emphasized. D'Holbach affirmed that the universe was given unity by its material basis. He had a monist vision of the oneness of the universe, and saw man as a part of the entirety of nature. He thought the idea of a metaphysical component of the universe was mere prejudice and error fostered by the clergy. He could become quite lyrical, if not literal, in his comparison between religion and nature:

> O Nature, sovereign of all beings, and your adorable daughters, virtue, reason, truth! be for ever our sole divinities; it is to you that the incense and homage of the earth are due. Show us, then, O Nature, what man must do to obtain the happiness which you have made him desire. . . . Inspire the intelligent being with courage; give him energy, that he can eventually love himself, esteem himself, feel his dignity; that he dares free himself, that he is happy and free, that he will never be a slave to your laws; that he perfects his fate; that he cherishes his fellow-beings; that he makes himself happy, that he makes others happy.

But it was d'Holbach's harangue against gods and priests which brought notoriety and condemnation from Parlement to the *System of Nature*. Voltaire thought it was dangerous and sorely tested the principle of tolerance, while Frederick the Great prepared a criticism of it, so that, as Voltaire wryly observed, 'God had on his side the two least superstitious men in all Europe – which ought to have pleased him immensely.' D'Alembert considered the *System of Nature* long-winded and 'too rigid and dogmatic'.

The criticism of long-windedness was met when two years later d'Holbach produced an abridged version called *Le Bons Sens* (*Good Sense*). It became a favourite with nineteenth-century freethinkers and is clear, sharp and forthright. The concluding paragraph gives the tone:

> Religion has ever filled the mind of man with darkness, and kept him in ignorance of his real duties and true interest. It is only by dispelling the clouds and phantoms of Religion, that we shall discover Truth, Reason, and Morality. Religion diverts us from the causes of evils, and from the remedies which nature prescribes; far from curing, it only aggravates, multiplies, and perpetuates them. Let us observe with the celebrated Lord Bolingbroke, that '*theology is the box of Pandora; and if it is impossible to shut it, it is at least useful to inform men that this fatal box is open.*'

D'Holbach also addressed himself to the question which had blunted the pen of many nascent atheists: 'The vulgar, it is repeatedly said, must have a Religion. If enlightened persons have no need of the restraint of opinions, it is at least necessary to rule men, whose reason is uncultivated by education.' D'Holbach was unimpressed by the power of religion to act as a restraint for the 'vulgar'. 'Do we see, that this religion preserves them from intemperance, drunkenness, brutality, violence, fraud, and every kind of excess?' However, he advocated caution in preaching atheism to the masses: 'It would be madness to write for the vulgar, or to attempt to cure prejudices all at once. We write for those only, who read and reason; the multitudes read but little, and reason still less. Calm and rational persons will require new ideas, and knowledge will be gradually diffused.' *Good Sense* had more impact upon men of action and campaigners against injustice than upon intellectuals, but Godwin was an admirer of d'Holbach and Shelley refers to him in his notes to *Queen Mab*, having once contemplated making his own translation of *Système de la Nature*. Another example of an English freethinker influenced by d'Holbach was Matthew Turner (*d.* 1788?) to whom is attributed An Answer to Dr Priestley's *Letters to a Philosophical Unbeliever*.

In the 1770s d'Holbach turned to moral and political questions, writing works which were moderate, liberal and based on a utilitarian morality: they caused much less stir than his attacks on religion, but were admired by his friends. Diderot praised the three-volume *Morale Universelle* (1776) and suggested that 'fathers and mothers recommend it to their children for their daily reading'.

D'Holbach and Diderot continued to collaborate in publishing the works of Seneca, but Diderot's health was declining and d'Holbach's force seems to have been spent. D'Holbach's final decade before his death in 1789 passed quietly: he outlived the *philosophes* whose host he had been. His intellectual curiosity was not dead and he was visited by Mesmer in 1780 – all his experiments failed before d'Holbach's sceptical eye. Among younger writers he knew Volney, an orientalist who studied comparative religion and visited the Near East. (Volney developed a passionate hatred of despotism and devout faith in progress and his *Ruins of Empire* became a freethought classic.)

In January 1789, only a few months before the start of a revolution whose development would have fascinated him, he died at the age of sixty-six. According to Naigeon he is said to have told a fellow-patient at a spa in Vosges, where he had been saving a peasant family from misery: 'Don't say anything about this to anybody. Any one would say that I am trying to play the good-natured philosopher. I am neither benefactor nor philosopher, but just a human being, and my charities are the pleasantest expense I have on these journeys.' He was buried a Catholic, as he had always, to outward appearances, remained.

Immediately after his death writers began to attribute authorship of his writings correctly and to comment upon his work. An example was Condorcet who published an analysis of a later work, *Politique Naturelle*. During the French Revolution religion became a matter of public policy as well as of intellectual debate: there was a hard battle to secularize society. There were numerous reprints of d'Holbach's works during the period of attempted Church reform known as 'the civil constitution of the clergy' and the religious rising in the Vendée. Later, following the Terror and then the Directorate, copies of *Contagion Sacrée* were sent by the Minister of the Interior to all prefects of departments to discourage a Roman Catholic revival.

The *philosophes* have been made scapegoats responsible for the excesses of the Terror. In fact, a reverse perspective shows that the period of panic, fear and war produced a reaction that did much to prevent the spread of the ideas of the Enlightenment. Although the complex series of events known as the French Revolution were bound to be influenced by the reformist ideas of some of the *philosophes*, the deification of the state and worship of the Goddess of Reason would have been anathema to the spirit of toleration, scepticism and open-mindedness that are part of the Epicurean-humanist-Enlightenment tradition. A hymn sung at the fête for the restoration of the Supreme Being proclaimed:

> Où sont-ils ceux qui t'osaient menacer?
> Qui sous le manteau de civisme,
> Vils professeurs de l'athéisme,
> Du coeur de l'homme espéraient t'éffacer!

(Where are those who dared to threaten you? who under the cloak of civism, vile teachers of atheism, have hoped to remove you from the heart of man!)

They were mostly dead, these atheists and *philosophes*: a few were in hiding or imprisonment.

Condorcet (1769–1794), a mathematician and *philosophe* who took an active part in the new Legislative Assembly was no exception. Robespierre, a disciple of Rousseau, hated Condorcet as a representative of the Encyclopedists. Condorcet became a victim of the the Terror and after eight months in hiding took his own life to avoid the guillotine. While expecting death he wrote *Esquisse d'un tableau historique des progrès de l'esprit humain*, a historical sketch, which saw the errors and prejudices which had halted history's march towards perfection as a consequence of the activities of priests, who served their own interests by preserving darkness and ignorance. Condorcet's *Sketch* is a testament for the *philosophes*. Condorcet calmly writing of progress while facing death is a symbol of the *philosophes* and their ideas, overwhelmed and traduced by the Revolution and Terror, yet of undiminished influence in the subsequent century. Condorcet contemplated human happiness as 'a refuge where the memory of persecutors cannot reach; where men, living by thought and re-established with rights and natural dignity, can forget the greed, fear and need which torment and corrupt him; there he can truly live with his fellows, in a paradise created by reason, and where his purest joys are crowned with his love of humanity.'

6
David Hume: The Saintly Infidel

The paradox of the virtuous infidel, for a paradox it seemed to many eighteenth-century minds, is excellently exemplified in the life of David Hume (1711–1776). 'Le bon David' as he was dubbed by the French, enjoyed study, company, food and drink, theatre, debate – but above all ideas and literature. He became one of the most admired and financially successful writers of his age. His philosophical ideas were not fully understood at the time, and his reputation rested on his history of England and political essays as much as his philosophical works. His writings did much to undermine the idea of God as 'the first cause', his chapter on Miracles, which was one of the most controversial and explicit of his writings, ended any widespread defence of miracles as a bolster to faith, and his *Dialogues Concerning Natural Religion* presented a brilliant and subtly ironic sceptical view. The latter was published posthumously, since Hume's friends advised caution during his lifetime. Many an anecdote testifies to his known infidelity and it certainly held back his career at some stages. He was so moderate in controversy and good-humoured in debate that he was friendly with fine minds of many outlooks; moderate clergy were on good terms with him.

David Hume was born in 1711 and brought up in Ninewells in Berwickshire. After the death in 1713 of his father, an Edinburgh advocate, he was brought up by his mother, a Presbyterian of great strength and charm. In his brief and lucid self-portrait *My Own Life,* penned shortly before his death, Hume said he was of 'good Family by Father and Mother' and claimed that his father was related to the Earl of Home. (He changed the spelling of his name to coincide with its pronunciation when he was in England.)

At the early age of eleven he went to study at Edinburgh University and for three years studied Greek, logic, metaphysics and natural philosophy. Edinburgh University had a high reputation, and was to be a centre of the eighteenth-century Scottish Enlightenment which made Edinburgh, temporarily, 'the Athens of the North'. Hume read Newton, Locke and Berkeley and his mind was stimulated by the new ideas fermenting in Edinburgh academic life – a marked contrast to the insipid dullness which Gibbon encountered at Oxford. It was presumably at this time that Hume lost his religious belief. Throughout his life he retained a love of study, referring to 'the two greatest and purest pleasures of human life, study and society'.

He returned to Ninewells uncertain how to combine his love of literature, 'which has been the ruling Passion of my Life' with a profession. He studied law but was constantly turning to a 'secret devouring' of works of literature. The classical writers Cicero, Seneca and Plutarch attracted him for their stoic virtues. While in his eighteenth year he entered what he described as 'a new Scene of Thought, which transported me beyond Measure, & made me, with an Ardor natural to young men, throw up every other Pleasure or Business to apply entirely to it'. This almost certainly refers to the ideas he was to expound in *A Treatise of Human Nature*. His ideas, which seemed to overturn the tradition of philosophy from Descartes to Berkeley, may at first have overwhelmed him; he suffered serious ill-health and depression from too much study and concentration. His wide reading included Bayle and Fénelon, and he copied out a motto from *Epicharmos*: 'Keep sober and remember to be sceptical'. He says that he cured himself by exercise and healthy diet, but his nervous disorder was for a while a serious affliction, a consequence of the enormous and daunting task of presenting his new ideas to the world, perhaps exacerbated by his uncertainty about his career. The early intellectual discovery seems to have come to him as a passionate experience – something which was outside the character of the abstract, equable, cool figure he presented for the remainder of his life.

Part of the medicine he prescribed for himself was 'Business and Diversion'. He left for London intending to consult a physician, but in due course found employment in Bristol as a clerk to a sugar merchant. In common with many Scots, Hume admired French culture and, after a quarrel with the Bristol merchant who employed him, he crossed the Channel to spend three years (1734–37) in France. He was introduced to the Chevalier Ramsay, a Catholic Jacobite with views diametrically opposed to his; he early showed his ability to sustain friendship with those whose views differed widely from his. Ramsay quickly discerned the young man's cast of mind: 'He seems to me one of those philosophers that think to spin out Systems, out of their own brain, without any regard to religion, antiquity or Tradition sacred or profane. . . .'

Hume spent a year at Rheims, then two years at La Flèche in Anjou, where he used the library of the same Jesuit monastery at which Descartes had been educated. All the while he was composing his *Treatise of Human Nature,* and he returned to London to arrange for its publication. In 1739 the first two books, *Of the Understanding* and *Of the Passions* appeared, and the third book, *Of Morals*, came out in November 1740. Hume described in *My Own Life* the lack of initial response to his first work: 'Never literary attempt was more unfortunate . . . It fell dead-born from the Press.' He always considered the failure was due to the lack of clarity with which his ideas were expressed, and much of the philosophical writing during the rest of his life was a re-expression of his first work.

Hume was not deterred from his literary ambitions by the reception of his first work and retired to Ninewells, to live with his mother and brother and to continue his studies. His next work, *Essays Moral and Political* (1741) was described as by 'a new author' to dissociate it from the *Treatise.* It was favourably received, as was a second volume which appeared in 1742. The essays covered subjects such as 'Of Superstitions and Enthusiasm', 'Of the Dignity of Human Nature' and 'The Sceptic', from which the following sentences show Hume putting his philosophical ideas into popular form: 'If we can depend upon any principle, which we learn from philosophy, this, I think, may be considered as certain and undoubted, that there is nothing, in itself, valuable or despicable, desirable or hateful, beautiful or deformed; but that these attributes arise from the particular constitution and fabric of human sentiment and affection.' His political essays made the most impact, and ranged over 'Of the Liberty of the Press' and 'Of the first Principles of Government'.

In Edinburgh Hume, whose reputation was slowly growing, had friends among academics, clergy and town dignitaries. When he was asked by the Lord Provost, John Coutts, if he was interested in applying for the chair of Ethics and Pneumatical Philosophy at Edinburgh University, his expectations were raised only to be disappointed, as on several occasions in his life, by the 'popular Clamour' raised against him 'on account of Scepticism, Heterodoxy & other hard names'. The delay in resignation of the occupant of the chair allowed time for his election to become a *cause célèbre* in the town council. Factions were organized against Hume: 'Heresy, Deism, Scepticism, &c. &c. &c. was started against me.' Hume's own campaign was fought vigorously, but 'the matter was brought to an issue, and by Cabals of the Principal, the bigotry of the clergy, and the credulity of the mob, we lost it'. Hume did not suffer the vilification and persecution of more polemical freethinkers (or some of the *philosophes*) but his career was certainly checked because of his known sceptical beliefs.

Requiring an income, Hume became tutor to the Marquess of Annandale in Hertfordshire, from where he conducted the unsuccessful final stage of his campaign to gain the chair of philosophy in Edinburgh. His tutorship was an unhappy experience, since his charge, the Marquess, was going mad. At the age of thirty-five, having failed to gain the academic position which he really wanted and disappointed with the impact of his major philosophical work, he may well have been pessimistic about his ambitions. His plan to return to Berwick was prevented by an unexpected opportunity to join a military expedition to America: 'Such a Romantic Adventure & such a Hurry, I have not heard before.' The expedition was a disaster and foundered off the French coast, nevertheless it marked a turn in his public life and he was made a Judge Advocate by the General in Command and received a small stipend. He wrote of his 'reluctance to leave my books and my leisure and retreat', but joined a military delegation to Turin and Vienna.

When he returned to Edinburgh he found his reputation had grown and his circle of friends widened. He failed to get another academic post of which he had hopes, the professorship of moral philosophy at Glasgow being denied him because of 'the violent and solemn remonstrance of the clergy'. The offer of another position, librarian to the Faculty of Advocates in Edinburgh, also caused controversy, but the 'violent cry of Deism, atheism and scepticism' raised against him did not prevent his appointment. Apparently popular knowledge of the 'contest betwixt Deists and Christians' led to a torchlight procession put on by porters and messengers to celebrate his success. As librarian he had not only an emolument but the use of the library, particularly valuable as he was now researching for his *History of England*.

His problems with bigots were not over. Three books which he purchased were censured as 'indecent'. They were the *Contes* of La Fontaine, a romantic novel *L'Écumoire* by Crébillon *fils*, and

L'Histoire amoureuse des Gaules by Bussy-Rabutin. Hume's authority to purchase books was challenged and he replied with indignation: '. . . if every book not superior in merit to *La Fontaine* be expelled the Library, I shall engage to carry away all the remains in my pocket . . . By the bye, *Bussy-Rabutin* contains no bawdy at all, though if it did, I see not that it would be a whit the worse. For I know not a more agreeable subject both for books and conversation, if executed with decency and ingenuity.' Eager to retain his position in the library without losing his honour, he renounced his salary and then resigned after five years.

In 1748 he published his next major philosophical work, a popular version of his first book, the *Treatise*. It was first called *Philosophical Essays Concerning Human Understanding,* but was later re-entitled *An Enquiry Concerning Human Understanding* by which title it is better known. It contains a criticism of the argument that God's existence is evident from the 'design' of the universe. Even more controversial was his chapters 'Of Miracles' in which he stated the famous maxim: 'That no testimony is sufficient to establish a miracle, unless the testimony be of such a kind, that its falsehood would be more miraculous, than the fact, which it endeavours to establish: And even in that case there is a mutual destruction of arguments, and the superior only gives an assurance suitable to that degree of force, which remains after deducing the inferior.' He ironically spelled out the consequences for believers of the Christian religion: 'So that, upon the whole, we may conclude, that the *Christian Religion* not only was at first attended with miracles, but even at this day cannot be believed by any reasonable person without one. Mere reason is insufficient to convince us of its veracity: And whoever is moved by *Faith* to assent to it, is conscious of a continued miracle in his own person, which subverts all the principles of his understanding, and gives him a determination to believe what is the most contrary to custom and experience.'

In the 1750s pamphlets and books arguing against Hume multiplied, but he resolved not to answer them 'not from Disdain (for the Authors of some of them, I respect) but from my desire of Ease and Tranquillity'. This desire for ease and tranquillity led him to push his arguments less forcefully than the French *philosophes*; prudence also led to a use of irony, which, while an enjoyable feature of some of his writing, has led to difficulty in interpreting his exact views.

One of the most thorough attacks on Hume came in the Rev. John Leland's *View of the Principal Deistical Writers* (1755 2nd edition) which said Hume was 'looked upon as one of the most subtil writers that had of late appeared against Christianity'. This reputation spread and the *Bibliothèque Raisonnée* referred to him as 'among the most subtle advocates of unbelief'; by 1761 his books were placed on the Catholic Index.

Hume's *History of England* was published in four volumes from 1754 to 1762 and was the work upon which his contemporary reputation rested. He was sensitive to the criticism that the *History* was irreligious, since he wrote a preface to the second edition claiming that the 'Mischiefs which arise from the Abuses of Religion' would naturally be more prominent than 'the salutary Consequences which resulted from true & genuine Piety'. He acknowledged the social usefulness of religion: 'The proper Office of Religion is to reform Men's Lives, to purify their Hearts, to inforce all moral Duties, & to secure Obedience to the Laws & civil Magistrate.'

There were further quarrels in Edinburgh, when the General Assembly pronounced against 'Infidelity and Immorality'. Hume was caught in a struggle between the old guard and the moderates in the Scottish Church. The following year the debate focused on Hume's infidelity in particular. Fortunately for the reputation of the Scottish Enlightenment, the moderates triumphed and no martyr was made of him; according to Ramsay of Ochtertyre 'this rash and feeble attempt to check the progress of freethinking, convinced the philosophers of Edinburgh that they no longer had anything to dread from the Church courts'. Hume, however, was always conscious that Scotland was 'too narrow a Place for me'. This did not prevent him from buying a house in St. James Court, Edinburgh, where he intended to settle quietly for the remainder of his days.

Before retiring to Edinburgh he was tempted to Paris by the prospect of an appointment as Secretary at the British Embassy. He arrived here in 1763 and his twenty-six-month stay was a triumphant success. His personal charm gave him the reputation of 'le bon David', his conversation delighted members of the salons and he exchanged ideas with many of the *philosophes*. High society and flattery embarrassed him: 'I am convinced that Louis XIV never, in any three weeks of his life, suffered so much flattery: I say suffered, for it really confounds and embarrasses me, and makes me look sheepish. . . .' Horace Walpole, also a visitor in Paris and never short on malice, said he was 'fashion itself, although his French is almost as unintelligible as his English'.

His contact with the *philosophes* was considerable. Diderot was attracted to Hume's ideas; the two were compared by Friedrich Melchior Grimm: 'M. Hume is comparable to a brook, clear and limpid, which flows always evenly and serenely, and M. Diderot, to a torrent whose impetuous and rapid force overwhelms whatever opposes passage . . .' There is a famous anecdote from Diderot's letters giving an account of the first time Hume found himself at the table of the Baron d'Holbach:

> The first time that M. Hume found himself at the table of the Baron, he was seated beside him. I don't know for what purpose the English philosopher took it into his head to remark to the Baron that he did not believe in atheists, that he had never seen any. The Baron said to him: 'Count how many we are here. We are eighteen.' The Baron added: 'It isn't too bad a showing to be able to point out to you fifteen at once: the three others haven't made up their minds.'

Hume differed from the *philosophes* in his complete scepticism, his lack of certain disbelief. Gibbon spoke of the 'intolerant zeal' of the *philosophes* who 'laughed at the scepticism of Hume, and preached the tenets of atheism with the bigotry of dogmatists, and damned all believers with ridicule and contempt'. Hume did not share their hopes for progress, for what he described as the 'agreeable and laudable, if not too sanguine hope, that human Society is capable of perpetual Progress towards Perfection. . . .'

After the Seven Years' War between France and England, Hume was genuinely an 'Ambassador of Good Will'. He was eventually, after the usual opposition on account of his non-religious beliefs, appointed Secretary with a stipend, although this position was to be short-lived, since he was the *protégé* of Lord Hertford who was moved to Ireland. He returned to Edinburgh, where he enjoyed a 'philosophical retreat' free from the burdens of office. He was only once more briefly tempted back into public affairs as Under-Secretary in the Northern Department for eleven months.

He settled in Edinburgh for a final nine years of autumnal serenity. A new house was built to his order in the new town, and, at first as a joke, the street was named St David's Street, a name which stuck and eventually gained official sanction. He resisted an invitation to continue his *History,* 'Because I am too old, too fat, too lazy, and too rich', but he made careful revisions for a new edition. Gibbon wrote to a friend, calling Hume 'the northern Epicurus': 'I hope you will not fail to visit the Stye of that fattest of Epicurus's Hogs, and inform yourself whether there remains no hope of its recovering the use of its right paw.' Though his writing days were over, friendship and reading kept him abreast of ideas; he admired the work of Gibbon and Adam Smith, and was visited by Benjamin Franklin. He still faced criticism and a vitriolic attack on him and his ideas was published in a work by James Beattie, Professor of Moral Philosophy and Logic at Aberdeen. Beattie's *An Essay on the Nature and Immutability of Truth; in opposition to Sophistry and Scepticism,* first published in 1770, went through five editions before 1776. Beattie also wrote a prose allegory, *The Castle of Scepticism*, in which Hume is portrayed as the despotic governor of the castle who enslaved and tortured all who entered. A famous painting by Reynolds, The Triumph of Truth, shows Truth (Beattie) pushing down the three demons of Hume, Voltaire and an unidentified figure.

In 1772, in his sixties, his health began to deteriorate with the bowel cancer from which he eventually died. He faced illness and death calmly, writing that 'Old age is but sorrow . . . may it be my fate . . . not to enter too far into that dismal region'. In 1776 he wrote the short *My Own Life,* in which he admitted, 'I now reckon upon speedy dissolution.' His affairs, papers and bequests were meticulously arranged. His friends hoped for recovery, but he was doubtful and conversed cheerfully about his impending end.

Among his last concerns were instructions relating to the posthumous publication of the *Dialogues Concerning Natural Religion.* The *Dialogues* is a key work in discussion of eighteenth-century attitudes to God, and it is his masterpiece, which he nurtured and polished for many years. The dialogue form and the use of irony left some readers unclear about his attitude – which may have been his purpose – but most modern commentators take the views of Philo, the Sceptic, to be those closest to his own.

Natural History of Religion (1757), his first work entirely devoted to that subject, was seen by Bishop Warburton as intended 'to establish *naturalism,* a species of atheism, instead of religion'. Hume's account of the growth of religions is set within the context of the deist assumption that 'the whole frame of nature bespeaks an intelligent author', but this is no more than a token gesture and the secondary passions which cause religious feeling are rather like Gibbon's secondary causes for the rise of Christianity – only secondary because of a prudent nod in the direction of prevailing beliefs. The main cause of religion was 'a concern with regard to the events of life, and from the incessant hopes and fears, which actuate the human mind'. Primitive man invented many gods to explain the seasons and storms (literal and metaphorical) in life. Hume noted that Hesiod had listed thirty thousand deities, and referred to the gods of sneezing, and also, of sexual activities: 'The province of copulation, suitably to the importance and dignity of it, was divided among several deities.' Polytheism gave way to monotheism with the development of abstract thinking. Hume did not see this as progress – unlike many eighteenth century historians, he saw history as only 'change and flux', with no particular direction. Polytheism was crude in its ideas but tolerant in practice, while monotheism led to more subtle thought, but also to persecution to enforce its claims to universality. He concluded: 'The whole is a riddle, an enigma, an inexplicable mystery. Doubt, uncertainty, suspense of judgment, appear the only result of our most accurate scrutiny concerning this subject. But such is the frailty of human reason, and such the irresistible contagion of opinion, that even this deliberate doubt could scarcely be upheld; did we not enlarge our view, and opposing one species of superstition to another, set them a-quarrelling; while we ourselves, during their fury and contention, happily make our escape into the calm, though obscure, regions of philosophy.'

Hume was more concerned to explain religion than to *écraser l'infâme* and he was not popular amongst radical freethinkers. Another reason why he was found less relevant in the nineteenth century was that his arguments were the final episode in the development from natural religion to deism: the *Dialogues* is concerned mainly with the argument from design, and this argument went out of fashion following increasing scientific study of the origins of the earth and the human race. The meat of the *Dialogues* is contained in arguments between Philo, the Sceptic, and Cleanthes, the deist. A third figure, Demea, interpolates a pious view of God as a great mystery, but he departs before the dialogues conclude, having pointed out that Philo's imagination was leading him into 'all the topics of the greatest libertines and infidels, and betraying that holy cause, which you seemingly espouse'. That 'seemingly' is crucial to the *Dialogues,* to its difficulty and pleasure, for Philo entices his antagonists into positions which he can then demolish, by presenting arguments which he has no intention of holding to. Philo, the Sceptic, slowly demonstrates the untenability of all arguments for the existence of God. To the argument by analogy, that if a house is put together it needs a builder, he counters that analogies do not always follow and the universe may, for example, resemble a vegetable more than a house. To the supporting argument from design he points out that a creative mind or principle is not a final explanation, for where does it originate? – an 'infinite progression' which has no answer. He also argues that we cannot learn of the whole from knowledge of a part: 'Would the manner of a leaf's blowing, even though perfectly known, afford us any construction concerning the vegetation of a tree?'

Hume died in 1776. In his last months he was visited by Boswell, who was puzzled by the contradiction, as he saw it, of the 'plain, obliging, kindhearted man' and the 'infidel writings'. He asked Hume whether his views on God and immortality had changed as he approached death. Hume answered directly: 'He said he never had entertained any belief in Religion since he began to read Locke and Clarke. I asked him if he was not religious when he was young. He said he was . . . He then said flatly that the Morality of every Religion was bad, and, I really thought was not jocular when he said that when he heard a man was religious, he concluded he was a rascal, though he had known some instances of very good men being religious. . . .'

Hume, no utopian or radical, placed man firmly within the reality of the natural world, seeking, as he did in his own life, what pleasures and consolations can be wrought from life, and wishing upon society that benevolence and happiness which he possessed to an unusual degree: 'Upon the whole, then, it seems undeniable, *that* nothing can bestow more merit on any human creature than the sentiment of benevolence in an eminent degree; and *that* a *part,* at least, of its merit arises from its tendency to promote the interests of our species, and bestow happiness on human society' *(Enquiry concerning the Principles of Morals).*

7
Gibbon: The decline of God's historic role

Gibbon and Hume, two intellectual giants of the eighteenth century, admired each other and were both influenced by European, especially French, ideas in a way unusual for British thinkers. They were both conservative rather than radical in politics and men of learning rather than action. Their writings were widely respected, and although Christian defenders launched attacks upon them, they escaped the censure of the law (but Dr Bowdler snipped away at *The Decline and Fall*). Unlike the pamphleteer, they wrote with scholarship and elegance for an educated audience. The full impact of their blows against Christianity was softened in the case of Gibbon by irony and of Hume by presenting ideas in veiled literary form.

Macaulay said that Gibbon wrote of Christianity like a man who had received a personal injury: his comment echoed the words of Gibbon's contemporary adversary, Porson, a divine who wrote that Gibbon sought to insult 'our religion, which he hates so cordially that he might seem to revenge some personal injury'. This was not the motivation that lay behind Gibbon's masterpiece, *The History of the Decline and Fall of the Roman Empire*. He was moved by his desire to be a great historian and by his admiration for the peaks of Roman civilization. As the tale of the decline of the Roman Empire unfurled in his mind it became apparent that he would simultaneously describe the rise of Christianity, and he determined to treat it as a historian, not a theologian. Chapters XV and XVI, in which he describes 'The Progress of the Christian Religion and the Sentiments, Manners, Numbers and Condition of the primitive Christian' and the 'Conduct of Romans towards Christians', became notorious and were much admired by later freethinkers, but in rescuing Christianity from the hands of the theologians on behalf of the historians his perspective was the olympian prospect of slow historical change, not the battlefield of freethought.

Edward Gibbon was born in Putney in 1737. His father was a gentleman and Member of Parliament, who had been disinherited for his marriage into a less well-to-do Putney family. His mother bore seven children, of whom only Edward lived – and his health was at times so precarious that survival seemed doubtful. His mother's death during his childhood caused his father to withdraw in grief to his estate in Buriton, Hampshire. Although he spent two years at Westminster School, Edward's formal education was neglected, but solitude and the encouragement of his aunt, Catherine Porten, enabled him to develop his powers of reading and imagination.

He went up to Magdalen College, Oxford, when only fifteen. No one has written more scathingly of the sorry state of learning and teaching at mid-eighteenth-century Oxford. The college fellows were lax: 'From the toil of reading, or thinking, or writing, they had absolved their conscience; and the first schools of learning and ingenuity withered on the ground, without yielding any fruits to the owners or the public.' However, at Oxford, an important intellectual development in Gibbon's life took place – his conversion to Catholicism. He had read Bossuet and the English Jesuit, Parsons; it is not known which arguments persuaded him, but he was fond of religious disputation and perhaps wanted a little excitement to contest with the tedium of Oxford life – 'Youth is sincere and impetuous', he declared in his own account of the event. Technically conversion to Rome was treason, an offence not rigorously punished, but taken sufficiently seriously for the London bookseller who introduced Gibbon to a Jesuit for instruction to be interrogated by the Privy Council. Certainly Gibbon could not stay at Oxford, where the Thirty-Nine Articles of the Church of England had to be assented to by all students, even if they were 'signed by more than read, and read by more than believed them', as Gibbon commented.

Among the works of religious dispute which Gibbon had read was that of Dr Conyers Middleton of Trinity College, Cambridge. He did not proceed, like Middleton, to query the evidence of the gospels but, as he later pointed out, 'he saw where his principles led; but he did not think proper to draw the consequences'. Gibbon's conversion and departure from Oxford caused his family much consternation. He went to stay in Putney with Mr David Mallet, a deistical, freethinking poet and friend of the family. Mr Mallet had published Bolingbroke's works and been the target of Johnson's famous quip about the 'beggarly Scotchman' who 'fired the blunderbuss against religion and morality' which Bolingbroke had charged.

Gibbon was moved from Putney to Lausanne into the safe hands of the good Calvinist minister, Daniel Pavilliard. Pavilliard was a patient, tactful and conscientious teacher of a kind which Gibbon had not yet encountered. He set about explaining the errors of popery and in 1754 Gibbon took the sacrament in the Protestant church of Lausanne. The struggle for his soul, at the early age of sixteen, gave him a lifelong taste for religious controversy, and a sceptical attitude towards the truth of any one religious position. It might be a mistake to assume that the experience of conversion and reconversion turned him immediately into a rationalist, but the thrust of his thought was henceforth in that direction.

The more enduring contribution of Pavilliard was not Protestantism but disciplined habits of study. Gibbon developed facility in French and Latin and studied carefully for ten to twelve hours a day. Life in Lausanne was at first austere, but he slowly entered Lausanne society and with good reports from Pavilliard his meagre allowance from England was improved. His reading encompassed Pascal, from whose style he learnt cutting irony, and Montesquieu, whose work introduced him to the idea that history may be influenced by impersonal forces. Soon his mastery of classical literature was sufficient to correspond with leading European authorities.

Among his social pleasures were visits to Voltaire's private theatre, set up in Lausanne outside the jurisdiction of the disapproving Calvinist fathers of Geneva. He saw *Zaïre*, and retained a life-long love of French theatre; he was briefly introduced to Voltaire, but the young man and the grand old sceptic of Europe made little impression on each other. Although Voltaire's work as a historian was significant in placing historical facts above fable, Gibbon was contemptuous of his carelessness: 'M. de Voltaire, unsupported by fact or probability, has generously bestowed the Canary islands on the Roman Empire.' There are numerous references to Voltaire in *The Decline and Fall*, but most are critical, and Gibbon thought that 'in his way Voltaire was a bigot, an intolerable bigot'.

A much more lasting impact was made by his meeting with the young Suzanne Curchod at Voltaire's theatre. Their relationship quickly became both playful and intense. Parental opposition and consciousness of lack of secure means prevented marriage, but they remained fond, and later in life as the wife of the French finance minister, Necker, and mother of a vivacious daughter to become Mme de Stael, Suzanne resumed a close friendship with Gibbon.

He returned to England in 1758 and his life was divided between Hampshire and rooms in Bond Street, London. He wrote (in French) his first work *L'Essai sur L'Étude de la Littérature*, which was a defence of learning and literature, a contribution to the European debate over the relative merits of the natural sciences and classical and literary studies. *L'Essai* began to establish Gibbon's reputation in France, but the publication of the English version made less impact.

Gibbon spent two years with the South Battalion of Hampshire, when the militia was called out to prepare for a threatened invasion during the Seven Years' War. He claimed that the experience made him 'an Englishman and a soldier', but he did not really enjoy it and found time for study, always carrying volumes of Greek and Latin with him.

He spent his twenty-sixth birthday in the militia and wrote in his journal a self-portrait, which seems as judicious an appraisal of his character as anyone could have given:

> . . . This was my birthday, on which I entered into the 26th year of my age. This gave me occasion to look a little into myself, and consider impartially my good and bad qualities. It appeared to me, upon this enquiry, that my Character was virtuous, incapable of a base action, and formed for generous ones; but that it was proud, violent, and disagreeable in society. These qualities I must endeavour to cultivate, extirpate, or restrain, according to their different tendency. Wit I have none. My memory is both capacious and retentive. The shining qualities of my understanding are extensiveness and penetration; but I want both quickness and exactness. As to my situation in life, tho' I may sometimes repine at it, it perhaps is the best adapted to my character. I can command all the conveniences of life, and I can command too that independence (that first earthly blessing), which is hardly to be met with in a higher or lower fortune.

With the conclusion of the war in 1763 he embarked on a long-delayed European tour. In Paris he enjoyed society and met figures such as d'Holbach, but as always in his life he was equally at ease with simpler environments. He revisited Lausanne, becoming acquainted with John Holroyd, who was to prove a lifelong friend, later taking from him much of the burden of managing his financial affairs and eventually, by then become Lord Sheffield, editing his manuscripts into what has become a famous autobiography.

Together they toured Italy and amidst all the thorough reading and sight-seeing came the famous moment which he recorded in his *Autobiography*: 'It was at Rome, on the 15th of October 1764, as I sat musing amidst the ruins of the Capitol, while the bare-footed friars were singing Vespers in the Temple of Jupiter, that the idea of writing the decline and fall of the city first started in my mind.' He returned to England, jettisoned other historical projects and set to work on his great *opus*.

By this time his rationalism was becoming more pronounced. As a country gentleman he attended church, but read the testaments in Greek and Latin. 'Since my escape from Popery I had humbly acquiesced in the common creed of the Protestant Churches', but his thoughts and reading were leading him in different directions. He read Grotius *On the truth of the Christian Religion* and found no truth for himself. In 1761 he still wrote of 'our Creator' and 'His works', but in the same paper he said, 'I shall continue to search for the truth, though hitherto I have found nothing but probability'.

While he progressed with *The Decline and Fall*, Gibbon found time for theatre-going and society. He settled in 7, Bentinck Street, London and became Member of Parliament for Liskeard. His parliamentary career was undistinguished, though commentators have noted that he failed to vote for American independence, thus supporting the perpetuation of one empire while describing the disintegration of another. He was an early riser and happily combined early morning study with a full social life: 'I never found my mind more vigorous or my composition more happy than in the winter hurry of society and Parliament.'

In 1776 the first edition of the first volume of *The History of the Decline and Fall of the Roman Empire* was published in an edition of five hundred copies. They were sold within a fortnight. He gained rapid esteem, and reported to his friend Georges Deyverdun: 'The ancient history of your friend has succeeded like the Novel of the day.' Measured praise came from Hume: 'Whether I consider the Dignity of your stile, the Depth of your Matter, or the Extensiveness of your Learning, I must regard the Work as equally the Object of Esteem . . .' Horace Walpole's accolade, 'Lo, there is just appeared a truly classic work', helped to establish the work's popularity.

He had anticipated controversy with Chapters XV and XVI, in which the rise of Christianity is delineated, and had rewritten them many times. He wrote, employing his favourite weapon of irony, to his friend Deyverdun:

> Would you imagine, my dear Sir, that injustice would be carried to the point of attacking my faith. The outcry of the Bishops and a great number of ladies respectable equally for their age and enlightenment has been raised against me. They dare to assert that the last two chapters of my pretended history are nothing but a satire on the Christian religion, a satire the more dangerous as it is disguised under the veil of moderation and impartiality and that the emissary of Satan after having entertained his reader for a long time with a very agreeable story leads him insensibly into his infernal trap. You perceive, Sir, the horrible nature of such conduct and you are well aware that I shall only present a respectful silence to the clamour of my enemies.

In due course he broke his resolve to remain silent in the face of his many critics, whose books and essays are now forgotten. The criticisms concentrated upon details, errors of scholarship, or scandalous phrases, but Gibbon's transfer of the history of Christianity from the divine to the secular world was irrevocable. The *Vindication*, his self-defence, was published in 1779 and showed Gibbon as a deft and sharp polemicist. But work on the ensuing volumes was of more importance.

Following the succesful publication of the first volume, Gibbon enjoyed a very sociable six months in Paris, where he was lionized, re-established contact with Mme Necker (Suzanne Curchod) and met people such as the Austrian Emperor Joseph II and Buffon. According to an account by Cobbett, he accidentally ran into Benjamin Franklin at an inn. When Franklin requested his company at dinner because of his admiration for *The Decline and Fall*, Gibbon declined to dine with a subject who had opposed the King and received the response from Franklin that he had such regard for *The Decline and Fall* that when Gibbon came to write the decline and fall of the British Empire, as he expected he soon would, he would be pleased to furnish him with ample material.

Back in England his continuous financial problems were eased by a position at the Board of Trade and Plantations. The Fox circle, with which he was briefly associated, accused him of being bought by the government. He was equable in the face of political mud-slinging and at the loss of office after Lord North's fall.

The second and third volumes of his history were published in 1781 with steady success. He gave himself a year's break, which he spent reading much Greek literature, before continuing with the fourth volume. His financial problems, his loss of office, and his decision not to stand for Parliament again all led to a plan to return to

Lausanne, which he had known so well as a young man. In 1783, he moved to set up house with Deyverdun in Lausanne. In Lausanne the two bachelors established a comfortable *régime*, which included much company, food and wine, and gave Gibbon the peace to conclude *The Decline and Fall*.

He approached completion: 'But let no man who builds a house, or writes a book, presume to say when he has finished. When he imagines that he is drawing near to his journey's end, Alps rise on Alps and he continually finds something to add and something to correct.' Eventually he reached the moment recorded in his *Autobiography:* 'It was on the day, or rather the night, of the 27th of June 1787, between the hours of eleven and twelve, that I wrote the last lines of the last page in a summer-house in my garden. . . . I will not dissemble the first moments of joy on the recovery of my freedom, and perhaps the establishment of my fame. But my pride was soon humbled, and a sober melancholy was spread over my mind by the idea that I had taken my everlasting leave of an old and agreeable companion, and that, whatever might be the future fate of my history, the life of the historian must be short and precarious.'

Gibbon's removal of God from an active role in history was of lasting importance for all historians, and also theologians who have long adopted his rigorous study of the facts and assumed that the spread of Christianity is best observed through what Gibbon described as 'secondary causes'. Gibbon allowed to Christian expansion the primary cause of 'the ruling providence of its great Author', but he did not leave much place for this other great Author. In a draft *Outline History of the World* which Gibbon wrote to clarify his ideas before composing *The Decline and Fall,* he wrote: 'The existence of a Supreme Being was indeed acknowledged; his mysterious attributes were minutely, and even indecently, canvassed in the schools; but he was allowed a very small share in the public worship, or the administration of the Universe.' This back-seat place for God – a common Greek or Roman view – was Gibbon's perspective in life and literature. He may have retained a belief in God as 'a working symbol of the inexplicable' (D. S. Low). But he favoured religion in inverse proportion to the extent to which it interfered with people's lives. The lax, orthodox clergymen who subscribed to the articles of faith 'with a sigh, or a smile' were less dangerous than the zealous early Christians or contemporary evangelicals.

In describing the rise of Christianity, Gibbon attributed it to the

Christian's zeal, their doctrines of immortal life, the miraculous powers which were ascribed to the early church, the pure and austere morals of the early Christians, and the organisation of Christian churches as an independent republic within the Roman state. It was his ironic comments on the unsullied purity of the early sect that aroused indignation more than his historical examination of the records. He wrote, referring to the wide variety of the early Christian sects: 'It has been remarked with more ingenuity than truth, that the virgin purity of the church was never violated by schism or heresy before the age of Trajan or Hadrian, about one hundred years after the death of Christ. We may observe with much more propriety, that, during that period, the disciples of the Messiah were indulged in a freer lattitude both of faith and practice than has ever been allowed in succeeding ages.' He indicated that the early Christians were not free from the usual foibles of human nature: 'Ambition is a weed of quick and early vegetation in the vineyard of Christ.' The worldly development of the churches and clergy did not escape his scathing pen: 'The primitive Christians were dead to the business and pleasure of the world; but their love of action, which could not be entirely extinguished, soon revived and found a new occupation in the government of the church. The laity was separated from the clergy – a celebrated order of men which has furnished the most important, though not always most edifying, subjects for modern history'.

In writing of the Roman persecution of Christians he claimed that history should never condescend 'to plead the cause of tyrants, or to justify the maxims of persecution'. However, he suggested that Christians, by refusing to acknowledge the Emperor, or join the libations or festivals which were the national aspects of religions, set quoted the proconsul Antoninus, who exclaimed to the Christians of Roman toleration of religious diversity. He also pointed out that Christians were not themselves advocates or practitioners of toleration. The scale of persecutions had been exaggerated, in his view, and the fervour of Christians for martyrdom was also a factor. He quoted the proconsul Antoninus, who exclaimed to the Christians of Asia: 'Unhappy men! unhappy men! If you are thus weary of your lives, is it so difficult for you to find ropes and precipices?'

Gibbon did not himself believe in an after-life, pointing out that 'a union of sensual and intellectual enjoyment is a requisite to complete the happiness of the double animal'. But he thought the credulous multitude were led by priests to believe in immortality. He wrote that the priests in India, Assyria and Egypt had gained power and 'employed the motive of virtue as the instrument of ambition', and pointed out that the immediate attraction of a kingdom of heaven on earth 'perfectly adapted to human desire' was abandoned once the edifice of the church was almost completed at the time of the Council of Laodicea.

His friend Deyverdun died in 1789, the year of the French Revolution. His perturbation at the French upheaval was no doubt increased by meeting French exiles in Lausanne. Threats of approaching war spread across Europe. Gibbon quietly composed fragments of his autobiography and planned further historical essays. The death of Lady Sheffield, wife of his lifelong friend, caused him to revisit England. His own health was poor; a hydrocele, apparent to his friends for many years, was tapped. He was in good humour and enjoying conversation; but his health declined with unexpected rapidity and he died in January 1794. There is no evidence, despite later stories to this effect, that he changed the view expressed in his *Autobiography:* 'The present is a fleeting moment, the past is no more; and our prospect of futurity is dark and doubtful.'

In the months of his final illness churches had been closed in Paris, and the Terror was approaching its peak. Gibbon admired Burke's stern disapproval of the French Revolution: 'I admire his eloquence, I approve his politics, I adore his chivalry, and I can almost excuse his reverence for church establishments. I have sometimes thought of writing a dialogue of the dead, in which Lucian, Erasmus, and Voltaire should mutually acknowledge the danger of exposing an old superstition to the contempt of the blind and fanatic multitude.' Members of the multitude, like Thomas Paine, saw hope not danger in exposing the 'old superstition'.

8

Thomas Paine: The age of reason

Thomas Paine (1737–1809), whose *The Age of Reason* profoundly influenced several generations of freethinkers, was a product of the age of Enlightenment. His writing sprang from a strong reaction to circumstances and a sturdy independence of mind which led him to think things out from first principles. The case for deism was put by him plainly and forcefully and with such vigour and wit that he quickly entered the demonology of orthodox Christians.

His writings were so castigated and feared that a black legend arose from propaganda attempts at character assassination. The early biographies by Francis Oldys and James Cheetham in 1791 and 1809 were not fully exposed until Moncure Conway's thorough vindication of Paine in his biography published in 1892. Paine is a classic example of the critic of orthodoxy, who was prominent in major events of his time and as well-known as any writer of his age, who was blackened and largely forgotten by historians for almost a century.

Thomas Paine was born and brought up in Thetford, Norfolk. His father was a Quaker staymaker and his mother an Anglican daughter of the Thetford attorney. He was educated at the local grammer school and was excited much more by the natural world than by classics or book learning: 'The natural bent of my mind was to science!' His Quaker upbringing had a lasting impression: 'My father being of the Quaker profession, it was my good fortune to have an exceedingly good moral education, and a tolerable stock of useful learning.' He recollected questioning conventional religious belief at an early age: 'From the time I was capable of conceiving an idea, and acting upon it by reflection, I either doubted the truth of the Christian system or thought it to be a strange affair.' He remembered at the age of eight having been read by an aunt a sermon on the subject of what is called *Redemption by the death of the Son of God* and being revolted at the idea of God acting like a passionate man and killing his son, for 'God was too good to do such action' (*The Age of Reason*). He retained a belief in a beneficent deity and his attack on the Bible stemmed from a view that God was too good to be associated with such 'a muddled catalogue of misdeeds'.

At the age of thirteen he left school and became apprenticed to his father to learn the trade of staymaker. In a brief bid for a more adventurous life at the age of seventeen he attempted to sail on a privateer but was rescued by his Quaker father, presumably aghast at his son embarking upon a career of war. The captain from whom he escaped is alleged to have been named Death. Two years later he went to sea on the privateer King of Prussia, but he did not stay aboard for long.

For the next eighteen years until he was thirty-nine, his life was uneventful and did not presage the fame he was to gain. He was a staymaker in Kent, and then an exciseman in Lincolnshire until he was discharged in 1765 for stamping a consignment which he had not examined, apparently a fairly common practice among overworked excisemen. He then stayed briefly in London, where he taught English at a private academy and perhaps first gained experience of metropolitan life. He appealed for re-appointment in the Excise, successfully being appointed officer at Lewes in 1768. During the next eight years in Lewes, he settled to a comfortable and sociable existence. There was as yet little indication of the rebel author, and his literary powers were confined to an election song for a Whig candidate and a patriotic song for the death of General Wolfe. But his civic sense was developed as he served on the Vestry (equivalent to parish council) and he was gaining a reputation for expressing strong views in debate at an evening club at the White Hart Inn.

In 1771 he married Elizabeth Ollive, a woman thirteen years younger than he was. The following year he prepared his first pamphlet, which was, like all his writing, a response to events. The conditions of excisemen were poor and, perhaps at the request of other officers, perhaps on his own initiative, he wrote *The Case of the Officers of Excise*, which was published and distributed by his own efforts. In 1774 he was again discharged from the Excise, the reason given being that he had quit without the Board's leave and 'gone off on Account of the Debts which he hath contracted'. The debts may have been due to the cost of printing and distributing his pamphlet, and the contents of the pamphlet may have been the real reason for his dismissal. At the same time the small grocery and tobacco business which he ran in Lewes failed and he separated from his wife. The reason for the separation is unclear, but there is evidence that it was quite amicable and, unusually at a time when women were regarded as the legal property of husbands, he abandoned all rights over his wife's income and property.

At thirty-seven he had lost his profession, his financial means, and his wife. He had demonstrated a modest pamphleteering talent and had shown himself a man of honesty, integrity and curiosity. But it could not have been predicted that his name would become renowned as that of a radical or that he would write the *Rights of Man* and *The Age of Reason*, two of the most searching and widely read books on political and religious thought of his time.

In London, where he had distributed his pamphlet, he met Benjamin Franklin and was given a letter of introduction to his son-in-law in Philadelphia. He sailed on the London Packet in September 1774 to a new world and a new life. In Philadelphia he was quickly involved in the flourishing trade of journalism. He edited the *Pennsylvania Magazine* and rapidly increased its circulation, including in it many of his own pieces under numerous pseudonyms, until he was refused a salary increase. Among the topics he covered were the oppression of autocracy and monarchy, the custom of duelling, cruelty to animals, slavery, the position of women, and scientific matters. His attack on slavery was based on the inconsistency of Americans complaining of their own subjection to England while they were depriving others of their freedom. He could not tolerate the moral inconsistency which is the norm for human behaviour.

The conflict between England and the American states was a growing issue during Paine's first two years in America. At first he favoured reconciliation, but after open hostility had broken out at Lexington he decided that separation was the only answer. During the autumn of 1775 he worked on a pamphlet in favour of American independence, and in the new year *Common Sense*, his first major essay, became the first printed pamphlet arguing for a complete break with England. A citizen in Massachusetts wrote that he believed that no pages were 'ever more eagerly read, nor more generally approved. People speak of it in rapturous praise.' The first edition sold a thousand copies within two weeks. Later editions included an Appendix written to persuade the Quakers of the justness of his arguments, and he acknowledged that the pamphlet was 'working a powerful change in the minds of men'.

Paine played an active part in the War of Independence and met Washington. A series of pamphlets, known as *The Crisis*, began with the famous phrase, 'These are times that try men's souls'. During the war he was Secretary of the Committee of Foreign Affairs, then clerk to the Pennsylvania Assembly, and sailed to France to gain financial support for the American side. His offer to Congress to write a history of the war was not accepted – regrettably, since his involvement in affairs, his clarity of mind and his critical sense would have eminently suited him for the task. Once the Peace Treaty was signed in 1783, he was left, as often in his life, with little means or reward for his efforts; he was still owed arrears for his work as Secretary to the Committee of Foreign Affairs. Then he was given the gift of a farm at New Rochelle by the Assembly of New York and a Congress grant.

Now he settled to a life of friendship and scientific enquiry. He sent a smokeless candle which he had invented to Franklin, and devoted the next few years to the design of an iron bridge of one single arch, a version of which was eventually built at Sunderland, but for which he was never paid. He settled in England again, but when the Revolution started in France in 1789, ever-anxious to see humanity improved, he returned to France. In the Spring of 1790 he was entrusted with the key to the Bastille by Lafayette, which he was to take to Washington. He described the key in a letter to Washington as 'an early trophy of the Spoils of despotism, and the first ripe fruits of American principles transplanted into Europe'. Paine always made comparisons between the French and American upheaval, believing that all Europe would in due course follow suit in creating societies free from enslavement to corrupt and autocratic governments.

He saw in Edmund Burke's *Reflections on the Revolution in France* an opportunity to outline his support for the revolution. Burke's rhetorical attack infuriated radical opinion. It lacked accurate information about events in France and surprised his Whig friends, who had known him as a supporter of the American colonies and of modest reform. He was essentially concerned to elaborate a conservative philosophy of the value of custom and tradition; but the force of his oratory underlined his passionate attack on the changes in France. He articulated irrational fears, predicting disaster several years before the Terror in France: 'Along with its natural protectors and guardians, learning will be cast into the mire, and trodden down under the hoofs of a swinish multitude.' For many years representatives of the multitude were to bristle under the insult 'swinish'.

Paine determined to answer Burke and did so from an entirely different political stance and with first-hand knowledge of events in France. The first part of *Rights of Man* was published in 1791. Paine was contemptuous of Burke's 'wild, unsystematical display of rhapsodies' and offered a cool description of events in France and analyses of how governments come between man and his maker. He vigorously attacked priestcraft and kingcraft, especially when linked as Church and State (a team which Burke particularly admired). In the second part Paine aimed to combine 'Principle and Practice' and advocated a vast range of social reforms including family allowances, universal education, universal suffrage, and pensions. The plainness of his language and the topicality of his account gave an immediate success to the book and there were many copies reprinted by republican and radical societies.

In 1791 he returned to France and wrote and had translated a republican manifesto. Even in revolutionary France republicanism was not yet widely proposed – Marat still favoured a constitutional monarchy. The manifesto was published in Brissot's journal *La Patriote Française* and nailed on the door of the National Assembly, with the result that there was some agitation for Paine's arrest. He was back in London in the summer and in much demand as a guest of honour at reform clubs. His great idealism was seen in his address at the Thatched House Tavern (published under the signature of Horne Tooke, the chairman of the Society for Constitutional Information): 'We live to improve, or we live in vain. . . .'

The following year, when he published Part II, he had difficulty in finding a publisher. His opposition to censorship is seen in his Preface to Part II: 'Mankind are not now to be told they shall not think or shall not read; and publications that go no further than to investigate principles of Government, to invite men to reason and to show the errors and excellencies of different systems, have a right to appear.' In May there was a royal proclamation against writing, printing and selling seditious works and in a parliamentary debate on the proclamation Paine's name was mentioned. In June the government issued a trial summons against him for seditious writings; he attended court but the trial was postponed until December by which time he had left England for the last time.

His departure for France on 15 September 1792 was probably due to an invitation to represent Calais in the National Convention more than his desire to escape prosecution. There is an unsubstantiated story that the poet Blake warned him that he was due to be arrested. Effigies of him had been burnt around England, but he was triumphantly greeted at Calais with a salute of guns and the cry of 'Vive Thomas Paine!'. Although he was optimistic that the French Revolution would lead to a Europe liberated from bondage, he entered the French Assembly at an inauspicious time. During the next year, under the pressure of war, internal conflict and food shortages, the revolutionary leaders were deflected from discussion and reform into panic and the guillotine.

Paine knew many of the politicians in the National Assembly. His participation in French politics was hampered by a lack of knowledge of French, but his voice was heard, and he was known as the author of *Rights of Man*, which had been translated by his friend Lanthenas. He was appointed one of a committee of nine to write a new constitution, but when completed in 1793 it was put in abeyance because of the war. He delivered an enthusiastic *Address to the People of France* before the Convention, which contained a warning indicating that he suspected the course of the revolution was moving awry: 'Let us punish by instructing rather than by revenge.' He made a memorable plea for the life of Louis XVI, arguing that he should be treated with compassion as a human being, and exiled to America rather than executed.

Meanwhile in England at the end of 1792 Paine, in his absence, was tried for sedition for publishing *Rights of Man*. He was brilliantly defended by Sir Thomas Erskine, whose speeches have become famous in the literature of defence of freedom of speech, but the case was lost chiefly as a result of a letter from Paine to the Attorney-General, which elaborated his fervent opposition to the King and government. (The authenticity of the letter has been questioned, since Erskine, strangely, was not aware of its contents.) Paine was baned from returning to England, and the trial marked the beginning of one of the worst periods of suppression of free speech in English history.

In France Paine took less and less part in public affairs during the increasing disorder in 1793. He must have been disillusioned and there is evidence that he was drinking heavily (an accusation that was often levelled at him, but which does not seem to have been true to an extent that ever impaired his effectiveness). In what he described as the 'tumultuous misconduct with which the internal affairs of the revolution are conducted', accusations and arrests abounded and he must have known that his own safety was endangered. At this time he embarked upon his last major literary work, *The Age of Reason*.

The arrest of the only two foreign deputies, Paine and Anarcharsis Clootz, was ordered by the Committee of General Security on 27 December 1793. The next morning, between three and four, Paine was arrested, but managed to convey the first part of *The Age of Reason* into the hands of an American friend, the poet Joel Barlow, before being conducted to the prison of the Luxembourg. He remained there for ten months and only narrowly escaped the guillotine. He contracted a severe fever which weakened his health for the remainder of his life. He was permanently embittered against Washington, who he thought could have secured his release, and later published a vitriolic attack on him. Such personal attacks were unusual from this fair-minded and generous man, but poor health and disillusionment have been offered as explanation of his hostility to a man he believed could have effected his release from prison.

Once out of prison, he returned to the Convention, although still in poor health. He opposed the new constitution of 1795 because it introduced property qualifications for voters and took no further part in the new government. He was now in his late fifties and ten months of imprisonment had left its mark upon him. Nevertheless, he went on to write Part II of *The Age of Reason*, substantiating his biblical criticism with detailed references.

The Society of Theophilanthropy which he founded in Paris was an endeavour at putting his religious ideas into practice. Theophilanthropy, 'compounded of three Greek words consisting of God, Love, and Man', was a forerunner of nineteenth-century ethical movements. The society published 'a collection of discourses, lectures, hymns, and canticles for all the religious and moral festivals of the Theophilanthropists' and their programme included readings from Confucius and 'divers moralists'. Paine's *A Discourse* delivered to the society of Theophilanthropists opened with the words: 'Religion has two principle enemies, Fanaticism and Infidelity, or that which is called Atheism. The first requires to be combated by reason of morality, the other by natural philosophy.' Something of the tradition of the Quaker meeting survived, and Paine who came to be regarded as the scourge of religion is seen to have had deep moral and religious concern.

He lived with Nicolas de Bonneville and his family; Bonneville was the young editor of the journal *Bien Informé* to which Paine frequently contributed. Many radicals from Europe visited him including Theobald Wolfe Tone, who had led the 1798 Irish rebellion. Tone thought Paine was 'vain beyond all belief', but he was himself a strong and prickly character. He noted that Paine 'seems to plume himself more on his theology than his politics, in which I do not agree with him'.

Paine was becoming impatient with his position in Paris, perhaps seen as an eccentric radical, and longed to return to America, where his career as a writer and campaigner had started. Eventually, with some help from Jefferson, with whom he had corresponded, he went back to America in 1802. Jefferson was personally considerate to him, but for political reasons was reluctant to express his own deist views or be too closely associated with him.

On his arrival in America every paper was filled with 'applause or abuse'. He found the excitement and the idealism of the formative period of the American nation had passed. He settled at New Rochelle and was soon joined by Madame de Bonneville and her two sons from France. Rumour incorrectly held that they were Paine's illegitimate children. Madame de Bonneville was an ineffectual housekeeper, but he took responsibility for the children, taking great interest in their upbringing. He continued with his journalism and scientific papers. Opponents continued to vilify him: James Cheetham, an editor with whom he had quarrelled, wrote a virulent biography, spreading rumours of drunkenness and immorality. Madame de Bonneville successfully sued Cheetham, but the judge praised the book because it 'served the cause of religion'.

Paine had the misfortune to live to see his reputation perish, his ideas lose ground, and his beliefs in morality, humanity and deity caricatured as crude militant atheism. Despite a disappointing old age, he remained mentally active, in contact with friends and acquaintances and unrepentant of his views. He had an apoplectic fit in 1806 from which he recovered, but the illness which he had suffered in France returned in 1809 and in his last few months he was confined to bed; his mind was clear and he received visitors. He wished to be buried in a Quaker graveyard, but this request was refused. On 8 June 1809 he died. He was buried in obscurity at New Rochelle. Opponents spread a rumour that he had made a death-bed recantation, and the Religious Tract Society circulated a pamphlet quoting a serving woman alleged to have witnessed the repentance. Cobbett investigated the rumour and found no truth in it.

Had Paine stuck to criticism of political systems and not taken the

Bible and Christianity apart with his engineer's mind, his reputation might have been comparable to that of Wilkes, Cobbett or Franklin. Had he not been a writer whose main impetus was a response to events, who outlived the events which inspired him, he might have experienced a more distinguished old age. Had he been more learned and acquainted with the ideas of the *philosophes*, his thought might have been taken more seriously by subsequent scholars. He worked out ideas from first principles and expressed them with the directness of a plain man. Therein lies his essential importance, for he laid the foundations of freethought among common men in the nineteenth century.

A sentence from *Common Sense* anounces his opposition to monarchy and the Churches: 'And as a man hath good reason to believe that there is as much of king-craft, as priest-craft in witholding the scripture from the public in Popish countries. For monarchy is in every instance the Popery of government' (*Common Sense*). The right to think for oneself which is part of the importance of the growth of a free press should not exclude scripture and *The Age of Reason* examined the Bible with devastating acuteness.

Paine was a devout deist, and his attack on orthodoxy came from a belief that the Bible was too violent and ridiculous to be the word of God and the Christian story made no sense of the universe. His Quaker childhood and love of science and nature gave him a reverence for the universe which he felt institutionalised Christianity betrayed.

It is perhaps surprising that he did not become an atheist; atheist writings, such as those of d'Holbach, were talked about, and he knew atheists in Paris during the Revolution. But he remained convinced that a deity was revealed through the natural world – thus sharing the views of the English deists who believed God was revealed through reason and the natural world. He was certainly aware of the argument that nature is unsatisfactory as a revelation of God, since it was propounded by Bishop Watson of Llandaff's reply to *The Age of Reason, An Apology for the Bible* (the work of which George III is said to have declared he was 'not aware any apology was needed for that book'). An innate optimism about the world may have exaggerated for him the beneficence of nature (and of political upheaval). He perhaps underestimated man's propensity for malicious actions; he saw the word of God in the works of creation and in the 'repugnance we feel in ourselves to bad actions, and disposition to good ones' (*The Age of Reason*). There is no evidence that the disillusion of his later years caused him to abandon his devout deism: his wish to be buried in a Quaker graveyard, leaving aside the obvious link with his childhood, indicates that his views remained firmly deist. It was a deism held by many Americans but rarely explicitly avowed. Elihu Palmer's *The Principles of Nature*, published in America in 1802, was a prime book in the tradition, but attempts to spread a deistic movement failed. More strength went into Unitarianism, which retained more of Christianity, although in a highly heterodox form.

Paine did not have the philosophical subtlety of Hume, the breadth of scholarship of Gibbon, or the polymathic mind of Voltaire; but he democratised religious unorthodoxy for that very reason. There was much less risk in attacking religion within the context of historical or philosophical enquiry than in the blunt, everyday language of the pamphleteer. He preferred thinking to reading and nothing could have pleased Paine more than to know that he provoked more than one generation of working men into thought.

Paine's biblical criticism attacked the Bible as revelation of the word of God. This was not new, but it was new to many of his readers. He was over-literal and unscholarly (as were most clergymen of his time). He laboured under the disadvantage of holding the current view that the Gospels were written by eye-witnesses. But he cannot be blamed for pre-dating German historical criticism. He understood the workings of history from first-hand experience. It was novel and shocking for those to whom the Bible had been propounded as God's truth to read of it as a *pot-pourri* of muddled history, poetry and violence. He was acutely aware that events could be transmuted by different tellers: 'It is not difficult to discover the progress by which even a simple supposition, with the aid of credulity, will in time grow into a lie, and at last be taken as a fact' (*The Age of Reason*).

Many writers have referred to the violence of Paine's language; he was witty and forceful, but never intemperate. He described the story of Jonah and the whale as 'a fit story for ridicule, if it was written to be believed; or for laughter, if it was intended to try what credulity could swallow; for if it could swallow Jonah and the whale, it can swallow anything'. He said at the end of his examination of the Old Testament: 'I have now gone through the Bible, as a man would go through a wood with an axe on his shoulder, and fell trees. Here they lie; and the priests, if they can, may replant them. They may, perhaps, stick them in the ground, but they will never make them grow.'

He attacked Christianity, having a particular dislike of the idea of the Resurrection, and speculated that if there were men in other worlds God would be busy sending his Son all over the universe to die in atonement. The debasement of man into a sinful creature in need of salvation affronted his view of human dignity. However, like the Unitarians, he admired the character and moral teachings of Jesus, which he thought were damaged by the inconsistencies and fabulous inventions of the New Testament, such as the story that Mary was 'debauched by a Ghost'. His sincere and moral deism placed him with the early eighteenth-century moralists, but the vigour of his attack on the Bible made him a favourite of nineteenth-century freethinkers. He wrote that 'it is the duty incumbent on every true deist that he vindicates the moral justness of God against the calumnies of the Bible'; but his defence of God against the defenders of the faith could not be separated from his insistence that the Bible 'is a book of lies, wickedness and blasphemy; for what can be greater blasphemy than to ascribe the wickedness of man to the orders of the Almighty'. Paine was not easily forgiven for ascribing the wickedness of the Church and the Bible to the clergy, and the hostility he aroused has often concealed the honesty and honourableness of his intentions.

9

Heine and Büchner: Atheism and revolution

'"I, Signora, was born on New Year's Eve 1800." "I already told you," remarked the Marquis, "he is one of the first men of our century."' Like this character in his satirical work *The Baths of Lucca*, the poet Heinrich Heine sometimes implied that his birth coincided with the dawn of a new century. It has now been established that he was born in 1797, but it was typical of him to prefer a symbolic to a factual version of his birthdate. He was a man who in his writings, quarrels and travels touched diverse and contradictory aspects of nineteenth-century thought. He was concerned with Jewish emancipation, but could make anti-semitic remarks; he championed freedom and greater equality, but feared proletarian rebellion and chaos; he castigated religion in some of the most caustic comments ever directed at priests, but was a rare example of a freethinker who returned in later years to belief in a personal God. Just as Shelley became best known for his lyrical poems, while the range of his ideas was neglected, so Heine survived in the many *Lieder* composed from his bitter-sweet love songs, while the span of his thought was forgotten.

Heine's mother was from a well-established family in the German Jewish community. She was strong-willed and ambitious and outlived her famous son. His father was a weak character who failed in business. An important relative was his paternal uncle, Salomon (1767 – 1844), a wealthy banker. Throughout his life Heine was disappointed in his hopes of a steady income from this source, but his waywardness and the uneasy combination of assertion and complaint with which he approached his uncle led to constant friction.

Heine was brought up in Düsseldorf. His childhood was apparently easy-going and provided no obvious foundation for that 'toothache in the heart' with which he said he was born. The Jewish influence was conventional, but relaxed; his deep ambivalence towards his Jewishness may have sprung from living in an era in which Jewish emancipation was discussed while anti-semitism thrived, and in which many Jews saw integration as a route to success. Spinoza, whose pantheism influenced Heine, had earlier tried to release Jews from a special religious destiny, writing that 'the Jews of today have absolutely nothing to which they can lay more claim than the rest of mankind'. Heine's anti-clerical agnosticism was a standard item in the intellectual equipment of a European student in the 1820s, but it must have been given especial impetus in his case by his ambivalence toward his Jewishness. One of his last poems, written when he had returned to some religious faith, was *Disputation*, a contest between a Capuchin friar and a Jewish rabbi which caricatures the arguments of both sides as vituperatively as any freethinking tract and concludes with the observation:

> I don't know which one is right –
> But I'll tell you what I think
> Of the rabbi and the friar:
> Both of them alike, they stink.

Heine's early poems concentrated upon frustrated love and their mood is more important than the disappointed infatuation, probably for a cousin, which provoked them. By the time he entered university in 1819, he had written some fine lyrics, unsuccessfully embarked upon a business career in Hamburg with the aid of his uncle, and been persuaded to study law. Commerce and law were half-hearted sops to society and relatives: he aspired to be a man of letters. He found himself in trouble after taking part in a student demonstration in Bonn; but, unlike Büchner, he was adapting to a student role and he was always to show greater enthusiasm for revolution in retrospect than in reality. He moved first to Göttingen and then to Berlin, which was a growing cultural centre where he found himself more at home than anywhere hitherto. Heine heard Hegel's lectures, but imbibed a vague current rather than any systematic ideas. He published the first version of his most famous volume of poems, *The Book of Songs*, and converted a visit to Poland into an early prose work, *On Poland*, which stated his view of writing as a 'holy struggle' against 'obsolete injustice, the dominant foolishness and the bad'.

He returned to Göttingen for the final phase of his law studies and in the following summer took a two-hundred-and-eighty-mile walking tour which was made famous in his first successful prose work, *The Harz Journey*. His prose works are a mixture of travel description, journalism, fictionalised autobiography and satirical comment; they bubble with ideas. Topicality, notoriety and a sardonic sense of humour gave them wide regard in his lifetime. The trek through the Harz mountains included a visit to Goethe, the grand old man of German letters, then in his seventies. Heine was disappointed that Goethe did not appreciate the rising young poet he considered himself to be and turned his pique into a 'war with Goethe and his writings'. In fact he was in tune with Goethe's Spinozist pantheism and shared his attraction to Hellenic paganism and distaste for Christianity. A bizarre incident is described in *The Harz Mountains*: on reaching a mountain top he grasped a cross erected there. Shortly afterwards he took instruction from a Protestant pastor and was baptized in 1825. Much speculation has failed to resolve the motive behind the sudden conversion. He was to write as early as January 1826: 'I very much regret that I had myself baptized.' His cynical explanation that it was 'the entrance ticket to European culture' cannot have been the complete reason. His search for identity and for religion were interlinked, and he never really acquired a stable position.

He had been awarded a doctorate in law, but this did not solve the problem of his career. On a holiday by the North Sea he wrote *The North Sea*, a volume of poems, and, soon after, Julius Campe, a liberal publisher committed to moderate but determined attempts to outwit censors, began to publish his work.

Heine's political and religious views were being crystallized in his writings. *Ideas: The Book of Le Grand* (1827) depicts a French drum major who passes on revolutionary principles to his son by drumming – an allegory of the writer's role. *English Fragments*, following a trip to England, showed his dislike of English dullness and his view that the victory of Wellington over Napoleon was the triumph of stupidity over genius. Many years later he wrote of the English: 'Their praying, their mechanical Anglican church-going with the gilded prayer-book under their arms, their stupid boring sabbath, their maladroit piousness is the most repulsive to me.'

Further *Travel Pictures* (IV) gave an account of a tour of Italy. His respect for Napoleon was modified as he began to appreciate the oppressiveness of the French Empire. In Italy he noticed the Christian-Austrian domination and undercurrents of rebellion and made a famous statement of belief: 'I have never placed great value on a poet's fame, and whether people praise or fault my songs concerns me little. But you shall lay a sword on my coffin, for I was a good soldier in mankind's war of liberators.'

The final part of the Italian *Travel Pictures*, *The City of Lucca*, contains some of his liveliest reflections upon religion. Much of the work consists of a dialogue between the caustic, freethinking Lady Mathilde and the unconventional, but more moderate, Heine. A religious festival and visit to a mass and a shrine are recounted with a running commentary from Lady Mathilde: 'Look there at Lady Eve *née* Rib, how she chats with the Serpent! It was a good idea of the painter to give the snake a human head with a human countenance; but it would have been much more sensible if he had adorned the face of the seducer with a military moustache. Look there, Doctor, at the angel announcing to the highly blest Virgin her blessed "situation", and who laughs at the same time so ironically. I know what the rascal is thinking of.'

Such sarcasm, which was a staple diet of some nineteenth-century freethinkers, aimed to break the aura of reverence surrounding religious themes and practices, rather than to prevent serious arguments against Christianity. Some of it seems tame – even pointless – in a secular age, but it was a significant part of the process which developed a climate of opinion where religious claims could not be accepted without question. Heine commented with words that were to be echoed by many earnest doubters who questioned, but did not mock, religion: 'It cannot be denied that the passion for ridicule and mockery, the delight in the incongruity of things, has something evil in it, while seriousness is more allied with the better feelings – virtue, the sense of liberty, and love itself are very serious.' The distinction between mocking and respectful criticism of religion was constantly raised in the nineteenth century; the acrimony and scorn of the Enlightenment were anathema at a time when religion was allied with respectability rather than respectable arguments.

One of the passages which most shocked Heine's readers indicates his view that Christianity banishes joy from the world. He quotes Homer's description of the 'immortals' sharing 'sweetest, pleasantest nectar' and 'an infinite laughter' and portrays the Greek gods threatened with the coming of Christianity:

> Suddenly there came gasping towards them a pale Jew, dripping with blood, a crown of thorns on his head, bearing a great cross of wood on his shoulder, and he cast the cross on the high table of the gods, so that

> the golden goblets trembled and fell, and the gods grew dumb and pale, and ever paler, till they melted in utter mist.
>
> Then there were dreary days, and the world became grey and gloomy. There were no more happy immortals, and Olympus became an hospital, where flayed, roasted, and spitted gods went wearily, wandering round, binding thier wounds and singing sorrowful songs. Religion no longer offered joy, but consolation; it was a woeful, bleeding religion of transgressors.

The semi-fictional nature of *The City of Lucca* makes his own position hard to define: he probably occupied a shifting ground somewhere between pantheism and atheism. As with many nineteenth-century revolutionaries, it was a position where animus was directed more against 'throne and altar' than against the arguments for the existence of God.

The revolution of 1830 in France produced no immediate response in Heine, though he was later to launder his revolutionary reputation with some retrospective enthusiasm. However, he was showing interest in France and French thought, and his problems with censorship made him fear for his freedom in Germany. A letter indicates that his interest in the ideas of Saint-Simon also attracted him to France: 'Every night I dream that I am packing my trunk and travelling to Paris to breathe fresh air, to give myself entirely to the sacred feelings of my new religion, and perhaps to receive the final consecration as a priest of it' (April 1831).

When Heine reached Paris in May 1831, the vitality of intellectual and cultural life, which made him feel like 'a fish in water', had a more lasting effect upon him than the beckoning priesthood of Saint-Simonism. Saint-Simon (1760–1825) was an early egalitarian who thought religion should be a human tool: his disciples developed a hierarchical and ritualistic secular imitation of religion which was one of the many attempts to give ritualistic shape to human hopes and fears while abandoning orthodox belief. Heine may have been attracted to some such ideas, but he was fully alert to the absurdities of Prosper Enfantin, the autocratic leader of the Saint-Simonists after their founder's death; Enfantin designed a tunic with buttons at the back so that another person was needed to remind the wearer of human interdependence, and Heine remarked that God in his incarnation as Enfantin had made the supreme sacrifice – he had made himself ridiculous.

In Paris Heine became acquainted with men such as de Nerval, Berlioz and Mignet, and enjoyed his own high reputation as a poet.

He did not develop intimate friendships and 'remained just as lonely in the world as before'. Mathilde, the affectionate peasant girl who became first his companion and then his wife, brought him domestic comfort, but not intellectual partnership.

The conflict between 'sensualism' and 'spiritualism' is one of the principal themes of *On the History of Religion and Philosophy in Germany*, one volume of a two-volume work designed to present German culture to France. His greatest accusation against Christianity was 'spiritualism', which he defined as being based on 'the principle that it is necessary to annul all the claims of sense in order to accord exclusive authority to the spirit; that it is necessary to mortify, to stigmatise, to crush the flesh that we may better glorify the soul: while the other system, *sensualism*, revindicates the rights of the flesh, which neither ought to be nor can be abrogated'. Heine's *Religion and Philosophy in Germany* is a colourful rather than an accurate account. He expresses admiration for Luther, who he thought transformed religion so that 'the most essential claims of matter are not merely recognized, but legitimized' and:

> religion once more becomes a truth; the priest becomes a man, and takes a wife and begets children as God has ordained . . . In fine from this time forward, especially since the natural sciences have made such great progress, miracles cease. Be it that God is chagrined to find natural philosophers watching His manipulations with such an air of suspicion, or be it from some other motive; certain it is that even in these latter days, wherein religion is in so great peril, He has disdained to support it by any striking miracle.

He thought that the essence of the German religious tradition was pantheism, damaged by Christianity and surviving in folklore. He enthused about the 'peculiar, indescribable fragrance' of the writings of Spinoza. He distinguished between deists and pantheists, and carefully protected them both from charges of atheism: 'The God of the pantheists, then, is distinguished from the God of the deists by being in the world itself, whereas the latter is outside of, or, what is the same thing, above the world.' The 'great deist' Lessing (1729–1781) was praised for his love of truth. Kant (1724–1804) was accused, in writing the *Critique of Pure Reason*, of drawing 'the sword that slew deism in Germany'. Such a 'catastrophe' for deism was compared to the French Revolution: 'As here [in France] the monarchy, the keystone of the old social edifice, so there, deism, the keystone of the old intellectual *régime* falls from its place.' Heine foreshadowed Nietzche's declaration that 'God is dead': 'Hear ye not the bells resounding? Kneel down. They are bringing the sacraments to a dying god.' Much of the debate about religion in the eighteenth century was conducted within a general deistic and sceptical framework; in the nineteenth century, clear rational arguments were accompanied by the alarm, excitement and *Angst* of the experience of the 'death of God'.

Heine misunderstood Kant, who refuted all the arguments for the existence of God based on reason, but re-introduced the necessity for a deity on the grounds of the certainty of a moral absolute. Kant's arguments are complex but the shift from rational arguments to appeal to experience and emotion is a major one. Christian apologists, having lost many of the arguments in the eighteenth century, also moved to an appeal to experience and emotion as is seen in Chateaubriand's *Génie du Christianisme* (1802). Heine did much to perpetuate an apocryphal story by recounting how Kant, having 'stormed heaven and put the whole garrison to the edge of the sword', saw his manservant, old Lampe, 'an afflicted spectator of the scene, tears and sweat-drops of terror dropping from his countenance' and then relented and said, 'Old Lampe must have God, otherwise the poor fellow can never be happy'. Kant's reasons for retaining belief in God are much more complex, but the anecdote illustrates an abiding view that religion was needed for the happiness and deference of ordinary people.

Heine concluded *Religion and Philosophy in Germany* with an ambiguous warning that German philosophy would bring about a terrible upheaval in Germany. This has often been misapplied as a prophetic picture of Nazi Germany, but in fact contains Heine's confused hopes and fears at the disorder which the undermining of deism and pantheism might unleash.

A more concrete threat to Heine came from the German Federal Decrees of 1833 banning political organizations and public meetings and a ban on writings of the Young Germans in 1835 in which Heine was mentioned by name. The Young Germans were radical and anti-Christian. Gutzkow, who was also mentioned by name in the ban, wrote an anti-Christian and semi-pornographic novel, *Wally the Sceptic*, and an uproar followed its publication. Gutzkow was imprisoned for two months. The radicals were divided by their differing degree of prurience and cowed by the decrees; the group lost its impetus. Heine, not personally associated with them, became even more strongly opposed to censorship and authoritarian rule. He began to write poems with greater political content, to attack

Germans for their subservience to authority and to castigate the greed of the wealthy. He differed from many younger radicals in his dislike of German nationalists, whom he described as 'sutler-women of freedom . . . washerwomen of Christian-German nationalism'.

For about eighteen months in 1843 and 1844 Heine and Karl Marx were regular acquaintances in Paris. Marx was twenty years younger than Heine, and less well known. They shared a hatred of tyranny and poverty, but Heine can have had no inkling of the revolutionary theories developing in Marx's mind at that time. Marx may have recalled Heine's description of religion (in a book about another German radical, Börne) as 'spiritual opium' soothing the wounds of deprived mankind when he came to write of religion:

> Religious suffering is at the same time an expression of real suffering and a protest against real suffering. Religion is the sigh of the oppressed creature, the sentiment of a heartless world, and the soul of soulless conditions. It is the opium of the people. (*Towards a Critique of Hegel's Philosophy of Right*)

They shared a belief that religion was a comfort for the downcast and regretted that harshness of life which made such solace necessary. Heine would not have continued as did Marx: 'The abolition of religion as the illusory happiness of the people is required for the real happiness. The demand to give up the illusions about its condition is the demand to give up a condition which needs illusion.' Heine's revolutionary enthusiasm was checked by his apprehension that disorder would release popular anti-semitism and his fear of the joylessness of puritanical egalitarianism.

The French revolution of 1848 coincided with the collapse of Heine's health. On a visit to hospital he became embroiled in fighting among the barricades and was dispirited by the experience. A few months later he wrote: 'About the current events I say nothing; it is universal anarchy, world hugger-mugger of God's madness made manifest. The Old Man will have to be locked up if this goes on – it is the fault of the atheists; they have driven him crazy.' How literal his references to God are, especially when jesting, cannot be easily determined. His distress was genuine. His health had been worsening for some years; headaches, eye trouble and temporary paralysis occurred between 1845 and 1848, but in April 1848 paralysis of the spine set in and he was never to walk again. He knew that he was on his death-bed, but did not know that he would live for almost eight pain-racked years, suffering what was almost certainly syphilis. Creeping paralysis made reading barely possible by attacking his eyelids. He surprised himself by his courage and calm and wrote some of his greatest poems while lying on his 'mattress-grave'.

His doubts about revolution solidified with the coincidence of the barricades and physical paralysis; similarly his religious views were to change as he lay meditating. Heine is unusual amongst those figures depicted in this book in that he returned to religion, declaring, not without a trace of self-mockery: 'When one lies on one's deathbed, one becomes very sentimental and soft-hearted, and would like to make peace with God and the world.' He was acclaimed by Christians eager for morality tales of death-bed conversions and accused of betrayal by freethinkers. This *volte-face* may not have been a total repudiation of early atheistic gestures, but there was a genuine transition from anti-clerical pantheism to a personal God. He wrote, in a Postscript to *Romancero*, his last published collection of poems, that he had no use for the God of the pantheists: 'This poor visionary being is intertwined and interwoven with the world, imprisoned in it as it were, and yawns in your face will-less and powerless.' He knew that the need for comfort while torn with pain motivated his change of view: 'When one longs for a God who has the power to help . . . then one must also accept his *persona*, his other-worldliness, and his holy attributes as the all-bountiful, all-wise, all just, etc.' There remained ambivalence in that trailing 'etc' and in the subsequent humorous comparison of the religious package to fine marrowbone which 'makes an excellent beef tea to regale the poor languishing patient and brace him up'. A very apposite comment on death-bed conversions was made much earlier by Heine himself in his *Religion and Philosophy*: 'So many free-thinkers are converted on their deathbeds – but make no fuss about it! These conversion stories belong at best to pathology and would yield poor witness for your cause. In the end they prove only that it was not possible for you to convert those free-thinkers so long as they went about with healthy senses under God's open sky and were completely in command of their reason.'

A more satisfactory consolation, from the point of view of freethinkers, was his brief love affair with a young woman, Camille Selden. Although their relationship was necessarily platonic, it raised deep and erotic emotion in Heine according to the evidence of his late poems.

In 1854, he described his terrible condition as that of 'A dead man who thirsts after the most vital pleasures of life!' The following year his condition worsened. His alleged last words, 'Write . . . paper . . . pencil', may be doubted, but he was lucid to the end. He was buried on 20 February 1856; as requested a simple ceremony without clergy took place at Montmartre cemetery.

The writings of the dramatist Georg Büchner (1813–37) have been much more admired in the twentieth century than those of Heine; he was certainly more atheistic in thought and revolutionary in deed. His play *Danton's Death* contains one of the most interesting discussions of atheism ever to be written for the stage.

Büchner was born near Darmstadt in Hesse. His father was a doctor, who had served in the Napoleonic army, travelling in Holland and France, being influenced by the ideas of the *philosophes* and enthusiastic about Napoleon's reforms. He tempered any early freethought and radicalism and paid prudent attention to his career, when he became a medical adviser to the Darmstadt court of Ludwig I. Georg's mother was from a well-to-do family and her own literary interests were passed on to her children. Physiology and literature were crucial to Büchner's short career; when he considered abandoning his anatomical studies, the Young German writer Gutzkow, with whom he had corresponded, commented that his particular strength lay in his 'unusual lack of inhibition, your autopsy, I almost want to say, that comes across in everything you write'.

Georg Büchner was given a conventional education at a private school and at the Gymnasium. He was talented but not outstanding as a youth and taught himself scientific subjects, since they were not included in the school curriculum. A school friend later recalled that he had said: 'Christianity does not please me: it makes you pious like a lamb.' His essay on suicide, in which he expressed the view that life is not a means but an end, 'for development is the end of life, life itself is development, therefore life itself is an end', suggests that his criticism of religion was more thoughtful than casual adolescent rebellion.

With the encouragement of his father, Büchner went to Strasbourg University to study zoology and anatomy. Strasbourg was a centre for radical exiles and Büchner's political commitment strengthened during his period there. He also met Minna Jägle, the daughter of a Swiss pastor in whose house he lodged for a while, and they fell in love and later became engaged. His early death prevented marriage and Minna remained single: shortly before her death in

1880 she destroyed letters, papers and probably the manuscript of a play, *Pietro Aretino*, to remove evidence of his unorthodox religious and political views.

A letter written while he was in Strasbourg illustrated his reaction to an unsuccessful rebellion in Frankfurt: 'If anything can help in our time it is *violence* . . . What do you call *a lawful state*? . . . A *law* that turns the great mass of citizens into serf-like cattle in order to satisfy the unnatural needs of an insignificant and decayed minority?' He gave an account of a Mass in Strasbourg in which he said 'I am not a Catholic' and that 'the music alone made more impression on me than the eternal commonplaces of most of our divines, who can think of nothing better to say than that God Almighty must have been a very clever man to allow His son to be born at this particular time of the year'.

Büchner was required by the German state rules to return to his native Hesse to complete his studies at Giessen University. He found Giessen a backwater in comparison with Strasbourg, and was ill and unhappy. He was restless, at odds with the world and himself and 'turned night into day': 'My mind is chaos – work has become impossible – I do nothing but brood. Everything turns inwards. If only I could escape from myself!'

At Giessen, Büchner met a radical pastor, Weidig, and began to reflect upon revolutionary action. He studied the French Revolution and 'had the feeling of being annihilated by the atrocious fatalism of history': 'The individual is merely a foam on a wave, greatness mere accident, the role of genius is puppetry, a ridiculous wrestling with an iron law in which the greatest achievement is simply to become aware of it, overcoming it is impossible.' Commentators have suggested that he foreshadowed Marx's view of the inevitability of history; as belief in the role of God in unfolding history declined, so people persistently sought secular explanations to give meaning to the passage of time.

Büchner, like many impressed with the impersonal movement of history, also wanted to give it a helping hand. He founded a branch of the Human Rights Society in Giessen and together with Weidig wrote a revolutionary tract, the *Hessian Peasant Courier* (1834). It contained figures demonstrating that the tax system transferred money from the poor to those at court, condemned the autocratic rule of Ludwig II, and called for action. Debate and pamphleteering were dangerous activities. An informer amongst the group caused the arrest of Büchner's close friend, Karl Minnigerode. Büchner managed to warn others and for reasons not known remained free from arrest himself. He returned to his family's house in Darmstadt. His rooms in Giessen had been searched and he knew that he was a prime suspect. For some months he lay low in his father's house, virtually in hiding. His mind was in a turmoil; he knew that he was at risk of arrest, torture and death. He was haunted by the fact that his friend Minnigerode was in prison while he was free.

Early in 1835, in a period of five weeks, he wrote his first play, *Danton's Death*. The vividness with which he portrayed the Terror after the Revolution is less surprising than the coolness with which he presented the process of history and Danton's fatalistic acceptance of death. His play, far from reinforcing the powerful myth that the Revolution and Enlightenment philosophy had led to the Terror, showed how disorder, fanaticism and belief in a Supreme Being undid the *philosophes* and revolutionaries. It was not well known or performed until the twentieth century.

Büchner hoped his play would earn him enough money to escape to freedom. He sent the manuscript to Gutzkow with an appeal for money. Gutzkow recognized the play's worth and it was published in the periodical *Phoenix* between March and April 1835.

Büchner longed to return to Strasbourg to rejoin Minna and resume his studies, but his family opposed flight. A summons to appear before a commission of inquiry in February 1835 determined him to delay no further. His brother kept a ladder ready in the back garden and he may have used it when he fled. The remaining two years of his life in Strasbourg and then Zürich were extremely productive. He replaced revolutionary activity with scientific study and creative writing: for reasons of safety he denied his revolutionary past. He wrote *Lenz*, a prose study of the poet's disintegration into madness, and the plays *Leonce and Lena* and the incomplete *Woyzeck*. *Woyzeck* examined the motivation of a murderer, showing the fascination for Büchner of the interplay between the individual and his environment. His scientific studies were serious and his work on the physiology of the barbel gained him a doctorate and, in due course, a lectureship in Zürich. He also worked at essays on Descartes, Spinoza and Greek philosophy and established contact with the literary world through Gutzkow.

In Zürich, early in 1837, he received news of the death of Minnigerode in prison; the news was incorrect but it deeply affected him. In February he became ill with a cold. It worsened and within three weeks he was dead, probably from typhus. Minna was at his death-bed and he was nursed by a friend, Caroline Schulz. Her notebooks written during his last weeks are full of poetical-religious fervour, so the accuracy of her record of Büchner's words may be doubted, but she wrote that he said: 'We can never have too much pain, we can only have too little. Through pain we come to God.' Nothing in his writing or letters suggests, however, that he was returning to religion. He had become known and respected in Zürich and a large congregation, including the mayor, attended his funeral.

Danton's Death contains a fascinating discussion of atheism. Thomas Paine, the deist, is mistakenly made the mouthpiece of atheism, in a conversation with Danton and others in the Luxembourg prison:

> There is no God – since either God made the world or He did not. If He did not make it, the world had its germ in itself, and there is no God – since God is only God if He holds in Himself the germ of all being. Now God cannot have made the world, since either creation is eternal like God, or it had a beginning. If it had a beginning, God must have made it at a given point in time. So that God, having rested for eternity, must have become active suddenly – and undergone a change in Himself, which made Him apply a new conception – Time. Both of which assumptions are contrary to God's essence. So that God cannot have made the world. Now since we know clearly that a world exists, or at least that we exist, and that, from what I have just said, that world must have its roots in itself or in some other thing that is not God there can be no God. *Quod erat demonstrandum.*

The prisoners continue their conversation about Spinoza, the first cause, and Voltaire, then 'Payne' asks why humans have wanted an eternal being:

> I prefer an earthly father to God. At least I don't have to say behind his back that he brought me up a galley slave or fed me at a pig trough. Remove our imperfections – then you can demonstrate your God; but not before. Spinoza tried it. God might satisfy your reason, but your feeling denies Him and rebels. We can deny evil, but never pain . . . Why do I suffer? There's my rock of atheism. The smallest stab of pain, if it only stirs an atom, cracks your creation from top to bottom.

This provides an interesting reversal of the common association of atheism with reason and religion with feeling.

All of Büchner's writings suggest he was as thoroughly materialistic and atheistic as any nineteenth-century writer. His brothers, though leading more conventional lives, also wrote from this viewpoint and *Force and Matter* (1855) by Ludwig Büchner was much admired as a work of rationalism. Ludwig, a scientist, lost his academic position at Tübingen after publication of the book, which gave scientific substance to naturalistic atheism.

Heine and Büchner provide a contrast between shifting scepticism larded with anti-clerical wit and clear-cut atheism allied to revolutionary fervour. Georg Büchner was forgotten for most of the nineteenth century, but Heine attained European fame and was, for instance, described by George Eliot in the *Westminster Review* as 'one of the most remarkable men of this age'.

10

Shelley and Carlile: Printing against the creed

The history of the freedom of the press is a long and fluctuating tale of the struggle for independent thought, linked with heresy and freethought, and inimical to any monolithic faith. One of those who risked prosecution by printing works sceptical of religion, Robert Taylor, the 'Devil's Chaplain', wrote in a note in his *Diegesis*: 'In the year 1444, Caxton published the first book ever printed in England. In 1474, the then Bishop of London, in a convocation of his clergy said: "If we do not destroy this dangerous invention, it will one day destroy us". After the Terror in France in 1793 and the growth of radical clubs, repressive laws were passed in Britain. *Habeas Corpus* was suspended in 1794 and leading members of the London Corresponding Society were tried, though acquitted for treason in the autumn of 1794. Severe restrictions were placed on the right of public meeting. There was a collapse of radical activity. A few individuals continued to print subversive work: Daniel Isaac Eaton, who had published a version of the *Rights of Man* in 1794, also published *The Age of Reason* and in the period up to 1812 suffered 15 months' imprisonment, and three years' self-imposed exile in America, for his printing activities. In 1812 he published the so-called third part of *The Age of Reason* as a separate tract and was tried for blasphemy and given a harsh sentence of eighteen months' imprisonment and two hours in the pillory every two months by Lord Chief Justice Ellenborough. (Eaton died in poverty in 1814. As J. M. Robertson comments: 'Militant atheism was obviously not a paying career'.)

As a result of the Eaton case a powerful defence of free speech was published as a pamphlet by Shelley in the summer of 1812 in the form of an open *Letter to Lord Ellenborough*. Shelley argues that truth may be reached by the public exchange of ideas: 'That which is false will ultimately be controverted by its own falsehood. That which is true needs but publicity to be acknowledged.' It has been suggested that Shelley did not fully appreciate the political dimension of the use of blasphemy law, but at the end of the *Letter* is a classic plea for toleration and freedom of ideas: 'The time is rapidly approaching, I hope, that you, my Lord, may live to behold its arrival, when the Mahometan, the Jew, the Christian, the Deist, and the Atheist, will live together in one community, equally sharing the benefits which arise from its association, and united in the bonds of brotherly love.'

Shelley's own writings were also suppressed and attacked. The youthful pamphlet *The Necessity of Atheism* was secretly printed in Sussex and distributed by Shelley and his undergraduate friend, Thomas Jefferson Hogg, in Oxford in 1811. It was produced in collaboration with his friend Hogg, and was based mainly on the ideas of Hume and Locke. The Oxford booksellers Slatter and Munday, who had earlier sold a Gothic novel by Shelley, were persuaded to display copies of *The Necessity of Atheism* around the shop. Within minutes the Rev. Jocelyn Walker came in, saw and read the atheist tract and ordered all copies except one, kept for evidence, to be burnt. Shelley and Hogg were expelled from Oxford; if their reaction to the incident had been less provocative they might have escaped expulsion and presented their essay as a piece of intellectual inquiry in the tradition of Hume. But Shelley had sent copies to bishops and heads of colleges and advertised the pamphlet in the *Oxford and City Herald*. He had also publicly advertised his support of an Irish journalist, Mr Peter Finnerty, who had been imprisoned for attacking the government's disastrous military policies. He had written to Leigh Hunt, editor of *The Examiner*, a respectable journal with radical leanings, outlining a plan for gathering together various dislocated radical groups in society to construct 'a form of methodical society which should be organized so as to resist the coalition of the enemies of liberty which at present renders any expression of opinion on matters of policy dangerous to individuals'.

Shelley's atheism and political radicalism were fired by his conflict with his father, an MP horrified at his son's 'dangerous' ideas. He had recently been abandoned by his cousin Harriet Grove with whom he believed himself in love, and imagined this to be due to his anti-religious opinions; he wrote to his friend Hogg: 'Oh! I burn with impatience for the moment of Xtianity's dissolution, it has injured me; I swear on the altar of perjured love to revenge myself on the hated cause of the effect which *even now* I can scarcely help deploring . . .' At his family home, Field Place in Sussex, his atheism had caused consternation: 'My mother fancies me in the High road to pandemonium, she fancies I want to make a deistical coterie of all my little sisters.'

Shelley's background was quite different from that of the working-class radicals who engaged in the practical struggle of printing and risking imprisonment. He was born in 1792 into the county aristocracy; his grandfather, Bysshe Shelley, was a fiery personality who had made his money in America and returned the family to England. His father Timothy Shelley was a conventional and conformist Whig MP. Shelley went to Eton, which he hated, and then to Oxford. He was a genius as a poet, essayist, polemicist, translator and thinker engaged in an astonishing breadth of ideas.

His religious unorthodoxy and political radicalism were played down by his Victorian admirers who preferred to emphasize his lyrical gifts, but they were an integral part of his thinking. The extent of his atheism has been a cause of argument. He went well beyond the familiar eighteenth-centry deist approach and was at least a thorough-going agnostic. *The Necessity of Atheism* is his most extreme statement, but arguments against theism recurred in his works, in the pamphlet *A Refutation of Deism* and in references in the first version of *The Revolt of Islam*. Later in his short life he publicly repudiated a pirated republication of *Queen Mab*: this was due to trouble it had caused his family and dissatisfaction with some immaturity of poetic expression rather than rejection of the poem which he still gave copies of to his friends. The first paragraph of the Note to the words 'There is no God' in *Queen Mab* sums up a recurring view: 'This negation must be understood solely to affect a creative Deity. The hypothesis of a pervading Spirit co-eternal with the universe remains unshaken.'

The long poem *Queen Mab*, with the framework of a fairy describing the past, present and future of earth from a remote point in the universe, contains an attack on established religion, political tyranny, the destructive forces of war and commerce, and the perversion of human love by the chains of marriage and prostitution. The growth of religion is described as a ghastly move towards the idea of God:

> The merciful, and the avenging God!
> Who, prototype of human misrule, sits
> High in Heaven's realm, upon a golden throne,
> Even like an earthly king; and whose dread work,

> Hell, gapes for ever for the unhappy slaves
> Of fate, whom he created, in his sport,
> To triumph in their torments when they fell!

The Spirit of Nature or necessity is praised in contrast as an impersonal force. There is a blasphemous passage (and it was prosecuted as such) in which God speaks of how he planted the tree of evil so that man 'might eat and perish, and My soul procure/ wherewith to sate its malice,' and sent his son to earth:

> . . . humbly he came
> Veiling His horrible Godhead in the shape
> Of man, scorned by the world, His name unheard,
> Save by the rabble of His native town,
> Even as a parish demagogue. He led
> The crowd; He taught them justice, truth, and peace,
> In semblance; but He lit within their souls
> The quenchless flames of zeal, and blessed the sword
> He brought on earth to satiate with the blood
> Of truth and freedom His malignant soul.

Shelley reinforced his rhetoric with carefully argued Notes, some of which are complete essays. The Note to 'there is no God', was an expansion of *The Necessity of Atheism*. He argued that the proof of the existence of a God can come from the three sources of the sense, reason, and the testimony of others. The 'God of the Theologians' is not experienced by the senses and 'is incapable of local visibility'. Reason suggests a beginning or a first cause, but we 'must prove a design before we can infer a designer'. Where two opposite propositions are put, the mind believes the 'least incomprehensible', and 'it is easier to suppose that the universe has existed from all eternity than to conceive a being beyond its limits capable of creating it.' As far as the testimony of others is concerned, we can only admit those views which are not contrary to reason, and those men 'who not only declare that they were the eye-witnesses of miracles, but that the deity was irrational' cannot be believed. Shelley sums up: 'It has been before shown that it (God) cannot be deduced from reason. They alone, then, who have been convinced by the evidence of the senses can believe it.' He adds that there is nothing reprehensible in disbelief, since belief is 'a passion of the mind' which people cannot be blamed for lacking. A lengthy series of quotations from Bacon's *Moral Essays*, d'Holbach's *Système de la Nature*, Pliny and Spinoza concludes the note.

The intellectual background to *Queen Mab* is the works of Lucretius and d'Holbach, linked with the scepticism of Hume and the militant anti-Christianity of Paine. Figures who also influenced Shelley were Count Volney, whose *Ruins of the Empire* gave a vision of a corrupt world, and the writings of Erasmus Darwin, who had written poems on science and society. Shelley read deeply and voraciously throughout his life, conducting a heated dialogue in his mind with many famous and obscure authors. As a student he had immersed himself in the works of Gibbon, Voltaire, Condorcet, Rousseau, Paine and Franklin. He quoted Voltaire's phrase 'Écrasez l'infâme' at the head of *Queen Mab*; Shelley also knew that it was the watch-word of the Illuminists, a secret international Jacobin society dedicated to world-wide revolution.

Godwin is often cited as another influence, and his affect was personal as well as literary, since Shelley married his daughter, Mary, whose mother Mary Wollstonecraft had died in childbirth. Godwin was an atheist at the time he wrote the *Enquiry Concerning Political Justice, and Its Influence on Morals and Happiness* (1793), a book which brought him both distinction and notoriety. 'No work in our time,' said Hazlitt in his essay on Godwin in *The Spirit of the Age* 'gave such a blow to the philosophical mind as the celebrated *Enquiry Concerning Political Justice*. Tom Paine was considered for the time as a Tom Fool to him, Paley an old woman, Edmund Burke a flashy sophist. Truth, moral truth, it was supposed, had here taken up its abode; and these were the oracles of thought.' Godwin modified his views, disapproved of his daughter's association with Shelley and quarrelled with him, and outlived the influential circle of friends who admired him. He questioned religion, criticized the churches, and linked reform with the questioning of religion; but perhaps his most enduring legacy was to present morals and happiness as a human aim, with no supernatural dimension.

Shelley's longest poem, *Laon and Cythna*, was toned down to iron out the incest and atheism and published in the new year of 1818 as *The Revolt of Islam*. The poem is structured within an allegory of the struggle between Revolution and Oppression; the incestuous love affair was at the heart of the celebration of moral and political revolution. Precise references to God, Hell, republicanism and atheism were changed to become vague; for instance: ' – therefore shall ye behold / How Atheists and Republicans can die' was changed to 'How those who love, yet fear not, dare to die' in a heroic death speech. Shelley compromised for his publisher at a moment when prosecutions of freethought publications were accelerating and when he was determined to gain some recognition from printing his works. Lines of Thomas Cooper, the Chartist Rhymer, spoke of Byron's *Childe Harold* and Shelley's *The Revolt of Islam* praising 'Freedom's fearless shout' when 'cold reward would be the frown / of power and priestcraft'.

Both *Queen Mab* and *The Revolt of Islam* were reprinted in pirated editions. *Queen Mab* was the subject of prosecutions brought as a result of pressure from the Vice Society and someone who defiantly reprinted it was Richard Carlile, an indefatigable opponent of censorship.

Richard Carlile was born in Ashburton, Devon, on 8th December 1790. His father was a cobbler, exciseman, schoolmaster and soldier and apparently published essays on mathematics. He was given to drink, perhaps the reason for his son's strong advocacy of sobriety, and died when Richard was only four. His mother and elder sisters sustained the family and Richard gained some education at Ashburton school. He was apprenticed in the tin-plate trade to a master who 'cared no further about me than as to the largest quantity of labour he could obtain from me upon the smallest quantity of food.' His rebellious temperament early showed itself in his conflict with his master. Later he wrote: 'I taught that master, as I shall teach my present oppressors, that mine is a temperament from which persecution can wring nothing but perseverance in resisting it.'

He was not yet interested in politics or religion and found work as a journeyman in London in 1811. After two years' wandering looking for work, he married in Gosport and then settled down in London. In 1815, at the end of the Napoleonic wars, the economic depression led to an upsurge of radical political writing. He began to write letters to the radical press which were not published because of their violence.

The two main curbs on publishing were stamp duties and the laws of libel, sedition and blasphemy. Cobbett published offprints of leading articles from the *Political Register* as *Twopenny Trash* and William Hone's *Reformist Register* and John Wooller's *Black Dwarf* were on sale. Carlile hawked these papers around the streets; they were illegal if they were classified as newspapers rather than pamphlets, for the tax differentiated in order to suppress popular political propaganda. Carlile was a successful salesman undeterred by risks: 'Of imprisonment I made sure; but I felt inclined rather to court than to shrink from it.'

In 1817 William Hone published some parodies of the Litany, Catechism and Prayer Book, which he withdrew on a threat of prosecution. In March of that year Lord Sidmouth, the Home Secretary, activated by a panic and rumour of rebellion, again suspended *habeas corpus* and introduced active measures against sedition. There was a flurry of prosecutions threatening radical journalism. Cobbett left for the United States. William Sherwin, who published the *Republican* and ran a book shop in Fleet Street was worried by the risks and first changed its title to *Sherwin's Political Register* and then offered Carlile the chance of taking over the shop and journal. Carlile leapt at the opportunity and restarted the paper under its original more provocative title of *Republican*.

Later in 1817, Carlile re-issued Hone's parodies, without his consent, and brought prosecution on them both for 'blasphemous libel'. In three successive trials Hone was acquitted by juries who laughed aloud at the wit of the parodies. Carlile spent eighteen weeks in gaol and was released on Hone's acquittal. He read *The Age of Reason* while in prison and was impressed with Paine's works and added deism and attacks on Christianity to his radical repertoire. When he left prison he immediately demonstrated his defiance by publishing a parody which he had written in gaol: 'The *Order* for the *Administration* of the *Loaves and Fishes*, or *The Communion* of *Corruption's Host* – Translated from an original Greek manuscript, lately discovered in the neighbourhood of a certain *Den of Thieves* in Westminster'. The political and religious overlap are seen in the mock prayer:

> Mighty Prince whose Kingdom may not be lasting; whose power is finite—; Have mercy upon the whole Host; and be so ruled by thy chosen servants, Liverpool, Sidmouth, Eldon, and their associates, that they (knowing whose Ministers they are) may above all things aggrandize themselves and dependents; and that we (duly considering under whose authority we are) may faithfully serve, honour, and humbly obey them, in view of, and hoping for further benefits, according to thy word and ordinance; through Castlereagh our Chief. Amen.

In 1818 Carlile published *Common Sense*, the *Rights of Man* and *The Age of Reason*. The sales of *The Age of Reason* were ensured when the Society for the Suppression of Vice began a prosecution in 1819. The Vice Society, as it was known, was associated with leading evangelicals such as William Wilberforce, and played a significant part in the numerous attempts to prosecute anti-religious literature during these years.

In the year of the Peterloo Massacre, 1819, Carlile threw down many challenges by printing controversial works. He started *The Deist* – 'a collection of all scarce and valuable Deistical Tracts, from both ancient and modern writers' and in the *Republican* he published an account of the Peterloo Massacre in the form of a *Letter to Lord Sidmouth*. Apart from Paine's books, he also reprinted Elihu Palmer's *The Principles of Nature*. He was charged with sedition for his account of Peterloo, but he was actually tried in October for blasphemy for publishing *The Age of Reason* and *The Principles of Nature*. The famous proceedings he called his Mock Trial since he did not recognize the laws against free speech. In defending himself he succeeded in reading aloud the whole of *The Age of Reason*, a manoeuvre which enabled him to print it in the verbatim report of the trial which sold ten thousand twopenny numbers. He had many arguments with Judge Abbott, defending the right to free discussion of religious questions. He quoted Archbishop Tillotson: 'If your religion be too good to examine, I doubt it is too bad to be believed', and claimed he had no wish to revile religion, only to examine it freely. He was found guilty and sentenced to two years' imprisonment and a £1,000 fine for selling *The Age of Reason* and one year in prison and £500 for selling *The Principles of Nature*. Since he had no money he was sent to Dorchester Gaol for an indefinite period. He passed the next six years in Dorchester Gaol, sometimes in solitary confinement, at times joined by his wife and sister, who had kept his Fleet Street shop functioning. Throughout the six years he never ceased reading, writing and publishing journals. Jane Carlile, with their baby, joined her husband for two years in gaol in 1821 after conviction for publishing an issue of the *Republican* in which Carlile had defended the right to assassinate tyrants. Carlile's sister, Mary Anne, took over the shop but also found herself in Dorchester Gaol. Until 1825, when he was released, a relay of men and women from throughout the country risked prosecution by keeping the shop open and the 'blasphemous' material on sale. Scores of ordinary people were prosecuted – not only in London – for their determination to sustain free discussion.

The devices to elude prosecution involved a special way of dealing with customers:

> Mr Carlile had formed a plan to sell the books down a spout, so that the person purchasing the books could not see the person that sold them. In this way it was accomplished:– There was a little door on the counter, which the person wanting a book had to rap at, when the

> door opened, and the purchaser asked for the book which he wanted. Then a small bag was lowered down for the money. When it was drawn up, the book with the change – if any was required – was lowered down to the purchaser. By this system informers were baffled; and Mr C. was enabled to carry on his business, and also to collect subscriptions from different parts of the country direct, without passing through the hands of the committee, which was of essential service to him, in case of his shop being closed. (B. B. Jones, 'The people's first struggle for free speech and writing. Led by Richard Carlile, in which they were completely successful.' *Reasoner*, xxiv, No. 680, 5 June 1859.)

The struggle created some of the first groups organized to publish and examine sceptical views of religion. The 'Edinburgh Freethinkers' Zetetic Society', led by James and Robert Affleck, was founded to give Carlile support. Other Zetetic groups followed, especially in London and the north, which sent collections to support Carlile, provided volunteer booksellers and kept the struggle alive.

Carlile was released in November 1825. He immediately took a larger book shop in Fleet Street, which he opened as the 'Temple of Reason', and formed the Joint Stock Book Company to finance publication of books which were suppressed, such as Shelley's *Queen Mab*, Byron's *Cain*, *Don Juan* and *The Vision of Judgment*, d'Holbach's *Bon Sens*, Palmer's *Principles* and Paine's works. The victory was not complete, the laws still had to be changed and the economic weapon of stamp duties challenged. But a decisive demonstration had been given that suppression could not succeed when prosecution increased demand and the persecuted refused to give in. The climate of opinion was slowly turning in favour of free critical discussion of religion.

Carlile's views had developed while he was in prison. From Paineite deism he had moved to thorough atheism; he wrote in one of his pamphlets *Address to the Reformers*: 'I advocate the abolition of all religions, without setting up anything new of the kind.' His most forcefully argued tract, *Address to Men of Science*, adopts two characteristic nineteenth-century themes of unbelievers: the power of education and knowledge to clear away superstition and misunderstanding, and the value of science in showing the absurdities of revealed religion.

Carlile set out his aim 'to lay down a sketch of what seems to me a more instructive and useful system of education. I submit this sketch to the Men of Science, with the idea that every schoolmaster ought to be a Man of Science, and not a parish priest.' The science which particularly impressed Carlile was chemistry, which he saw as important in underlying a materialist attitude to the mind. If the human mind could be explained by chemistry (and the brain seen as part of the nervous system as with other animals), where was the soul? and what was mind? A chemical examination of matter also led to questions about Creation:

> Creation is an improper word when applied to matter. Matter never was created – matter never can be destroyed. There is no superior power: it has no rival. It is eternal both as to the past and future. It is subject to continual chemical analysis, and as continual a new composition. For a full comprehension of these assertions it is necessary to have a knowledge of the elements of Chemistry.

Carlile, however, concerned himself less with the details of scientific development than with the principle that scientists should express their speculations freely, even if they conflicted with theology. He expostulated: 'Shame on that man who can tacitly submit to such a system. . . . I am anxious to sound a loud blast in the cause of Truth, of Reason, of Nature and her laws. I will give every Man of Science an opportunity of publishing his sentiments without any direct danger to himself: I will fill the gap of persecution for him, if a victim be still necessary to satisfy the revenge of dying Priestcraft.' He stated clearly themes which were to be elaborated with greater complexity but to remain of crucial importance: 'I trust I have sufficiently shown that superstition and science can never amalgamate, which also justifies the inference that morality and religion can never amalgamate.'

Like many who thought that religion and morality could be separated, Carlile had a sober, almost puritanical attitude to moral conduct. He always urged temperance and expressed doubts about Shelley's attitude to marriage. A periodical which he had produced from Dorchester Gaol in 1823 called the *Moralist* urged reformers to follow a high standard of moral conduct. However, most people at the time considered his publication of birth control literature as quite immoral. It was consistent with his outlook on freedom of speech. He published the text of a handbill giving contraceptive advice in the *Republican* and in 1826 published *Every Woman's Book* which sold several thousand copies within months and was the subject of prosecutions later in the century. Birth control, or neo-Malthusianism as it was euphemistically called after Malthus' theories about population expansion, thus became linked with radical and freethought causes but it was to remain controversial among freethinkers until late in the century. Carlile was one of the first not only to support the use of contraceptives, but to take the practical step of publishing information about it. There was no doubt about the demand for such information.

In 1826, the year following his release from gaol, his health broke down, probably as a consequence of the hardship of prison life. But he was back in the fray at the beginning of 1828, when he espoused the cause of Robert Taylor, who had been imprisoned for blasphemy. Taylor was prosecuted for delivering thirty-eight lectures on ethics examining and demolishing the basis of scriptural authority. During Taylor's year in Oakham Gaol, Carlile started a periodical, the *Lion*, to print Taylor's lectures, and the two men became friends and fellow campaigners.

Robert Taylor (1784–1844) is a curious figure in the history of freethought, in that he had been an Anglican clergyman and retained an elaborate allegorical interpretation of Christianity. He was born into the fairly well-to-do industrial classes, his father being a prosperous ironmonger in Edmonton. Although his father died when he was very young in 1791, his mother was left an adequate income to bring him up without hardship. He was a talented pupil at the boarding school in Edmonton and says in his autobiographical fragment *Life and Opinions of Talaisphron* that he very soon became distinguished as 'possessing the most extraordinary memory in the school'. He was sent by his uncle at the age of fourteen to Samuel Partridge, the house surgeon of the General Hospital near Birmingham, to be brought up in the medical profession.

Towards the end of his apprenticeship, he was converted by a Calvinist preacher, to the dismay of Mr Partridge, who 'often admonished him almost with tears – "My dear Poet, whatever you do for God's sake never give your mind to religion"'. He successfully completed his medical training in London and gained some work as a surgeon – but work was intermittent and a clergyman friend persuaded him to train for the ministry. At twenty-five he went to Cambridge, received his BA degree in 1813 and was ordained Deacon. After delivering a sermon in the church at Edmonton, he went as a curate to the Rev. Richard Lloyd at Midhurst in Sussex. He was highly thought of and set for a successful Anglican career, aided by personal charm and obvious scholarship.

After four years he began 'the drama of his life' and his views began to alter so that he became, in his own words 'convinced "in his heart's core, aye, in his heart of hearts" that the Christian religion – rather let us say the existence of religion in *any* modification – is the greatest curse that ever befell the human race – the bane of all social affection, and the destruction of wisdom, virtue, and happiness, from among men'. The change was initiated by reading copies of Gibbon and Paine lent by a sceptical parishioner. After reading *The Age of Reason* and enduring a 'paroxysm of prayer to God', he decided he was a deist. He left his parish and went to London. But he decided to recant and return to the Church. The Rev. Lloyd at Midhurst persuaded him to resign his curacy and seek another parish. Lloyd later wrote a pamphlet attacking Taylor's infidel beliefs under the guise of an account of his 'miraculous' return to the faith, which effectively finished all possibility of advancement in the church for Taylor. Taylor evidently could not easily wrench himself from the Church and was a born preacher, whatever he preached. He was briefly successful in a few other parishes until his past infidelity led the Church authorities to dismiss him. Once embarked upon a sceptical path, he was sped on his way by the uncharitable attitude of the ecclesiastical hierarchy and his knowledge of the hypocrisy of many who preached views they did not hold. In his last parish, Yardley near Birmingham, he decided to deliver sermons of the utmost irony so that he could heave 'the anchor of religious convictions of the whole parish and set 'em all afloat'. Crowds came to hear the infidel priest, and he was barred from ever again entering a pulpit as a consequence of a sermon about Jonah and the Whale, which told the biblical story so as to make it appear comic and ridiculous.

He was persuaded to go to the Isle of Man, but when the Bishop there heard an infidel was lecturing, even though the subject was philology, he was warned that he was unwelcome. Penniless in England again, he was lent money by his former friend and medical teacher, Mr Partridge, which enabled him to travel to Dublin. Again he could not resist the lure of the pulpit and was denounced for his irreligious preaching. He produced a series of deistical tracts called the *Clerical Review* and started a Universal Society of Benevolence, somewhat akin to Paine's Theophilanthropic religion. At the second Sunday meeting students from Trinity College caused a riot and Taylor returned to London.

In 1824 he started the Christian Evidence Society, the aims of which were the opposite of the other organization still surviving under that name: it was to examine the reasons for not believing in

Christian evidence. He survived by lectures and meetings, using an infidel 'liturgy' and 'service'. His position was similar to that of many nineteenth-century figures who attempted to purvey a non-Christian religion at various points between deism and universal brotherhood; none were of permanent success, but the attempts indicate the need some felt to propagate a moral stance and hold fast to a 'religious' organization despite their rejection of Christianity.

Taylor was imprisoned for blasphemy in 1828 and there wrote his two books *Syntagma* and *Diegesis*. The *Syntagma* was a reply to a Christian attack on him by John Pye Smith, *An Answer to a Printed Paper Entitled 'Manifesto of the Christian Evidence Society'*. *Syntagma* dealt with the historicity of Jesus, for Taylor thought that there was no evidence for the books of the New Testament being written by persons whose name they bore, that they did not appear in the times to which they referred, that the person and events they refer to never existed or took place.

The historical accuracy of the Bible was a subject of great importance in freethought, since it challenged the authority of Christian doctrine and the churches. Alexander Geddes, a Scottish Roman Catholic, had produced a new translation of the Bible in 1793, in which the Pentateuch was dated from the time of King Solomon; he treated the Mosaic account of the creation as myth in a later work, *Critical Remarks on the Holy Scriptures* (1800). He was an isolated figure who was censured by his bishops. New Testament scholarship was advanced by German scholars who began to examine the gospels and epistles as individual documents, suggesting, for instance, that the Gospel according to St John was not written by St John the Apostle. In England several important works appeared at about the same time as *Syntagma*. E. B. Pusey's *An Historical Enquiry into the Probable Causes of the Rationalist Character of Germany* (1826–1830) brought some German ideas to England, and H. H. Milman's *History of the Jews*, published anonymously in 1829, caused an outcry.

Diegesis, the other work which Taylor wrote in prison, is more idiosyncratic, covers a vast range of obscure knowledge, and though its main thesis that Christianity sprang from the same mythology as Egyptian and other Eastern religions is questionable, it gave free-thinkers an insight into the concept of comparative mythology. Taylor thought that Christianity originated from the Essenes. He made a dubious link between Christ and the Hindu god Krishna on the ground of word similarity and emphasized the idea that early Church Fathers may have tampered with texts.

When Taylor emerged from prison in 1829, he and Carlile set off on an infidel mission across the country to meet their supporters and debate with believers. An unsuccessful start in Cambridge, in which a challenge in Latin and Greek to heads of colleges pinned to the university library door was ignored, was followed by greater support in the textile towns of the north. After returning to London they planned another such tour, but other events intervened. They were now united in determination to uphold free speech, especially in discussion of religion. They were also both broadly concerned with political sympathy for the unrepresented masses in a period of considerable radical activity leading up to the first Reform Bill. Carlile wrote a defence of the agricultural revolt in his journal the *Prompter* (1830) and was tried for seditious libel, found guilty and sentenced in January 1831 to two years' imprisonment and a £200 fine. Taylor was tried for blasphemy in 1831 for two of his Astronomico-Theological lectures at the Rotunda, and given sentence of two years' imprisonment with a £100 fine. His prison conditions seem to have been much harsher than previously and he produced no further writing.

Taylor's other main publications were *The Devil's Pulpit*, published two years after his release from gaol in 1831, and a journal which included a serial autobiography which appeared under the title *Life and Opinion of Talaisphron* in 1833–1834 after another spell in prison. *The Devil's Pulpit* printed forty-six 'Astronomical-Theological Discourses', which Taylor had delivered in full ecclesiastical garb at the Rotunda in South London. They were largely based on C. F. Dupuis' *The Origin of All Worships*, produced in France at the end of the eighteenth century, and detailed the now discredited idea that the Bible was not based on history at all but created from myths and fables relating to the constellations of the stars.

Not long after, in 1833, he married a rich widow, abandoned public life, moved to Tours in France and worked as a surgeon until his death (1844). Unfortunately no papers survive from this last phase of his life to indicate if his ideas changed. He was an idiosyncratic and untypical figure, but Carlile and he, as partners propagating infidelity, shared popularity and prominence for a short period, and his books remained known, if not widely read, among freethinkers.

Eliza Sharples, an admirer who had first heard him while on his infidel mission to the north, had followed him to London. She helped keep the Rotunda open and read lectures written by Carlile and Taylor, becoming known as 'Isis'. When Carlile was released their friendship developed into a partnership and they lived together for the rest of his life. Eliza Sharples played an integral part in his campaigning and writing from now on. Under the influence of Taylor and 'Isis', Carlile, to the embarrassment of freethinking friends, abandoned his atheism and adopted an allegorical-mystical interpretation of Christianity. He remained opposed to the Church as it was and wanted to reform it. In the journal *Isis* in May 1832, he wrote: 'I declare myself a convert to the truth as it is in the Gospel of Jesus Christ. I declare myself a believer in the Christian religion. . . . I declare for the spirit, the allegory, and the principle, and challenge the idolatrous pretenders to Christianity to the field of discussion.'

A final four months in prison came in 1834 as a result of his opposition to the collection of church rates from his shop in Fleet Street. He had protested by erecting in the shop window an effigy of a bishop and a distraining officer; a devil was then added to the arm of the bishop, and crowds gathered, so that he was charged with causing a public nuisance. His attacks on the Church now took the form of pleas for reform; while in gaol he wrote an open letter to Peel, entitled *Church Reform*, urging the regeneration of the Church as a 'School of Moral Science,' and this became the theme of his remaining writings.

Carlile's sporadic later activities included opening a Hall of Science in Manchester (1838) and taking over the Bristol Hall of Science from the Owenites in 1842. The periodical *Christian Warrior* and the tract *Carlile's Railroad to Heaven* were typical of his later writing. He was out of touch with the radicals of the 1840s whose activities were being channelled into Chartism. His weakness as a political thinker was his belief in personal regeneration, eventually to develop into a moralism akin to Dickens' belief in the need for a 'change of heart'. In this he was unlike Robert Owen who placed all his hope on a change of environment rather than of the individual. His central contribution was to the freedom of the press (and freedom of information on birth control) and that was an enormous contribution to the free discussion of religious matters. The campaign against the stamp duty continued and it was reduced to a penny in 1836 and finally abolished in 1869. But there were many further blasphemy trials in the nineteenth century.

The influence which Carlile and Taylor had is indicated by a quotation from the evidence of a Bolton employer, *S.C. on Hand-loom Weavers' Petition* (1834):

> If it had not been for Sunday schools, society would have been in a horrible state before this time. . . . Infidelity is growing amazingly. . . . The writings of Carlile and Taylor and other infidels are more read than the Bible or any other book. . . . I have seen weeks after weeks the weavers assembled in a room, that would contain 400 people, to applaud the people who asserted and argued that there was no God. . . . I have gone into cottages around the chapel where I worship, I have found 20 men assembled reading infidel publications.

That came partly from the press freedom which Shelley was denied and Carlile demanded. Carlile had written in the *Republican*, rather prematurely, but triumphantly:

> The work is done – The press is free
> The manner how – here look and see.
>
> (*Republican*, Vol XIV, 1826)

11

Bradlaugh and secularism: 'The province of the real'

George Jacob Holyoake (1817–1906) was prosecuted for blasphemy in 1842. Richard Carlile was present at his trial and over-enthusiastically described Holyoake's nine-hour speech in defence of his case and freedom of speech as 'the most splendid of its kind ever delivered in this country'. In 1851 Holyoake adopted the word 'secularism' to mean a positive alternative to atheism and to delineate 'the province of the real, the known, the useful, and the affirmative' (*Reasoner*, 1853). Secularist groups and the National Secular Society were to become active in a campaign for the rights of atheists and in promoting anti-Christian views. The most powerful secularist leader was Charles Bradlaugh (1833–1891), whose struggle to enter Parliament became a national *cause célèbre*. Holyoake and Bradlaugh were very different personalities and their relationship was often strained: Holyoake's pedantry and constant self-justification contrasted with Bradlaugh's thorough forcefulness. They also differed in their attitude towards the existence of God, Holyoake preferring the label 'agnostic' and Bradlaugh choosing 'atheist'. They debated their differences in 1870 at the Hall of Science in London, when the propositions included 'The principles of Secularism do not include Atheism' and 'Secular Criticism does not involve Scepticism'.

Secularist groups were formed around the nuclei of earlier Owenite and Zetetic freethought groups. Robert Owen (1771–1858) is best known for his contribution to the Co-operative Movement and trade unionism, but his utopian views were highly individual and not widely accepted by the growing working-class movement. His decisive rejection of religion was intrinsic to his view of human nature. He claimed in his autobiography that he had early decided that contending Christian sects were all wrong and that the differences between them were due to social circumstances: 'Thus I was forced, through seeing the error of their foundation, to abandon all belief in every religion which had been taught to man. But my religious feelings were immediately replaced by the spirit of universal charity – not for a sect, or a party, or for a country or a colour – but for the human race, and with a real and ardent desire to do good.'

The single idea which dominated his life was that man and society could be remade if upbringing and environment were changed. He put this belief successfully into practice at his model factory at New Lanark and attempted to influence men of power by expounding his ideas in essays, pamphlets and at public meetings. *A New View of Society* was a series of 'Essays on the Principle of the Human Character and the application of the principle'. He read parts of it to the Archbishop of Canterbury, sent copies to the Prime Minister, many European leaders, and the governors of all the states of America. A plan to solve British social and economic problems which involved model Villages of Co-operation was received less enthusiastically; the Establishment realized that he was proposing a radical change of society, and workers feared that he wanted to turn the whole country into a workhouse. In 1817 Owen addressed large public meetings to persuade the public of his views. He saw this as a turning-point in his life and feared that the public expression of his views on religion had created opponents: in fact his autocratic paternalism and impractical utopianism did more to deter individual followers. On 21 August 1817 he denounced religion as a prime source of error and distress:

> Then, my friends, I tell you that hitherto you have been prevented from even knowing what happiness really is, solely in consequence of the errors – gross errors – that have been combined with the fundamental notions of every religion that has hitherto been taught to men. And, in consequence, they have made man the most inconsistent, and the most miserable being in existence. By the errors of these systems he has been made a weak, imbecile animal; a furious bigot and fanatic or a miserable hypocrite; and should these qualities be carried, not only into the projected villages, but *into Paradise itself, a Paradise would no longer be found*!

The remainder of Owen's long life was devoted to public debates, writing and editing and to the creation of utopian communities, such as the one established by his son Robert Dale Owen in Indiana, or the community of Harmony Hall at Queenswood, Hampshire. His attempts to create a form of 'rational religion' were of limited appeal to working-class groups where his ideas were gaining currency. The title of the journal which he edited, *New Moral World*, sums up the interest of the later stages of his life. *The Book of the New Moral World*, published in three volumes from 1836 to 1844, became the Bible of Owenite groups and was read like scripture at meetings. A succession of groups were devoted to his ideas: the Universal Community Society of Rational Religionists eventually became the Rational Society. There were paid Owenite missionaries, the so-called 'socialist Bishops' with headquarters in different towns. The unorthodox teaching made it difficult to hire rooms and Halls of Science were built – not without opposition; for instance, in Bradford the local gas company refused to supply the Owenite Institute, and when premises were planned in Manchester in 1839 a local clergyman formed a committee for 'the counteraction and suppression of that hideous form of infidelity which assumes the name of Socialism'.

Owen himself became a sad figure, ineffective but tireless; he never despaired of convincing the world of the truth of his ideas and he never seemed to understand why his reforms at New Lanark could not be successfully transferred to the world at large. Finally, at the age of eighty-three, he found support for his ideas in another world and learned, via a medium, that the spirit world eagerly awaited the earthly world's conversion to Owenism. He continued to lecture, and published a lively *Life* the year before he died in 1858 with the last words, 'Relief has come'. His yoking together of social reform and rational religion was a prime influence on G. J. Holyoake and nineteenth-century secularism.

G. J. Holyoake abandoned the metal foundry in Birmingham, where he had worked as a youth with his father, for the Mechanics' Institute to which he had been introduced by Unitarian acquaintances. After failing to gain a teaching post there he obtained a position as an Owenite lecturer in Worcester. The title of his first lecture, 'An Enquiry into the Incentives Offered by present Society in the Practice of Honour, Honesty and Virtue' suggests a worthy rather than an exciting lecture style and his audiences were small. In 1841 he moved to the larger Sheffield group, where he also had responsibility for a school, but 'neither my School nor my lectures were well attended'.

Infidelity and Owenism frightened the clergy and the Tory bishop of Exeter, Henry Philpott, lambasted the Owenites in a speech in the House of Lords in 1840. An attempt was made to persuade Owenite lecturers to take the oath of a Dissenting preacher. The Central

Board of Owen's movement, because of financial problems, was disposed to ask lecturers to take the oath to avoid trouble, but some supporters chafed at any compromise. One such was Charles Southwell, an adventurer and fiery open-air speaker. After criticizing Owen, he resigned his lectureship and set up his own paper in rivalry to *New Moral World*. Southwell's *Oracle of Reason* attacked religion vehemently. The Bible, for instance, was condemned vigorously: 'That revoltingly odious Jew production, called BIBLE, has for ages been the idol of all sorts of blockheads, the glory of knaves, and the disgust of wise men. It is a history of lust, sodomies, wholesale slaughtering and horrible depravity; that the vilest parts of all other histories, collected into one monstrous book, could scarcely parallel!' Not surprisingly, he was arrested for blasphemy and sentenced to one year's imprisonment. *Oracle of Reason* was kept going and after a couple more issues Holyoake agreed to become editor; the tone immediately became less belligerent.

In 1842 Holyoake set out to walk from Sheffield to Bristol. According to some accounts he had resigned his post in Sheffield and was looking for work, according to others he was travelling to visit Southwell in gaol. He gave a lecture at Cheltenham *en route*. His subject was 'Home Colonisation as a means of superseding Poor Laws and Emigration', and controversial religious matters might have been avoided had not a local clergyman asked him what place God was assigned in the new community. His reply is famous: 'If I could have my way I would place the Deity on half-pay as the Government of this Country did the subaltern officers.' He went on his way, but on reading a Cheltenham newspaper which announced that his arrest was sought, he decided to return to face the authorities. It was a moment of defiance which was not typical; for most of his life he took a compromising attitude towards authority.

Holyoake was duly arrested and placed in Gloucester Gaol. Only after protest that he was being denied due process of law was he released to prepare his defence. For the first time in his life he visited London and contacted Richard Carlile, secured the services of the liberal lawyer, W. H. Ashurst, and spoke at a public meeting at the Rotunda. At his trial he spoke in his defence for a full nine hours; but he seems to have been better at irritating the judge than inspiring the jury with the justice of his case and was sentenced to six months in gaol.

He experienced real hardship in gaol, and though he was prone to over-emphasize the experience throughout his life, as a means of boosting his radical credentials, the death of his young daughter, weakened because he lacked the funds to keep his family well fed, was a bitter wound. He was an industrious prisoner and wrote over two thousand letters and two pamphlets, one of which was a refutation of Paley's arguments from design entitled 'Paley Refuted in His Own Words'. He was consolidating his position as an unbeliever.

On release he found, as he ruefully put it in his memoirs, that 'graduating in gaol was not a recommendation afterwards', although he was at first in demand lecturing as the 'Liberated Blasphemer'. For a number of years he made ends meet with teaching and secretarial posts and with help from middle-class liberal friends. Slowly he established a reputation as a lecturer and journalist. The Owenite groups were in decline and his post with small groups such as the London branch of the Rational Society or the Glasgow Rational Society were neither lucrative nor fulfilling. He founded a paper, the *Movement*, which proposed to 'maximize morals and minimize religion' and then for nearly twenty years edited the *Reasoner and Herald of Progress*, which announced its ambition to be 'Communistic in Social Economy – Utilitarian in Morals – Republican in Politics – and Anti-Theological in Religion'.

The failure of the Chartists in 1848 led to disarray and depression among radical groups. At this time Holyoake founded a society to oppose the 'vast organized error of religion' which became the Society of Theological Utilitarians. In 1851 a group of three hundred freethinkers gathered at the London Hall of Science for an address by Holyoake: the Society of Reasoners was founded and shortly changed its name to the Secular Society. Holyoake developed the use of the word 'secularism' and was influenced by Comte's positivism; he liked to quote Comte's words, 'Nothing is destroyed until it is replaced'. Some unbelievers preferred straightforward attacks on religion and complained that 'Secularism should not shroud itself in refined obscurities'. The number of secularist groups slowly increased, and he attended a conference of secularist groups in Manchester. At a meeting of the London society in 1853, Holyoake, its President, was presented with £250. Thornton Hunt, the radical journalist, and Louis Blanc, the French socialist, were present, and messages were received from Owen and Harriet Martineau. The money enabled Holyoake to buy premises in Fleet Street where he could establish a freethought publishing business.

Holyoake was a poor administrator and lacked force as a leader.

Bradlaugh ousted him as President of the London Secular Society in 1858. For the remainder of his life he remained active within secularism hoping to be a focus for those who agreed with him that 'To make Atheism the Shibboleth of the Secular Party would be to make Secularism an atheistic sectarianism as narrow and exclusive as any Christian sectarianism'. He devoted much time to the Co-operative Movement and attempted to acquire eminence as a journalist and campaigner.

Under Charles Bradlaugh the secularists became a notable pressure group. Bradlaugh's father was a conscientious but unexceptional legal clerk, who found it difficult to earn enough to keep his family in times of economic depression. They moved from Hoxton to Hackney to Bethnal Green, and the young Bradlaugh saw enough of the worst side of Victorian urban squalor to gain an abiding concern with sanitation, birth control and temperance. His education was rudimentary and finished when he was eleven, but an early political awareness is seen in his purchase of a copy of the Charter for a precious half-penny when he was ten. He felt a responsibility to contribute to the family budget, and was first an office boy then a clerk and cashier for a small coal merchant. He made a short speech at a rally in support of the Charter and obtained a lesson in political education when he witnessed the spectacular failure of Chartism to muster its threatened march on Parliament in 1848.

His religious education was gained at Sunday school, where he became a student teacher. The Rev. John Graham Packer gave him the Thirty-Nine Articles to study before his confirmation. He examined them so thoroughly that contradictions became apparent and he wrote to the Rev. Packer asking for an explanation. The clergyman reacted with unreasonable alarm to Bradlaugh's adolescent doubts and suspended him from his Sunday School duties for three months. Although Bradlaugh still considered himself a Christian, he went to hear speakers critical of religion and became acquainted with sceptical literature. He later recounted how he had 'flung himself down and prayed aloud to God, if God there were, to give him light and help, and how no answer came from the void above him, from the empty air around'. The *Diegesis* by Robert Taylor (see p.152) was one of the books acquired by Bradlaugh and he sent a copy to the Rev. Packer. Packer did not take kindly to this study of Christianity as a mythical structure; Bradlaugh's father and employers were contacted and the youth was told he must either change his beliefs or lose his job. Before the three days' ultimatum had expired, he left home. No doubt his future militancy stemmed in part from the bigoted reaction to his sincere early doubts.

Bradlaugh needed a roof over his head, and he gravitated to the nearby home of Eliza Sharples, former companion of Richard Carlile (now dead). He continued his self-education and learnt Hebrew. He began to speak in public, was known as 'Baby' and was admired for his ability to hold an audience's attention. He wrote pamphlets, the first published being *A Few Words on the Christian Creed* which was addressed to the Rev. Packer. At the Hall of Science he met Holyoake and a collection was taken for the 'victim of the Rev. J. G. Packer'. He was developing that 'Self-Reliance' of which Emerson wrote in an essay which so impressed Bradlaugh that he copied out a large part of it:

> To believe your own thought, to believe that what is true for you in your private heart, is true for all men – that is genius. . . . Whoso would be a man must be a nonconformist. . . . What I must do, is all that concerns me; not what the people think. . . . Nothing can bring you peace but the triumph of principles.

An early attempt to start his own coal merchant business failed because he lacked sufficient capital. Attracted by the idea of foreign travel, he signed up with the army and, with the prospect of secure employment, was reconciled with his family. In 1851 he set sail for Dublin. His three years' experience of army life taught him that he was well able to defend himself with his fists against other soldiers or with wit and legal astuteness against authorities. He was popular for his ability to write letters and defend his colleagues' rights. Observation of the army's purpose of suppressing the Irish peasantry made him a life-long champion of Irish freedom. He obtained leave to visit his dying father and then bought himself out of the army with a small legacy from a great-aunt.

For many years he combined attempts at a legal and commercial career with freethought campaigning. He rapidly gained recognition as a speaker. In 1855 he led a group of demonstrators to Hyde Park to oppose a restrictive Sunday Trading Bill. The demonstrations had been banned and Bradlaugh, not for the last time, resisted arrest by the police. As a lecturer throughout the country he often had to contend with local opposition. In Devonport he was forbidden to speak at an open air meeting by a police constable. He defiantly announced a further date and time, but when the mayor and soldiers set out to stop him they found that his platform was a boat on water just outside the jurisdiction of the town authority. His skill at using the legal system to his own advantage was to be one of his greatest strengths.

He continued to write and began to publish *The Bible, What It Is!* in serial form; Holyoake and others stopped its publication from the Fleet Street headquarters, because it was thought dangerous and improper – the Garden of Eden story was seen as a sexual allegory. In fact Bradlaugh was a model of Victorian virtues, dressing with the respectability of a non-conformist clergyman. He settled with his wife in Tottenham, and their house was visited by famous refugees, such as Herzen.

Bradlaugh was amongst those who criticized Holyoake's management of the Fleet Street premises, and his election as President of the London Secular Society marked the beginning of recognition by secularists of his leadership qualities. The *National Reformer* was started in Sheffield in 1860 by Joseph Barker and Bradlaugh was invited to be co-editor. The two disagreed over the introduction of material related to birth-control – a moral question which often divided secularists – and Bradlaugh became sole editor. Apart from a break in 1863, caused by poor health, he remained editor until 1890, and the *National Reformer* was to become 'a sort of personal diary' which covered his public life. Freethought journalists were often divided about how far to stick exclusively to an anti-theological programme and how far to embrace wider political issues: Bradlaugh took the broad approach, deciding that the *National Reformer* should be 'an *avant-courier* on political, social and theological questions, but that it should never deal with one to the entire exclusion of others'. It took much of his energy for most of his life.

In the *National Reformer* Bradlaugh described his position as that of an atheist, a stance from which he never wavered:

> I do not deny 'God', because that word conveys to me no idea, and I cannot deny that which presents to me no distinct affirmation, and of which the would-be affirmer has no conception. I cannot war with a nonentity. If, however, God is affirmed to represent an existence which is distinct from the existence of which I am a mode, and which it is alleged is not the noumenon of which the word 'I' represents only a speciality of phenomena, then I deny 'God', and affirm that it is impossible 'God' can be.

To those who said that criticism of religion was a destructive task and that something must be put in its place, he replied:

> Tell the backwoodsman, who, with axe in hand, hews at the trunks of sturdy trees, that his is destructive work, and he will answer: 'I clear the ground, that plough and reaping-hook may be used by and by'. And I answer that in many men – and women too, alas! – thought is prison-bound, with massive chains of old church welding; that human capacity for progress is hindered, grated in by prison bars, priest-wrought and law-protected; that the good wide field of common humanity is over-crowded with the trunks of vast creed frauds, the outgrowth of ancient mythologies. . . . Atheist, without God, I look to humankind for sympathy, for love, for hope, for effort, for aid.

Among his business ventures was involvement in a company set up to obtain iron and coal from Southern Italy. Occasionally able to combine his business and political career, he acted as a link between Mazzini and England on his travels to Italy.

His inability to work through ill-health in 1863 and the financial crisis in 1866 left him in severe financial difficulties. But leadership was his natural role and when the National Secular Society was founded in 1866, he became its first President and remained so for over twenty years. His energy ensured that most secularist groups joined the national organization. He campaigned for the right of atheists to affirm and supported the work of the Reform League to extend the franchise. After the Reform Bill of 1867, he decided that Parliament was the best place to continue his work and was adopted as candidate at Northampton for the general election of 1868. There was much opposition and, although he did his best to separate his political campaign from his atheism, the *Daily Telegraph* wrote deploring the candidature of a man who encouraged Englishmen to 'revile the sublime moralities of the New Testament'. During his campaign, as frequently in his career, he had to deal with libellous attacks on his character. He was not averse to litigation but found himself in a dilemma: 'If when I am libelled I take no notice, the world believes the libel. If I sue, I have to pay about one hundred pounds' costs for the privilege, and gain the smallest coin the country knows for recompense.'

During the 1870s, the secularist groups were for several years quite inactive. Much of his energy went into republicanism, which was aimed not just at the monarchy, but at land reform, hereditary privileges and reform of the House of Lords. Even so conservative an institution as the University of Cambridge had a republican club with a young mathematics don, W. K. Clifford, as secretary. One of the most famous of Bradlaugh's publications was *The Impeachment of the House of Brunswick*. His fame extended beyond Britain and some European observers tipped him as the most likely man to be the first president of a British republic. He twice visited America on lecture tours as a means of earning money and met celebrated freethinkers such as Ludwig Büchner and Emerson.

Having failed to be elected in 1874, Bradlaugh acquired a further handicap to his electoral image by adding to atheism and republicanism the defence of birth control – an issue tainted with suspicion of obscenity and immorality. By 1876 Annie Besant had risen rapidly to a prominent position as a secularist lecturer and become a close friend of Bradlaugh. She was a woman of more enthusiasm than judgement or consistency and her long career spanned secularism, socialism and theosophy. She and Bradlaugh were for over ten years extremely close but, although scurrilous rumours hinted at adultery, there is no evidence of it. (The monotonous sexual probity of English nineteenth-century freethinkers compares oddly with the hedonistic pleasures of the eighteenth-century European *philosophes*.) Bradlaugh and Mrs Besant stood trial after republishing *The Fruits of Philosophy; or the Private Companion of Young Married Couples* by Charles Knowlton. The jury found them guilty but exonerated them from 'any corrupt motive' and the verdict was quashed on a technicality on appeal.

In 1880, having been accepted as an official candidate of the Liberal Party, Bradlaugh was finally elected to Parliament. His stuggles were not over, and he spent six years fighting to take his seat in the House. He was not the first openly unbelieving MP, for John Stuart Mill and others had preceded him. He thought the Evidence Amendment Acts of 1869 and 1870, which he had done much to bring into law and which gave atheists the right to give evidence in court, allowed him to affirm rather than take the oath when he formally entered Parliament. There was doubt about the legal position and a Select Committee decided, by the casting vote of its Conservative chairman, against his right to affirm. He therefore prepared to take the oath. However, since he had made statements indicating that he thought the oath was 'idle and meaningless' and 'a form less solemn to me than the affirmation I would have reverently made', a parliamentary caucus led by Randolph Churchill opposed his taking the oath on the grounds that he could not be bound by it. Another Select Committee, set up to decide whether Bradlaugh should be allowed to take the oath, ruled against. A motion that he be allowed to affirm put forward by his Northampton colleague, Labouchère, was defeated. Bradlaugh made a speech at the bar declaring that 'there is a court to which I shall appeal: the court of public opinion'. The Speaker asked him to withdraw, he refused, and after a struggle was taken to the Clock Tower. He was the last political prisoner to spend a night there. An amnesty was granted. Gladstone successfully moved a motion that unbelievers be allowed to affirm and in a moment of tense excitement Bradlaugh affirmed and took his seat. Within hours, an opponent, the reactionary Newdegate, took legal steps to bring a writ against him declaring his affirmation was void.

For the subsequent five years Bradlaugh faced complex legal cases, was more than once forced to return to Northampton for re-election, and several times tried to administer the oath to himself. Throughout the country supporters and opponents rallied their forces. In 1881 he publicly declared his intention of taking his seat, arrived in Parliament Square by coach, was cheered by supporting crowds, climbed the steps of the House and was forcibly ejected by the Serjeant at Arms after a physical struggle. His daughter was prevented from studying at University College and Annie Besant was banned from teaching at the Hall of Science. Bradlaugh rightly assumed that his opponents wanted 'to weary and ruin me'.

Another famous case against a freethinker came as a result of Bradlaugh's Parliamentary struggle. G. W. Foote had founded the militant atheist paper *The Freethinker* in 1881. It was provocatively anti-Christian and contained cartoons ridiculing biblical texts. Bradlaugh was thought, wrongly, to be implicated in the publication of the relevant issues of *The Freethinker* and in a further attempt to wear him down a blasphemy prosecution was brought against *The Freethinker* in 1882. One of the most notorious offending cartoons was 'Moses Getting A Back View of God' which depicted the rear side of an elderly gentleman wearing baggy pants. Although Bradlaugh, now expert at threading his way through any legal labyrinth, was able to prove himself not involved in the publication, G. W. Foote was sentenced to a full year's imprisonment – a punishment the severity of which shocked even leading Christians.

Bradlaugh found time for much parliamentary activity, even though technically not seated in the House. In 1883, in a further attempt to pass a Bill giving atheists the right to affirm, Bradlaugh made one of his finest speeches from the bar. He pleaded:

> The House, being strong, should be generous . . . but the constituents have a right to more than generosity. . . . The law gives me my seat. In the name of the law I ask for it. I regret that my personality overshadows the principles involved in this great struggle; but I would ask those who have touched my life, not knowing it, who have found for me vices which I do not remember in the memory of my life, I would ask them whether all can afford to cast the first stone . . . then that, as best judges, they will vacate their own seats, having deprived my constituents of their right here to mine.

Ministers cheered and his opponents were impressed.

By a strange irony Bradlaugh eventually took his seat in a Conservative-dominated parliament. In 1886, after a general election brought in a new Conservative government, the Speaker, Sir Arthur Wellesley Peel (son of the former Prime Minister) said that a new parliament need not be bound by previous resolutions and quickly allowed Bradlaugh to take the oath before there was any opportunity to oppose it. By this time, Bradlaugh had become a national figure seen, like Wilkes, to be a champion of the parliamentary rights of the people. The fight had gone out of his opponents.

Bradlaugh was prematurely aged by the experience, but in his remaining five years he was a tireless and original Member of Parliament. Ironically, he did not live long enough to benefit from his greatest parliamentary achievement – the passage of the Oaths Act, 1888, which finally gave all MPs the right to affirm. The many causes which he championed in the House included the rights of the Irish, of miners, of labourers and of Indians. He took such an interest in Indian affairs that he became known as 'the member for India'. He was received in Bombay with acclamation and presentation of scrolls and banners, when, following a doctor's recommendation of rest and a long sea voyage, he travelled to India in the winter of 1890–91.

In the last few years he was not free from the litigation and conflicts which had so sapped his energy. His relationship with Annie Besant became distant as her enthusiasm flitted from socialism to theosophy. His disagreement with socialism was serious, for he was profoundly individualistic, preferring people to 'rely more on themselves and look less for salvation to paper statutes'. Socialists were often atheists, and their programme of social reform overtook the secularists; in dealing with a limited range of anti-religious themes the secularists had remained a pressure group and failed to become a political party. However for a decade the sceptical atheist views of the many individuals in this book grew into a popular – albeit small – movement. Whether secularists were a cause or a symptom of the gradual secularization of society, they were superseded not by a return to religion but by what they often scornfully termed 'Indifferentism'. Atheism was becoming respectable; Huxley's neologism 'agnosticism' was gaining currency and even if militants like Bradlaugh saw it as 'a mere society form of Atheism', it was a mark of the extent to which sceptical views had penetrated all levels of society. When a Conservative MP friendly to Bradlaugh said to him, 'Good God, Bradlaugh, what does it matter whether there is a God or not?' he was as much a herald of the twentieth century as Bradlaugh himself.

Bradlaugh's last pamphlet was *Humanity's Gain from Unbelief*, published in 1888. It is imbued with an optimism and belief in progress that the most ardent humanist could not sustain in the twentieth century. Bradlaugh looks to a period when religion will wither away. This, he thought, would be a gradual progress:

> No religion is suddenly rejected by any people; it is rather gradually outgrown. None sees a religion die; dead religions are like dead languages and obsolete customs: the decay is long and – like the glacier march – is perceptible only to the careful watcher by comparisons extending over long periods.

He thought that the 'ameliorating march of the last few centuries has been initiated by the heretics of each age' and, although he admitted that 'many eminent servants of humanity have been nominal Christians', he considered their services 'have not been in consequence of their adhesion to Christianity, but in spite of it'. The improvement of the human condition was due to the 'modern study of the laws of health, experiments in sanitary improvement, more careful application of medical knowledge', which 'have proved more efficacious in preventing or diminishing plagues and pestilence than have the intervention of the priest or the practice of prayer'. He also saw a gain in freeing the mind from 'the terrible doctrine that eternal torment is the probable fate of the great majority of the human family' and 'the faith that it was the duty of the wretched and the miserable to be content with the lot in life which providence had awarded them'.

It was a measure of Bradlaugh's own progress that by the end of his life he was accepted and respected throughout the House of Commons. During the struggle to gain his seat, Gladstone had declared: 'I have no fear of Atheism in this House.' Bradlaugh's integrity had dispelled the fear of atheism as a threat to morality.

In 1890, failing health caused Bradlaugh to resign as President of the National Secular Society. In January 1891 the kidney disease which had weakened him for many years worsened. Much sympathy was expressed in the House, where members were debating a motion to expunge the record of his expulsion from the Journals of the House. But his strength was fading and he did not hear the news that the motion had been passed. He died on 29 January. In a will of 1884 (not his last) he had directed that 'my body be buried as cheaply as possible and no speeches be permitted at my funeral'. His daughter believed this was his last wish and endeavoured to carry it out; so many people, from working men to MPs, wished to pay their respects that a special train was laid on from Waterloo to Brookwood (where he was buried with his family). The young Indian student Gandhi was among the mourners. A group of Nottingham secularists sent an inscription with their flowers: 'Brave, honest, incorruptible, thorough'.

12

John Stuart Mill and George Eliot: A religion of humanity

John Stuart Mill (1806–1873), who was dubbed 'the Saint of Rationalism' by Gladstone, supported Bradlaugh's efforts to enter Parliament. But he dissociated himself from Bradlaugh's militant atheism, proclaiming: 'If anyone tells you that I am an atheist, I would advise you to ask him how he knows, and in what page of my numerous writings he finds anything to bear out the assertion.' Mill was more the product of Enlightenment views on education than the struggle of working men. His father, James Mill, believed, like Helvétius, that all children started with the same *tabula rasa* and that everyone could be educated to the level of a genius given a sufficiently energetic input.

His first son, John Stuart, became the subject of one of the most famous of all educational experiments almost as soon as he was born. At the age of three he started to learn Greek and progressed rapidly from Aesop's fables to Xenophon. When he was eight, Latin and mathematics were added to his programme. Although his childhood was happy, it was not playful: his walks with his father were opportunities for analysis of his reading, for James Mill was determined to stimulate the critical faculties rather than induce parrot learning. At home he interrupted his father's work, *A History of India*, to ask about Latin grammar and by ten he was helping his father read the proofs.

James Mill was encouraged in his educational experiment by his close friendship with Jeremy Bentham. Mill was a frequent visitor at Bentham's Westminster house, and his family stayed in houses out of London rented by Bentham. Bentham's principle of 'the greatest happiness of the greatest number' and his attempt to give meaning to life in purely social terms inspired the Utilitarians or Philosophic Radicals, whose principles nurtured and eventually dissatisfied John Stuart Mill. Bentham had invested in Owen's New Lanark scheme and was interested in Owen's educational ideas. The intense opposition which they all met from churchmen, appalled at general education without their involvement, led Bentham to write a systematic attack on religion. In the *Analysis of the Influence of Natural Religion on the Temporal Happiness of Mankind* (1822), he launched an assault on 'Jug' (Juggernaut) his private nickname for religion: he thought it was irrational, explicable in naturalistic terms and so damaging that it created the 'greatest unhappiness for the greatest number'. Even if God did exist, Bentham thought, religion would be 'impotent for the purpose of resisting any temptation, and efficient only in the production of needless and unprofitable misery'.

John Stuart Mill was deeply influenced by Bentham's writing, but he did not acquire his father's animosity towards religion, which he described in his *Autobiography*:

> . . . his aversion to religion, in the sense usually attached to the term, was of the same kind with that of Lucretius: he regarded it with the feelings due not to a mere mental delusion, but to a great moral evil. He looked upon it as the greatest enemy of morality: first, by setting up fictitious excellences, – belief in creeds, devotional feelings, and ceremonies, not connected with the good of human-kind, – and causing these to be accepted as substitutes for genuine virtues: but above all, by radically vitiating the standard of morals; making it consist in doing the will of a being, on whom it lavishes indeed all the phrases of adulation, but whom in sober truth it depicts as eminently hateful. I have a hundred times heard him say, that all ages and nations have represented their gods as wicked, in a constantly increasing progression, that mankind have gone on adding trait after trait till they reached the most perfect conception of wickedness which the human mind can devise, and have called this God.

The consequence was that Mill was not someone who had thrown off religious belief, but someone who had never had it. He sometimes accompanied his mother to church and had good literary knowledge of the Bible, but his attitude to religion was always analytical: feeling and enthusiasm, which he came to consider Bentham and his father had neglected, he preferred to find in poetry and a 'religion of humanity'.

John Stuart Mill obtained a year's respite from his father when, at the age of fifteen, he stayed with Bentham's brother in France: his sympathies were widened to include love of music and nature, and he gained a permanent interest in French affairs. On return he studied Bentham's *Treaty on Legislation*. He reacted enthusiastically:

'I now had opinions; a creed, a doctrine, a philosophy; in one among the best senses of the word, a religion; the inculcation and diffusion of which could be made the principal outward purpose of life. And I had a grand conception of changes to be affected in the condition of mankind through that doctrine.'

At an early age J. S. Mill employed his pen and his energies in the service of social reform. His first appearance in print was in 1823, when he wrote five letters to the *Morning Chronicle* on the subject of freedom of the press, provoked by one of the occasions upon which Richard Carlile had been given a prison sentence for his defiant printing programme. In the same year he took up employment in the East India Company, where his father was a senior employee. The post gave him a secure income and his swiftness at dealing with the paper work left him ample time to pursue his own activities.

His apprenticeship to Bentham was completed by the mammoth task of collating and editing the three drafts of his *Rationale of Judicial Evidence*. Doubts about the adequacy of utilitarian theories and a reaction against his relentless intellectual upbringing led to an emotional crisis in 1826. He was depressed and found the pursuit of happiness impossible as a direct aim. He could not discuss his feelings with his father, since the crisis was in part an attempt to break free from his influence. He emphasized this period in his *Autobiography* and claimed to have restored his health and hopes by reading Wordsworth and Coleridge and by modifying Bentham's principles so that 'the only chance is to treat, not happiness, but some end external to it, as the purpose in life'. Henceforth, he was to stress the necessity for 'the internal culture of the individual', always to see the truth as 'complex and many-sided' and to open himself to 'the reaction of the nineteenth century against the eighteenth' – by which he meant the Romantic movement and an emphasis on individual emotion.

Mill was so ready to consider all points of view that others, for example Thomas Carlyle and Auguste Comte, mistook his sympathetic interest for agreement and he was forced to repulse their efforts to turn him into a Transcendentalist or Positivist. He responded to the ideas of Saint-Simon, whose follower, d'Eichthal, tried to convert Mill. He was impressed by Saint-Simon's attempt, in *Le Nouveau Christianisme*, to transform Christianity into an ethical social theory and to organise society so as to alleviate poverty. But, later, he could not approve the Positivists' attempt to create their own ritual and hierarchy. Although deeply sympathetic to the attempt to create a social religion of humanity, he always saw the dangers of putting the 'human race as a collective being' before 'those who compose it'.

In 1826, he met Harriet Taylor. She was married to Robert Taylor (not related to the Robert Taylor of Chapter 10), who ran a drug business and moved amongst the Unitarians of Finsbury Chapel. Mill and Harriet rapidly developed a close relationship, which was wrongly assumed by society to be adulterous. Until Robert Taylor's death in 1849, they sustained a *modus vivendi* in which Harriet continued to be a dutiful wife and mother while also frequently travelling and spending weekends with Mill. He always claimed that Harriet had contributed the finer part of all his subsequent writings and there can be no doubt that their persistent discussion led to a creative partnership. Two years after Robert Taylor's death they 'sank into matrimonial intimacy', sadly to be cut short after five years by Harriet's death from consumption while they were in Avignon.

Mill's career in the years between meeting Harriet in 1826 and her death in 1858 was highly successful. He rose to the position of Chief Examiner at India House and welcomed the substantial pension and early retirement brought about by the transfer of Indian affairs to the government. His journalism made a significant contribution to the political and intellectual currents of the period. In 1835 the *London Review* (to become *The London and Westminster Review*) was established largely as an attempt by Mill to provide support for a group of radicals in the reformed Parliament. An article in the second issue by his father, in which the doctrine and ceremony of the Church and character of the clergy were forthrightly attacked gave the *Review* a taint of atheism, but Mill's subsequent editorial direction made it a forum for moderate and diverse views.

Mill's major works, which gave him fame as a philosopher and sold much more widely than he expected for such weighty works were *A System of Logic* (1843) and *The Principles of Political Economy* (1848). *A System of Logic* became the foundation of university philosophy courses for the rest of the century and its attempt to examine human behaviour in a logical and scientific way alarmed some Christians: an attack from the Puseyites in the *British Critic* said that if his 'principles be adopted as a full statement of truth, the whole fabric of Christian Theology must totter and fall'. A section in *Principles of Political Economy* on the working class, in which egalitarian tendencies had been emphasized after pressure from Harriet

Taylor, was reprinted as a serial in G. J. Holyoake's periodical *The Reasoner*. Holyoake's inaccurate description of Mill as a 'militant atheist' brought a reproof from Harriet, who wrote in a letter to Mill: 'I am disgusted with the mixture of impudence and imbecility of the *foolish* creature Holyoake. . . . I fancy I should say that the morality of the *Reasoner* appears to me . . . to be as intolerant, slavish and selfish as that of the religion which it attacks.'

Two of Mill's most important works were not published until after Harriet's death, because only then was he able to admit that the process of revision must come to an end: *On Liberty* (1859) and *The Subjection of Women* (1869) have remained two of his most widely read and influential essays.

After Harriet's death, Mill bought a house at Avignon and erected a substantial monument to her. He slowly returned to public life, entertaining Victorian liberals such as the Grotes, the Amberleys (Bertrand Russell's parents) and Moncure Conway. He was persuaded to stand for Parliament and from 1865 to 1868 was MP for Westminster. He saw his role as that of a catalyst stimulating new ideas such as the rights of women.

Mill elaborated his views on religion in *Three Essays on Religion* published posthumously. In *On Liberty* he had compared Socrates and Jesus as two admirable thinkers who were persecuted for their beliefs and argued that there was no good reason for the prohibition of the freest discussion of religion. He noted that 'the introducers of new opinion' were no longer put to death, and condemned the imprisonment of Thomas Pooley for 'writing on a gate some offensive words concerning Christianity' and the rejection of Holyoake and Truelove as jurymen 'because they honestly declared they had no theological belief'. He considered it no business of the law to restrain 'intemperate discussion, namely invective, sarcasm, personality and the like', although it was his view that 'opinion contrary to those commonly received can only obtain a hearing by studied moderation of language'.

One of Mill's *Three Essays on Religion*, the *Utility of Religion*, concentrates upon an important area of nineteenth-century discussion of religion. Mill was much concerned with the 'utility of religion' regardless of its truth and he knew that such a discussion indicated the acceptance of widespread doubt: 'The utility of religion did not need to be asserted until the arguments for its truth had in a great measure ceased to convince.' Mill thought it possible to demonstrate that some benefits conferred by religion on society could be equally gained from education and public interchange. He allowed that religion, like poetry, supplied 'ideal conceptions grander and more beautiful than we see realized in the prose of human life'. But he thought that the Religion of Humanity retained 'the essence of religion' which is 'the strong and earnest direction of the emotions and desires towards an ideal object, recognized as of the highest excellence'.

Mill assumed a naturalistic explanation of religion: 'A sufficient explanation will, I conceive, be found in the small limits of man's certain knowledge, and the boundlessness of his desire to know.' He was critical of Christian morality as too negative and disliked its use of rewards and punishments to motivate behaviour; he warned of the danger of 'ascribing a supernatural origin to the received maxims of morality'. However, he also granted that 'some of the precepts of Christ as exhibited in the Gospels – rising far about Paulism, which is the foundation of ordinary Christianity – carry some kinds of moral goodness to a greater height than had ever been attained before'. Mill thought the Christian concept of God was illogical and unpleasant, especially objecting to 'ascribing absolute perfection to the author and ruler of so clumsily made and capriciously governed a creation as this planet and the life of its inhabitants'. He added: 'The author of the Sermon on the mount is assuredly a far more benignant being than the Author of Nature.' Mill himself believed in the value of a conception of the ideal, but was not a deist. In his *Autobiography* he describes those, presumably like himself,

> whose belief is far short of Deism. Though they may think the proof incomplete that the universe is a work of design, and though they assuredly disbelieve that it can have an Author and Governor who is *absolute* in power as well as perfect in goodness, they have that which constitutes the principal worth of all religions whatever, an ideal conception of a Perfect Being, to which they habitually refer as the guide of their conscience; and this ideal Good is usually far nearer to perfection than the objective Deity of those who think themselves obliged to find absolute goodness in the author of a world so crowded with suffering and so deformed by injustice as ours.

Mill differed from his father in respecting the value of religion for personal gratification and his sympathy for 'an ideal conception of a Perfect Being' tempered his criticism of religion.

He died suddenly in Avignon in 1873, having tramped fifteen miles on one of his frequent botanizing walks a few days earlier. He was buried beside Harriet after an address and prayer from a local pastor. He may have longed to rejoin his wife, but cannot have expected to meet his maker.

George Eliot (1819–1880) shared Mill's belief that mankind needed large aspirations and high ideals. She arrived at a position similar to Mill's from an opposite direction, having been profoundly influenced by evangelical Christianity in her youth. 'George Eliot' was the name chosen by Mary Ann Evans when she wished to begin her career as a novelist anonymously. She was born in 1819 in Warwickshire and her father was a successful estate manager. Miss Maria Lewis, a teacher at a school in Coventry which she attended, was strongly evangelical and exercised a deep influence upon the serious young girl. The death of her mother in 1836 may have encouraged an intense and self-denying allegiance to evangelical Christianity; this was a period when such religion was disconcerting conventional Anglicans. After school she combined housekeeping for her father, acts of charity such as organizing a clothing club for unemployed ribbon weavers, and serious theological reading. On a visit to London with her brother, she preferred reading the *History of the Jews* by Josephus to a visit to the theatre.

George Eliot moved with her father to the outskirts of Coventry on his retirement and she became acquainted with Mr Charles Bray and his wife Caroline Hennell. They were Unitarians, philanthropic, progressive and sufficiently liberal for Charles Bray to have read his wife some of the writings of d'Holbach on their honeymoon. Caroline's brother, Charles Christian Hennell, published *An Inquiry into the Origin of Christianity* in 1838; his orthodox conclusions could not disguise the fact that to embark upon such an inquiry itself implied doubt. The Bray circle freely discussed social reform, phrenology, Owenism and religion, and visitors included W. J. Fox (the reformer and minister of South Place Chapel in Finsbury) and Emerson. George Eliot abandoned her evangelical Christianity and told her father that she could no longer with honesty join him in worship at church on Sunday. He was a conventional Anglican and was so shocked that she was forced to leave home temporarily and to stay with a married sister.

She explained her position very clearly in a letter to her father:

> I wish entirely to remove from your mind the false notion that I am inclined visibly to unite myself with any Christian community, or that I have an affinity in opinion with Unitarians more than with other classes of believers in the Divine authority of the books comprising the

> Jewish and Christian Scriptures. I regard these writings as histories consisting of mingled truth and fiction, and while I admire and cherish much of what I believe to have been the moral teaching of Jesus himself, I consider the system of doctrines built upon the facts of his life and drawn as to its materials from Jewish notions to be most dishonourable to God and most pernicious in its influence on individual and social happiness.

A family row was patched up by a compromise whereby she agreed to attend church on condition that she could think what she liked while she was there.

She responded enthusiastically to Charles Bray's suggestion that she might translate D. F. Strauss's *Leben Jesu*. This was a key work for nineteenth-century rationalists, being a seminal work of the so-called 'higher criticism' in Germany; Strauss examined the New Testament life of Jesus from an entirely historical perspective exposing inaccuracies and mythical elements. Her translation, which was published in 1846, was very influential. The sceptical poet, Arthur Hugh Clough, in his poem *Epi-Straussium*, wrote:

> Matthew and Mark and Luke and Holy John
> Evanish all and gone. . . .

After the strain of nursing her father in his last illness, in 1849 George Eliot travelled to Europe with Caroline Hennell. She spent half a year in Geneva, taking stock of her life and working upon a translation of Spinoza's *Tractatus Theologico-Politicus* (never published). On her return to England her publisher, John Chapman, asked her to write an article on the Strauss book. She stayed with him in the Strand in London and began to meet other writers.

A wealthy Norfolk freethinker, Edward Lombe, offered Chapman financial support for a liberal journal or an abridgement of the Strauss book: this enabled Chapman to purchase the *Westminster Review* and George Eliot assisted him in compiling a prospectus for the quarterly. From 1852 she was editor in all but name and under her guidance it attained a high standard of writing. At this time she began work on a translation of Feuerbach's *Das Wesen des Christenthums* (published in 1854 as *The Essence of Christianity*) which was a thorough critique of Christianity and theism from a naturalistic viewpoint. The *Westminster Review* covered politics, literature and science, upon which Huxley was a contributor. An attachment to Herbert Spencer, who had published *Social Statics, or the Conditions Essential to Human Happiness Specified, and the First of*

Them Developed brought her no personal happiness. Her friendship with G. H. Lewes, one of whose publications was *A Biographical History of Philosophy*, based on lectures given at Finsbury Chapel, was to ripen into a profound and passionate partnership.

Lewes and she left for Germany, where he intended to undertake research for a biography of Goethe. When they returned they set up house together – an arrangement which shocked their friends, since Lewes was still married. Eventually esteem for her writing outweighed the stigma of their partnership, but this was not for many years.

In 1858 they moved to a house in Wandsworth, where their neighbours, Mr and Mrs Congreve, became close friends. Richard Congreve was to become the chief English exponent of Comte's positivism: Lewes had met Congreve while he was translating Comte's *Philosophy of the Sciences*, but he did not admire the development of Positivism into a pseudo-religion. George Eliot was attracted to the idea of a religion of humanity and her animosity to religion, which had arisen from her reaction to her evangelical phase, was abating. However, although she gave the Positivists small donations, she declared she was 'never a Comtist, but as they were a poor unfortunate sect, she would never renounce them'. She developed an eclectic interest in religions, attending a Mass or a Unitarian chapel in a spirit of respectful curiosity.

Evangelical Christianity was the one form of religion for which her distaste always remained, and she provided a perceptive analysis of it in her first work of fiction, *Scenes of Clerical Life* (1857). Throughout her career as a novelist the encouragement of Lewes and of her publisher, Blackwood, were crucial in sustaining her, for she was morbidly sensitive to the possibility of failure. It was primarily for this reason that she was at first extremely anxious to retain her anonymity. Her career as one of the finest of all novelists is not relevant here, but aspects of her novels do, of course, reveal her beliefs. In an aside to the reader in Chapter Seventeen of *Adam Bede* she explains her determination to give as truthful an account of the world as possible: the dictum 'Falsehood is easy, truth so difficult' is characteristic of a sceptic as well as a realistic novelist. Her interest in religious people and attempt to understand the psychology and institutions of belief systems she did not share was apparent from the portrayal of Methodism in *Adam Bede* to the study of Jewish beliefs in *Daniel Deronda*. While, like Mill, she rejected a supreme force of goodness in the form of a supernatural being, she longed to foster an ideal of goodness among the hearts and minds of frail human beings. Dorothea, the central character in her masterpiece *Middlemarch*, is compared in the Introduction to St Theresa with her 'rapturous consciousness of life beyond self' and the novel studies the problems of her finding fulfilment for 'loving heart-beats and sobs after unattained goodness' in provincial England.

Two of George Eliot's essays also displayed her intellectual interest in religion. 'The Influence of Rationalism: Lecky's History' was written for the first number of the *Fortnightly*, an influential literary review edited by Lewes. She writes as someone critically aware of the 'spirit of rationalism' and, in suggesting that Lecky gave insufficient attention to the development of science, gives a clear statement of her own perception of the impact of scientific observation upon belief:

> The great conception of universal regular sequence, without partiality and without caprice – the conception which is the most potent force at work in the modification of our faith, and of the practical form given to our sentiments – could only grow out of that patient watching of external fact, and that silencing of preconceived notions, which are urged upon the mind by the problems of physical science.

An earlier essay, 'Evangelical Teaching: Dr Cumming' in the *Westminster Review* displays her deep dislike of evangelical preachers and provides fascinating detail of the nature and content of mid-nineteenth-century arguments about religion. She castigated this popular preacher for his 'unscrupulosity of statement': 'Experience has so long shown that the human brain is a congenial nidus for inconsistent beliefs, that we do not pause to inquire how Dr Cumming, who attributes the conversion of the unbelieving to the Divine Spirit, can think it necessary to co-operate with that Spirit by argumentative white lies.' Her own position is revealed in her comment on Dr Cumming's inability to recognize the sincerity of non-Christians: 'It [the experience of his own religion] has not enabled him even to conceive the condition of a mind "perplext in faith but pure in deed", craving light, yearning for a faith that will harmonize and cherish its highest powers and aspirations, but unable to find that faith in dogmatic Christianity.' She includes a comment upon what she saw to be the failure of religion:

> Fatally powerful as religious systems have been, human nature is stronger and wider than religious systems, and though dogmas may hamper, they cannot absolutely repress its growth: build walls round

> the living tree as you will, the bricks and mortar have by-and-by to give way before the slow and sure operation of the sap. But next to the hatred of the enemies of God, which is the principle of persecution, there perhaps has been no perversion more obstructive of true moral development than this substitution of a reference to the glory of God for the direct promptings of sympathetic feelings.

By the time that she published her last great novel, *Daniel Deronda*, in 1876, she was famous and Lewes had to cope with her admirers: 'Lords and Ladies, poets and cabinet ministers, artists and men of science crowd upon us.' Among her many visitors were Matthew Arnold and Arthur Hugh Clough's widow. Both Clough and Arnold were poets who expressed doubt as a feeling of anguished loss very different from the confident ironies of Enlightenment critics of religion or the angry tirades of radical secularists. Arnold's *Dover Beach* regrets the ebbing of the Sea of Faith:

> The Sea of Faith
> Was once, too, at the full, and round earth's shore
> Lay like the folds of a bright girdle furled.
> But now I only hear
> Its melancholy, long, withdrawing roar,
> Retreating, to the breath
> Of the night-wind, down the vast edges drear
> And naked shingles of the world.

Clough, whose scruples severely damaged his career, described his contemplation of the fact that 'Christ is not risen' in *Easter Day* (Naples 1849):

> Eat, drink, and die, for we are souls bereaved:
> Of all the creatures under heaven's wide cope
> We are most helpless, who had once most hope,
> And most beliefless, that had most believed.

When Lewes died in 1878, George Eliot at first detached herself from society and worked on a manuscript which Lewes had left and on the revision of her final work, *Impressions of Theophrastus Such*, a collection of character sketches and essays. She slowly resumed contact with friends, and Johnny Cross became invaluable to her in dealing with her business correspondence. Somewhat to the surprise of their friends, who commented on the disparity of age between the forty-year-old Cross and sixty-year-old Eliot, they married in 1880. At the end of the year she died suddenly from heart failure during a bout of laryngitis. Cross was disposed to plead for her burial in

Westminster Abbey, but the case was not pressed. Huxley pointed out the contradictions involved since:

> George Eliot is known not only as a great writer, but as a person whose life and opinions were in notorious antagonism to Christian practice in regard to marriage, and Christian theory in regard to dogma. How am I to tell the Dean . . . to do that which, if I were in his place, I should most emphatically refuse to do? . . . One cannot eat one's cake and have it too.

George Eliot was buried at Highgate Cemetery, after an Anglican service with 'discreet Unitarian omissions'.

George Eliot's deeply serious, but sceptical, attitude to religion is summed up in an oft-quoted remark of hers which, according to F. W. H. Myers, was made to him in the Fellows' Garden at Trinity College, Cambridge:

> She stirred somewhat beyond her want, and taking as her text the three words which have been used so often as the inspiring trumpet-calls of men, – the words, *God*, *Immortality*, *Duty*, – pronounced, with terrible earnestness, how inconceivable was the *first*, how unbelievable the *second*, and yet how peremptory and absolute the *third*.*

*Bertrand Russell in his *Autobiography*, however, recalled the remark of a friend whom he had introduced to the garden: 'Oh yes! This is where George Eliot told F. W. H. Myers that there is no God and yet we must be good; and Myers decided that there is a God and yet we need not be good.'

13
Thomas Huxley: Religion and science

In June 1860 the British Association held a meeting in Oxford and, since Darwin's *Origin of Species* had been published in the previous year, controversy on the theory of evolution was in the air. On the last day of the conference, rumour led a large audience to expect a confrontation between 'Soapy Sam' Wilberforce, Bishop of Oxford, and the scientists. The afternoon began with an unremarkable lecture by the American Dr Draper on 'The Intellectual Development of Europe considered with reference to the Views of Mr Darwin'. Dr Draper later published the unsubtle and anti-Catholic *History of the Conflict between Religion and Science* (1874) – a title which sums up what many people thought was the tension crystallized by Darwin's theories. The simplified antithesis was confirmed when Bishop Wilberforce turned to Huxley and asked 'whether it was through his grandfather or his grandmother that he claimed descent from a monkey'. Huxley rose to reply, confident that 'The Lord hath delivered him into mine hands'. In his own words: '– If, then, said I, the question is put to me "would I rather have a miserable ape for a grandfather, or a man highly endowed by nature and possessed of great means and influence, and yet who employs these faculties and that influence for the mere purpose of introducing ridicule into scientific discussion?" – I unhesitatingly affirm my preference for the ape. Whereupon there was unextinguishable laughter among the people – and they listened to the rest of my argument with the greatest of attention.'

As 'Darwin's Bulldog', Huxley (1825–1895) was thorough and combative in spreading Darwin's ideas. He was himself a scientist of note and was also an instinctive educator, who ensured a place for science in the expanding education system. The importance of Darwinism to a history of scepticism lies less in the hypothesis of natural selection, which has proved so fruitful a framework for scientific research ever since, than in the questions raised about the beginnings of life and man's place in the cosmos. In his first popular work, *Evidence as to Man's Place in Nature* (1863), Huxley wrote:

> The question of questions for mankind – the problem which underlies all others, and is more deeply interesting than any other – is the ascertainment of the place which Man occupies in nature and of his relations to the universe of things. Whence our race has come; what are the limits of our power over nature and of nature's power over us; to what goal are we tending; [these] are the problems which present themselves anew and with undiminished interest to every man born into the world.

Such matters fascinated those whose knowledge of paleontology, embryology, taxonomy (and, later, genetics) was non-existent.

Huxley's father was an ineffective teacher at Great Ealing School, a school of some note. Thomas disliked it intensely and later wrote that his 'regular school training was of the briefest, perhaps fortunately'. In 1835, when he was ten, his father left the school and moved to Coventry where he scraped an existence running a savings bank. Huxley claimed that he owed his intellectual enthusiasms to the vivacity of his mother. Certainly, his scientific curiosity was active at an early age and he claimed that he read Hutton's *Geology* in bed by candlelight at the age of twelve. His enormous capacity for hard work ensured the success of his self-education; in writing, later, of his prodigious output, he commented that 'the secret is to preserve the power of working sixteen hours a day if need be'. Between the ages of fifteen and seventeen he kept a notebook which records his experiments at making a galvanic battery and his questions about the colour of the sunset and the difference between matter and the soul.

Engineering was Huxley's first choice of career, but his brother-in-law offered to start training him in medicine. He moved to Rotherhithe in 1841 and saw enough dockland starvation and misery to prime his social conscience for life. His medical apprenticeship continued with a doctor in North London and he also studied at a college in Chelsea. After entering an open competition he was awarded the Silver Medal of the Apothecaries' Society for botany and a free scholarship at Charing Cross Hospital. As a medical student he obtained prizes and published his first original scientific research on the structure of human hair at the age of nineteen. His scholarship came to an end after two years, before he was fully qualified, and he then became an Assistant-Surgeon in the Royal Navy.

Darwin's voyage on the Beagle has been made famous by his account of it. Huxley's voyage, of comparable interest, was on HMS Rattlesnake and the captain allowed him to spend much of his time on his scientific studies. The Rattlesnake set sail in December 1846 to explore the waters north of Australia and around New Guinea. One of the key aspects of study of the natural world was the classification of species, which had been given impetus by the eighteenth-century naturalist Linnaeus. Huxley chose to study the non-preservable creatures from the sea and his careful observations and detailed drawings enabled him completely to revise the classification of molluscs. He 'sent home communication after communication to the Linnaean Society with the same result as that obtained by Noah when he sent the ravens out of the ark'. In Sydney he met Henrietta Heathorn and they immediately fell in love. He had to wait eight years until he was confident he could support a family, but their marriage was then so loving that they wrote poems to each other until Huxley's death.

When he returned to Plymouth in 1850, Huxley was amazed to discover that knowledge of his work had spread amongst distinguished scientists. However, the career of a professional scientist was not easy and he hated 'fighting and scratching to keep your place in the crowd'. He continued his researches indefatigably and made a significant contribution to knowledge of invertebrate development and anatomy. He was elected a Fellow of the Royal Society before his twenty-sixth birthday and was awarded the Society's Royal Medal in the subsequent year. At moments he considered abandoning science so that he could earn more money and marry, but 'science alone seems to me to afford this scope – Law, Divinity, and Politics being in a state of chaotic vibration between utter humbug and utter scepticism'.

When it became clear that he had no intention of returning to sea the Admiralty ceased to pay him. For a brief period he was without income or a position, but he was then invited to substitute as a lecturer at the School of Mines in Jermyn Street, gained temporary work with a Geological Survey and obtained part-time teaching work at St Thomas's Hospital. His lecturing skills had already been seen when he gave his first public lecture at the Royal Institution on 'Animal Individuality'. Throughout his life both his students and the general public were impressed by the clarity and force of his scientific exposition. He was equally successful with Working Men's Colleges and Royal Societies, giving lectures 'full of high seriousness, but with no suspicion of pedantry; lightened by an occasional epigram or flashes of caustic humour, but with none of the small jocularity in which it is such a temptation to a lecturer to indulge' (T. J. Parker: 'Reminiscences of Huxley'. *Natural Science*. 1895. vii. 297).

In 1859 Darwin, who admired Huxley's 'quickness of apprehension or wit' sent him an advance copy of *On The Origin of Species by Means of Natural Selection, or the Preservation of Favoured Races in the Struggle for Life*. The idea that complex life forms had evolved from simpler ones in an immense time-scale was not new, but, as Huxley had earlier written, there were no 'clear and definite conceptions which could be brought face to face with facts and have their validity tested'. Huxley duly read his copy of the *Origin* and declared: 'How exceedingly stupid not to have thought of that.'

Earlier thinkers had proposed an alternative development of earth and its life to that given in Genesis and dated by Archbishop James Usher, the seventeenth-century divine, as commencing on 23 October, 4004 B.C. Leonardo Da Vinci had suggested that the earth's past could be explained by natural forces, and the botanist John Ray (1627–1705) had speculated about a fern-leaf fossil which seemed 'to shock the Scripture History'. Darwin's ancestor, Erasmus Darwin, a Unitarian, doctor and poet, had put forward evolutionist ideas in his long poem *Zoonomia* (1794). Lamarck's theory that acquired characteristics could be inherited and produce species change, though unproven, set naturalists thinking about a possible mechanism of evolution. Darwin's theory stood in a long tradition of speculation on evolution and he was not alone in making the imaginative leap into the theory of natural selection, for it was Alfred Wallace's intention to publish his reflections on the matter that forced Darwin, who was still cautiously accumulating his evidence, into publication in 1859. Darwin knew that this theory would not only concern scientists, for the claim that man had evolved slowly from lower forms of life directly confronted the Christian view that all species were created in their final form by God and that man was in a quite different category from the rest of the animal kingdom. So nervous was Darwin of upsetting the scientific and religious establishment that the implications of his ideas on the position of man were shrouded in the discreet phrase 'Light will be thrown on the origin of man and his history . . .'.

Huxley was much bolder. He anticipated conflict and prepared to defend Darwin: 'And as to the curs which will bark and yelp, you must recollect that some of your friends, at any rate, are endowed with an amount of combativeness which (though you have often and justly rebuked it) may stand you in good stead. . . .' The *Westminster Review* of April 1860 contained an enthusiastic and detailed review by him, with a comment on the impact the book had made: 'Everybody has read . . . or, at least, has given an opinion upon its merits and demerits; pietists, whether lay or ecclesiastic, decry it with the mild railing which sounds so charitable; bigots denounce it with ignorant invective; old ladies of both sexes consider it a decidedly dangerous book, and even savants, who have no better mud to throw, quote antiquated writers to show that its author is no better than an ape himself; while every philosophical thinker hails it as a veritable Whitworth gun in the armoury of liberalism.'

Huxley was no uncritical adulator of Darwin's work. He understood the scientific process, and nearly twenty years later said in a lecture to the Royal Institution, 'On the Coming of Age of the Origin of Species', that 'it is the customary fate of new truths to begin as heresies, and end as superstitions'. He had doubts about the gradualness of the process of evolution, wondering whether it did not proceed by sudden jumps. His defence of Darwin's *Origin* threw him fully into public life and his careful examination of the evidence for Darwin's theory directed his own researches for two decades.

The Oxford debate with 'Soapy' Sam Wilberforce symbolized the conflict between science and Church, but other public occasions made possible a more thorough presentation of Darwin's theories and other clashes were equally sharp. A lecture at the Philosophical Institute in Edinburgh on 'The Relation of Man to the Lower Animals' was well received in the lecture-hall but scathingly attacked in the Presbyterian *Witness* as a 'blasphemous contradiction to biblical narrative and doctrine . . . the vilest paradox ever vented in ancient or modern times amongst Pagans or Christians' with the caustic rider that those attending the meeting should have formed a Gorilla Emancipation Society.

Huxley gathered together his lectures and accounts of his debates to produce his first popular book, *Evidence as to Man's Place in Nature* (1863). The very title challenged readers to think about 'the place which Man occupies in nature and of his relations to the universe of things'. He was in much demand as a lecturer and his next collection of essays about evolution, *On Our Knowledge of the Causes of the Phenomena of Organic Nature*, was a best-seller. Darwin, who was regularly visited by Huxley, commented: 'What is the good of my writing a thundering big book, when everything is in this little green book so despicable for its size?'

In the subsequent two decades Huxley's career and fame advanced steadily. When he was awarded an honorary doctorate by Cambridge University, he complained that he had become 'a person of Respectability' – 'I have done my best to avoid that misfortune but it is no use.' Despite offers of posts at Oxford and in America, he remained with the Royal School of Mines in Jermyn Street, and slowly transformed the college so that it covered 'all Science applicable to Industry' with 'a special organization as a Training College for teachers'. He was made dean of the college in 1881 and was much amused to find that a letter to him would correctly be addressed 'The Very Revd —'. An aspect of his work which exhausted much of his energies was his part in merging the college with other institutions to become Imperial College and, at the very end of his life in the 1890s, to bring about a federal University of London.

The importance which Huxley attached to education and the popularization of scientific ideas puts him in line with men such as Carlile and Owen who valued humanity's potential for thought more highly than its need for guidance from a deity. He contrasted his own view of education for the masses as a means of self-fulfilment with that of politicians, churchmen and industrialists:

> The politicians tells us 'You must educate the masses because they are going to be masters'. The clergy join in the cry for education, for they affirm that the people are drifting away from church and chapel into the broadest infidelity. The manufacturers and the capitalists swell the chorus lustily. They declare that ignorance makes bad workmen; that England will soon be unable to turn out cotton goods, or steam engines, cheaper than other people; and then, Ichabod! Ichabod! the glory will be departed from us. And a few voices are lifted up in favour of the doctrine that the masses should be educated because they are men and women with unlimited capacities of being, doing and suffering, and that it is as true now, as ever it was, that the people perish for lack of knowledge.

After the 1870 Education Act, Huxley stood for election to the London School Board. Unlike the members of the religious sects and the secularists clamouring for a say in the content of future education, he conducted no campaign and left it to his friends, including J. S. Mill, to publicize his candidature for the district of Marylebone. He was elected on the strength of his reputation rather than his campaigning skills, and was almost immediately chosen to be chairman of the Board. The role of religion was very contentious. He took a moderate line: when it was proposed that the Board should open its meetings with a prayer, Huxley recommended that a separate room be provided for those who wished to pray. He supported the inclusion of Bible readings in schools, because of its literary and moral content and accepted a part for religious instruction in schools as a compromise: 'For the sake of the enormous advantage of giving the rudiments of a decent education to several generations of the people, they accepted what was practically an armistice in respect of certain matters about which the contending parties were absolutely irreconcilable.'

Huxley's health broke completely in 1872. His frequent spells of melancholy or headaches were usually dispelled by vigorous walking or mountaineering holidays – a fact which suggests, as with Darwin's many ailments, a psychosomatic cause. On this occasion it took a three month's tour of the Mediterranean and Egypt and much rest for the remainder of the year before he was restored to his usual energies. As head of a growing family he held many responsibilities, but was a typical Victorian paterfamilias, never happier than with his wife and children.

He continued his serious research. His work on *The Crayfish* is a classic of biological writing and contains a characteristic description of nature as 'nowhere inaccessible' and 'everywhere unfathomable'. His lectures continued to cause controversy. When he arranged to lecture at Edinburgh's Mission Hall 'On the Physical Basis of Life', the hall booking was cancelled at the last minute and another venue had to be found. He acknowledged the dismay with which others watched 'what they conceive to be the progress of materialism, in such fear and powerless anger as a savage feels, when during an eclipse, the great shadow creeps over the face of the sun'. Although loathing bigotry, he had some sympathy for the distress of those in what Tennyson called the 'sunless gulfs of Doubt'. This did not staunch his public speculations and, for instance, a lecture he gave to the British Association in 1874 was entitled 'On the Hypothesis that Animals are Automata, and its History'.

In his last fifteen years of public life up to 1885 academic distinctions and public positions were regularly bestowed upon him. He was invited to America to lecture at the opening of the John Hopkins University in Baltimore; there was much criticism of the omission of a religious ceremony of dedication and Huxley's 'Address on University Education' contained the provocative remark:

> I am not in the slightest degree impressed by your bigness or your material resources, as such. Size is not grandeur; territory does not make a nation. The great issue, about which hangs a true sublimity, and the terror overhanging fate is – 'What are you going to do with all these things?' . . . The one condition of success, your sole safeguard, is the moral worth, and intellectual clearness of the individual citizen.

In the latter part of his life morality and the ethical implications of evolution theory became a prime preoccupation for him. He had abandoned his religious faith as a young man. He was profoundly grieved by the death of his four-year-old son, Noel, in 1860, and gave an account of his feelings at the funeral in a reply to Charles Kingsley, who had written him a letter of sympathy:

> As I stood behind the coffin of my little son the other day, with my mind bent on anything but disputation, the officiating minister read, as part of his duty, the words, 'If the dead rise not again, let us eat and drink for tomorrow we die'. I cannot tell you how inexpressibly they shocked me. Paul had neither wife nor child, or he must have known that his alternative involved a blasphemy against all that was best and noblest in human nature. I could have laughed with scorn. What! because I came face to face with irreparable loss, because I have given back to the source from whence it came, the cause of a great happiness, still retaining through all my life the blessings which have sprung and will spring from that cause, I am to renounce my manhood, and, howling, grovel in bestiality? Why, the very apes know better, and if you shoot their young, the poor brutes grieve their grief out and do not immediately seek distraction in a gorge.

Huxley's estrangement from religion was a continuous progression from his metaphysical speculations while aboard the Rattlesnake to his harsh criticism of Christianity in his essay on agnosticism written in his retirement. Speculation about religion was one of the principle activities of the Metaphysical Society, of which he was an active member. This debating group was instigated by James Knowles and others at Tennyson's house in Clapham, and from 1869 to its disbandment in 1880 men such as Gladstone, Manning, Fitzjames Stephen, Huxley, Ruskin and Froude regularly exchanged views. Huxley insisted that all views, including those of non-Christians, should be allowed expression, but without personal animosity. Huxley did not approve of those who saw ridicule as a valuable weapon in undermining Christianity, such as Winwood Reade, who wrote in *The Matyrdom of Man*: 'Ridicule is a destructive instrument, and it is my intention to destroy. If a man is cutting down a tree, it is useless asking him not to strike hard.' Huxley wrote to C. A. Watts, the founder of the Rationalist Press Association: 'It is quite hopeless to fight Christianity with scurrility. We want a regiment of Ironsides.'

The Metaphysical Society's discussions provided the occasion for him to coin the word 'Agnosticism'. Some years later in an article on 'Agnosticism' he gave an account of his choice of label:

> I, the man without a rag of a label to cover himself with, could not fail to have some of the uneasy feelings which must have beset the historical fox when, after leaving the trap in which his tail remained, he presented himself to his normally elongated companions. So I took thought, and invented what I conceived to be the appropriate title of 'Agnostic'. It came into my head as suggestively antithetic to the 'Gnostic' of Church history, who professed to know so very much about the very things of which I was ignorant; and I took the earliest opportunity of parading it at our society to show that I, too, had a tail like other foxes (*Nineteenth Century*. February, 1889).

The essay on agnosticism was provoked by an attack on agnostics at the Church Congress in which the principal of King's College declared of those such as Huxley: 'He may call himself an Agnostic; but his real name is an older one – he is an Infidel; that is to say an unbeliever.' (A criticism also made by Bradlaugh and other militant atheists.) Huxley protested that he did 'not care much what I am called by other people, and if I had at my side all those who since the Christian era have been called infidels by other folks, I could not desire better company'. His intellectual development had led him to ask whether he was 'an atheist, a theist, or a pantheist; a materialist or an idealist; a Christian or a freethinker', and he came to the conclusion that 'the one thing in which most of these good people agreed was the one thing in which I differed from them. They were quite certain they had attained a certain "gnosis" had, more or less successfully, solved the problem of existence; while I was quite sure I had not, and had a pretty strong conviction that the problem was insoluble.' He proceeded to give a very clear definition of Agnosticism:

> Agnosticism, in fact, is not a creed, but a method, the essence of which lies in the rigorous application of a single principle. That principle is of great antiquity; it is as old as Socrates; as old as the writer who said, 'Try all things, hold fast by that which is good'; it is the foundation of the Reformation, which simply illustrated the axiom that every man should be able to give a reason for the faith that is in him; it is the great

> principle of Descartes; it is the fundamental axiom of modern Science. Positively the principle may be expressed: In matters of the intellect, follow your reason as far as it will take you, without regard to any other consideration. And negatively: In matters of the intellect, do not pretend that conclusions are certain which are not demonstrated or demonstrable. That I take to be the agnostic faith, which if a man keep whole and undefiled, he shall not be ashamed to look the universe in the face, whatever the future may have in store for him.

The respectability achieved by the word is seen by essays such as 'An Agnostic's Apology' (1893) by Sir Leslie Stephen, the brother of Fitzjames Stephen, the famous judge and member of the Metaphysical Society.

Huxley was particularly indignant at the comment of a Church journal that it would be 'an unpleasant thing for a man to have to say plainly he does not believe in Jesus Christ', and retorted: 'That it ought to be unpleasant for any man to say anything which he sincerely, and after due deliberation, believes, is, to my mind, a proposition of the most profoundly immoral character.' He continues with an indictment of Christianity more robust than might have been expected from so respectable a figure:

> I verily believe that the great good which had been effected in the world by Christianity has been largely counteracted by the pestilent doctrine on which all the churches have insisted, that honest disbelief in their more or less astonishing creeds is a moral offence, indeed a sin of the deepest dye, deserving and involving the same future retribution as murder and robbery. If we could only see, in one view, the torrents of hypocrisy and cruelty, the lies, the slaughter, the violation of every obligation of humanity, which have flowed from this source along the course of the history of Christian nations, our worst imagination of Hell would pale beside the vision.

He denied that Christianity had a monopoly on morality and disputed that science was responsible for a decline in moral behaviour in an essay on 'Science and Morals'. One of his last lectures, the Romanes lecture at Oxford in 1893, covered the topic 'Evolution and Ethics':

> If there is any generalization from the facts of human life which has the assent of thoughtful men in every age and country it is that the violator of ethical rules constantly escapes the punishment which he deserves; that the wicked flourishes like a green bay tree, while the righteous begs his bread; that the sins of the father are visited upon the children; that, in the realm of nature, ignorance is punished just as severely as

wilful wrong; and that thousands upon thousands of innocent beings suffer for the crime, or the unintentional trespass, of one.

The Metaphysical Society's symposium on 'The Influence upon Morality of a Decline in Religious Belief' was a key subject for Huxley and his contemporaries. A contribution to the Symposium, published in the *Nineteenth Century* was by W. K. Clifford, who firmly separated religion and morality, seeing 'the moral sense . . . as arising indeed out of a universal principle, but not as personified in a conscious being'. Clifford (1845–1879) was a brilliant young Cambridge mathematician who had been excited by the ideas of Darwin and, as his friend Frederick Pollock wrote in a memoir after his death, 'Clifford was not content with merely giving his assent to the doctrine of evolution: he seized on it as a living spring of action, a principle to be worked out, practised upon, used to win victories over nature, and to put new vigour into speculation.' His essays on 'The Ethics of Belief', the 'Ethics of Religion' and 'Cosmic Emotion' are among the finest, though least known, writings on science and religion of the period. His essay 'Virchow on the Teaching of Science' took up the arguments of a German scientist and was a forceful defence of Darwin's theories and of the value of teaching science to children. Virchow had delivered an address 'On the Liberty of Science in the Modern State' to a meeting of scientists at Munich in 1877. He urged moderation in not proclaiming new scientific theories while they remained controversial for fear of damaging the stability of the state. One of his chief opponents was Ernst Haeckel, who had played a similar role to that of Huxley in Britain in propagating Darwin's ideas in Germany.

Haeckel (1834–1919) was a naturalist at Jena University who was profoundly influenced by the publication of Bronn's German translation of the *Origin* in 1860. He spoke about the implications of Darwin's theories at a Scientific Congress in 1863 and was very conscious of a conflict between science and religion, while being anxious to find an intellectual reconciliation. His *History of Creation* was published in 1868, amidst much controversy. Darwin commented that he would have had no need to write the *Descent of Man* if he had known of Haeckel's work. Haeckel's later popularization of scientific and philosophical ideas, *The Riddle of the Universe* (1899), became a rationalist classic. In it he claimed that a connecting link between religion and science was to be found in a 'monistic religion'. In his chapter on 'Science and Christianity' he highlighted the reaction of the Roman Catholic Church to the scientific age, especially the Encyclical of 1864 which he saw as 'an absolute condemnation of the whole of modern civilization and culture' in which the Pope 'excommunicated and anathematized all the rational theses and philosophical principles which are regarded by modern science as lucid truths'. In his chapter on 'Our Monistic Religion' he sought to show how 'religion and science would indeed blend into one if we had a perfectly clear and consecutive system of monism' – for which he acknowledged his debt to the 'pure and lofty conception of Spinoza and Goethe' – and which he saw as springing from the unity of matter and spirit (energy). The 'central unity of the cosmos' ruled out 'the three central dogmas of metaphysics – God, freedom, and immortality'. He thought it was 'of the first importance that modern science not only shatter the false structures of superstition and sweep their ruins from the path, but that it also erect a new abode for human emotion on the ground it has cleared – a "palace of reason", in which, under the influence of our new monistic views, we do reverence to the real trinity of the nineteenth century – the trinity of "the true, the good, and the beautiful"'. Though this trinity goes back at least to Plato, Haeckel had his finger on a widespread nineteenth-century aspiration grounded as much on faith and hope as science and observation. The *Riddle* was widely translated, sold 180,000 copies in Germany alone, and prompted 5,000 readers to write to the author – all of whom received replies. At an International Congress of Freethinkers in Rome in 1904, Haeckel called for the formation of a new church, the Great Association of Monists. But this strange attempt to weld religion and science had no staying power.

Another less well-known writer deeply influenced by Darwin and forming for himself his own unorthodox blend of religion was Winwood Reade (1834–1875). At first he unsuccessfully attempted to follow in the footsteps of his uncle, Charles Reade, as a novelist. Then he visited Africa, first as an individual explorer, secondly with the support of the Royal Geographical Society and finally as *The Times'* correspondent for the Ashanti war. He desired to study 'religion and morality' among the natives and to collect materials for a work which he intended to call *The Origin of Mind* in acknowledgement of his debt to Darwin. He found Darwin's *Descent of Man* 'left little for me to say respecting the birth and infancy of the faculties and affections' and instead wrote *The Martyrdom of Man* an epic, rhapsodic history of mankind shifting the pivot of history from Europe to Africa and combining anthropological and historical research with such narrative thrust that the book gained a popular readership.

Reade was one of those post-Darwinians who mistakenly assumed evolution must be travelling towards human perfection: 'Finally, men will master the forces of Nature; they will become themselves architects of systems, manufacturers of worlds. Man then will be perfect; he will then be a creator; he will therefore be what the vulgar worship as a god.' Christianity would be discarded as a false and primitive religion, 'pernicious to the intellect', which 'demands that the reason shall be sacrificed upon the altar' and 'places a hideous image, covered with dirt and blood, in the Holy of Holies; it rends the sacred Veil of Truth in twain'. In its place Reade envisaged that 'those who desire to worship their Creator must worship him through mankind. . . . To develop to the utmost our genius and our love – that is the only true religion.'

Huxley kept his feet more firmly on the ground. In his essay on 'Agnosticism' he had been very scathing about Frederick Harrison's promotion of positivism as a religion of humanity, suggesting that 'when the positivist asks me to worship "Humanity" – that is to say, to adore the generalized conception of men as they ever have been and probably ever will be – I must reply that I could just as soon bow down and worship the generalized conception of a "wilderness of apes"'. He anticipated the worst excesses of social Darwinism, pointing out that Darwinian ideas were as consistent with 'gradual retrogression' or 'indefinite persistence of one state' as with 'gradual progress'. He was particularly critical of attempts, such as those of Herbert Spencer with his discussion of the 'struggle for existence in human society', to use the idea of 'survival of the fittest' to justify unrestricted economic competition. Although he lectured on 'The Natural Inequality of Man', he cautioned that 'individualism pure and simple – if carried out logically, is merely reasoned savagery, utter and unmitigated selfishness, incompatible with social existence'.

Darwin's own views on religion were very cautious and rarely expressed. In reply to a Dutch student he wrote:

> I may say that the impossibility of conceiving that this grand and wondrous universe, with our conscious selves, arose through chance, seems to me the chief argument for the existence of God; but whether this is an argument of real value, I have never been able to decide. I am aware that if we admit a First Cause, the mind still craves to know whence it came and how it arose. Nor can I overlook the difficulty

> from the immense amount of suffering through the world. I am, also, induced to defer to a certain extent to the judgement of the many able men who have fully believed in God; but here again I see how poor an argument this is. The safest conclusion seems to me that the whole subject is beyond the scope of man's intellect; but man can do his duty.

But he added:

> The old argument from design in Nature, as given by Paley, which formerly seemed to me so conclusive, fails, now that the law of natural selection has been discovered. We can no longer argue that, for instance, the beautiful hinge of a bivalve shell must have been made by an intelligent being, like the hinge of a door by man. There seems to be no more design in the variability of organic beings, and in the action of natural selection, than in the course which the wind blows.

Compared with Clifford, Haeckel and Reade, Huxley, like Darwin, held to a realistic, almost bleak, view of the universe:

> Whether astronomy can or cannot be made to agree with the statements as to the matters of fact laid down in Genesis – whether the Gospels are historically true or not – are matters of comparatively small moment in the face of the impassable gulf fixed between the anthropomorphism (however refined) of theology and the passionless impersonality of the unknown and unknowable which science shows everywhere underlying the thick veil of phenomena. (*Letters*, ed. Leonard Huxley.)

Weary of 'society and societies – committees, councils', Huxley had retired in 1885. In retirement he remained a controversialist: one of his most heated exchanges in the pages of *Nineteenth Century* and the correspondence columns of *The Times* arose from his attack on Gladstone's attempt to demonstrate that scientific evidence supported the order of creation in the Genesis story.

In his last few years he moved to Eastbourne, where he walked six or seven miles a day over the Downs and conversed with his children and grandchildren. His eldest surviving son was Leonard, father of Julian and Aldous, who were to explore their grandfather's ideas in quite new realms in the twentieth century. Leonard wrote: 'Like the old Greek sage and statesman, my father might have declared that old age found him ever learning.' A few months before his death at the age of 70, he was preparing a reply to A. J. Balfour's attack on agnosticism. After an attack of influenza and several months' weakness he thought he was recovering, but in June 1895 his heart failed. His son Leonard wrote of the family's interception of letters written to him by religious opponents during his last illness: 'Some of them, of an almost incredible malignity, arrived from the religious of all denominations, saying how glad they were to learn that he was dying and how happy to think that he was going to Hell.'

Huxley, as the loudest, clearest mouthpiece of Darwinian theories, had lived at the centre of the conflict between science and religion. Some scientists formed their own unorthodox religions. Many liberal Protestants increasingly found it possible to accommodate scientific research as part of God's method of revealing his cosmos to man. But Huxley best summed up the transformation of humanity's consciousness of its place in the universe: 'The phraseology of Supernaturalism may remain on men's lips, but in practice they are Naturalists . . . even parish clerks doubt the utility of prayer for rain, so long as the wind is in the east; and an outbreak of pestilence sends men, not to churches, but to the drains.'

14

Emerson, Ingersoll, Twain: Three secular preachers

Emerson (1803–1882), Ingersoll (1833–1899) and Mark Twain (1835–1910) all gained fame and income as public speakers on the American lecture circuit, which developed from haphazard arrangements with burgeoning adult education institutions like the Lyceums and Mechanics' Institutes in the early part of the century to an organized professional form of public entertainment by the end of the century. Each in their different ways could hold and inspire a crowd. Emerson, who began as a preacher, gave listeners a secular sermon retaining uplift and mysticism while eschewing formal religion. Ingersoll became the best-known agnostic in the land and outraged and enchanted his audiences as he calmly took an axe to the roots of Christianity. Twain, more of a humorist and pure entertainer, was a closet sceptic and, like many a clown, harboured a dark almost nihilistic vision of a savage meaningless universe.

Ralph Waldo Emerson's father and maternal grandfather were Unitarian ministers. Unitarianism absorbed much of the rationalism of the Enlightenment, and contained a range of views from broad deism and reverence for the teachings rather than the divinity of Jesus to rather more orthodox Christian dogma. William Emerson, Waldo's father, knew the writings of Joseph Priestley, the Unitarian, radical and scientist, and probably possessed a copy of Thomas Paine's *The Age of Reason*. His premature death, when Waldo was eight, left his pious wife the task of bringing up six children on her own. Much of Waldo's childhood was spent moving from place to place as his mother tried to make ends meet by running different boarding houses. Two influential figures were his maternal step-grandfather, Ezra Ripley, a minister, and his aunt, Mary Moody Emerson. Aunt Mary was a Calvinist eccentric, half-recluse half gad-about, whose letters show a quirky originality in their language and theology. Between prayer and preparing her shroud in constant readiness for death (which she was given more than eighty years to do) she was a frequent visitor and helper to Waldo's mother and corresponded with her nephew for many years, growing sourer and sourer towards him as he substituted nature for the Church. She had, however, foreseen this trend and correctly predicted that the emphasis of the so-called 'humanitarians' amongst the Unitarians upon reform and right living would lead them away from God and heaven.

Waldo Emerson (he dropped Ralph as an adult) was a diligent schoolboy but he preferred walking on the heath or verse-writing to serious study. He entered Harvard at fourteen helping to pay his way by working as a waiter and coaching. He was an undistinguished student, acquiring a taste for wide, unsystematic reading, an admiration for the essays of Montaigne, and the habit of writing a journal which was to prove a source-book for his lectures and essays. Upon leaving Harvard at the age of nineteen, he assisted his elder brother as a teacher in his school for young ladies. A dislike of teaching and the pressure of family tradition rather than a burning faith pushed him in the direction of the ministry. His elder brother had travelled to Germany to study theology at Göttingen University: he was profoundly influenced by the Higher Criticism, and communicated his excitement in his letters to Waldo. He returned to America determined to abandon divinity for the Law. Waldo was not deflected from his ambition to be ordained and enrolled in the School of Divinity at Harvard in 1825. His studies were desultory and interrupted by ill-health, but in 1826 he obtained a licence to preach and in 1829 he was ordained. While travelling south for the sake of his health he became friendly with a nephew of Napoleon, Achille Murat, who 'is, yet, that which I had ever supposed only a creature of the imagination – a consistent atheist – and a disbeliever in the existence, and, of course, in the immortality of the Soul'. Their exchanges were amicable and Murat always excepted Unitarianism from his general disgust with religions, while Emerson found he could 'love and honour this intrepid doubter'.

He was diverging from Aunt Mary, with her sweeping condemnation of the German 'atheists'. As a pastor at the Second Church in Boston his admired sermons emphasized ethical behaviour not Christian dogma. He had to face personal tragedy when his beautiful but consumptive first wife died after only seventeen months of marriage. A sense of personal crisis entered his beliefs: gradually he had been feeling that 'the Bible has no force but what it derives within us' and 'that, in order to be a good minister, it was necessary to leave the ministry'. In sentences which sum up his move towards heteredox, pantheistic 'Transcendentalism', he wrote: 'The profession is antiquated. In an altered age, we worship in the dead forms of our forefathers. Were not a Socratic paganism better than an effete, superannuated Christianity?'

He wrote to the church committee saying that he could no longer administer the Lord's Supper as a rite and after weeks of ill health preached a sermon which stated that the observance of the Lord's Supper gave him an authority which he did not and should not want. His resignation was accepted. His state of mind is seen in his notes while pondering the sermon:

> Religion in the mind is not credulity, and in the practice is not form. It is life. It is the order and soundness of man. It is not something else *to be got*, to be *added*, but is a new life of those faculties you have. It is to do right. It is to love, it is to serve, it is to think, it is to be humble.

He was conscious that he stood in a tradition of heretics, quoting in his letter of resignation the example of Luther, who said: 'It is neither safe nor prudent to do aught against conscience.' He moved towards the ultimate consequences of Protestant belief – a humanism in which reverence for life and moral intensity stand independent of God or a supernatural level of existence.

After his break with the Church, friends helped him raise enough money for a tour of Europe. The sea voyage restored his health and he met Walter Savage Landor in Italy and Coleridge, Wordsworth and Carlyle in Britain. On his return to America he took temporary preaching jobs, but the settlement of his deceased wife's estate gave him the means to embark on a career as a lecturer and writer. His income was modest and throughout his lecturing career the need for money spurred him on. The growth of education and travelling libraries led to an increased audience prepared to pay for an evening's serious enlightenment.

His first series of lectures was at the Mechanics' Institute in Boston on the topic of 'The Uses of Natural History'. His pondering on German Idealism and botanic life led him into an effort at 'humanizing & Transcendentalizing science'. He developed his ideas into his first published book, *Nature* (1836), which attempted to demonstrate the unity of nature, God and the soul. It contains more rhapsodic lyricism than philosophical clarity, but it was very influential in suggesting an individualistic, mystical alternative to orthodox religion. It possesses something of Shaftesbury's belief in the beneficence of nature and d'Holbach's reverence for nature as the stuff of the universe (minus the divinity). Nature seemed to Emerson, like the New England countryside, full of beauty and uplift for the human 'soul'. In the Jardin des Plantes in Paris he had had an intuition of 'the full and regular series of animals from mites and worms up to man' and, although not completely blind to the harshness of the natural world, he detected an overall unity behind any apparent savagery and drew ecstasy from his personal observation: 'Extacy! Extacy! . . . The striped fly that eats our squash and melon vines, the rosebug, the corn worm, the red old leaf of the vines that entices the eye to search for the lurking strawberry, the thicket and little bowers of the pea-vine, the signs of ripeness and all the hints of the garden, these grave city writers never knew.'

His second marriage, to Lydia Jackson, who shared his serious interest in religion and love of literature, was in comparison with his first love 'a very sober joy', but it brought him lasting domestic happiness. They settled on the edge of Concord and he established a life of lecturing, writing, tending his orchard and entertaining neighbours. Among his local friends were Amos Alcott, a reformer who set up a Utopian community at Brook Farm, influenced by Robert Dale Owen and visited by his father Robert Owen in 1845, Margaret Fuller, an adventurous intellectual, and, in due course, Thoreau, who as Emerson's disciple lived on his land observing his pond at Walden. With the spread of Emerson's ideas the group became known as the 'Transcendentalists', though Emerson always denied attachment to a sect or party. A journal, *The Dial*, was edited at first by Margaret Fuller and then by Emerson; its poetry and articles were associated with the Transcendentalist Group.

Emerson's concept of Transcendentalism permeates his essays and lectures, for he was less a systemizer than an essayist constantly juggling his thoughts into a series of mosaics. His lecture 'The Transcendentalist' was first read at the Masonic Temple in Boston in 1842. He rejected materialism and claimed that the Transcendentalist was the contemporary form of Idealist, who 'takes his departure from his consciousness and reckons the world an appearance'. The essential value of the Transcendentalist, who will be criticized for avoiding society and good works, is his love of 'Truth, marketable or perishable'. His Idealism set him poles apart from the materialist and atheist critics of religion, but his substitution of truth, goodness and beauty for God, immortality and the churches put him outside the conventional faith.

The break was made quite clear when he addressed the Divinity School at Harvard in 1838. His audience were about to become ministers of religion, and his words shocked the authorities there. He had written in his journal that he ought to write an address to the American clergy 'showing them the ugliness and unprofitableness of theology and churches at this day, and the glory and sweetness of the moral nature out of whose pale they are almost shut'. Here was his opportunity. He said, with the sentiment of a heretic as much as an infidel, that 'historical Christianity has fallen into the error that corrupts all attempts to communicate religion'. The communication is better served by the moral sense open to the continual revelation of nature than by the Church which 'seems to totter to its fall, almost all life extinct'. Emerson influenced Unitarians and other liberal Christians as well as freethinkers; yet once preaching became simply 'the expression of the moral sentiment in application to the duties of life', as he urged, preachers could become humanistic counsellors not intermediaries between people and God.

A pamphlet war followed the publication of the address. There was Presbyterian denunciation of his 'nonsense and impiety' and one animadversion was entitled 'A Discourse on the Latest Form of Infidelity'. Even his friends had urged caution over publication of the Address lest he be, as his uncle wrote, associated with infidels like 'Kneeland, Paine & bespattered & belied'.

Abner Kneeland (1744–1844) was a more typical freethinker: a Universalist clergyman, friendly with Robert Dale Owen, his pantheistic views had been expounded in the *Boston Investigator*, one of the earliest American rationalist journals. As a consequence of a piece published in 1833 he was charged with blasphemy and after several trials and appeals sentenced to sixty days in prison. Emerson had signed a petition on his behalf. Kneeland, a man of great calm and courtesy, continued his propaganda in the Mid-West on release and unsuccessfully entered politics on an 'infidel ticket'.

Emerson was chary of sects, of propaganda, of activism. But the justice of the anti-slavery cause stirred him so deeply that he spoke on political platforms during the period leading up to the Civil War. By now a figure of international fame, he visited Europe in 1848, talked to Clough and Arnold, and lectured to the Mechanics' Institutes. He was much impressed with young Mary Ann Evans when he was the guest of Charles Bray in Coventry. In Paris, like Heine, he was 'caught in a Revolution as one might be in a shower'.

After the Civil War his popularity as a lecturer increased while his powers diminished. As he entered old age his mind failed, and he slipped serenely into senility. While still fairly coherent, he paid another visit to Europe, accompanied by one of his daughters. He wanted to see the temple of Osiris at Phylae and sailed down the Nile. He did not study myths in detail, but the desire to find a common pattern in all religious mythology, as for example in James Frazer's *The Golden Bough* (first published in 1890), was attractive to those searching for a universalist religion as well as those rejecting all religion.

Eastern religion had always fascinated him, the *Bhagavad Gita* at one stage being his favourite text. He was delighted when Max Müller of Oxford University, who had done much to promote understanding of eastern religion in Europe, dedicated his book *Introduction to the Science of Religion* to him. In Paris he met Renan, whose *Life of Jesus* depicted him as a historical person but not the son of God.

In his last years the churches attempted to reclaim Emerson. He slipped back into churchgoing to accompany his family, but as Heine pointed out (p.134) it is no compliment to Christianity to make converts of those approaching senility. Emerson's son refuted accounts that he was returning to orthodox religion, presumably after conversations with him in his more lucid moments. The deterioration of his mind did not diminish his pleasure in life. Until a few weeks before his death he enjoyed walking in the countryside, and when he caught pneumonia after walking in the rain he quietly slid into his last few weeks' illness, dying just short of his seventy-ninth birthday.

Transcendentalism was criticized for its rapturous vagueness: Emerson's neighbour, the novelist Nathaniel Hawthorne, said it was 'a heap of fog and duskiness' and Charles Kingsley caricatured Emerson as Mr Windrush in *Alton Locke*. However, the emphasis on intuition and experience was an important development in the history of heterodoxy. Once personal experience becomes the touchstone, the authority of religion as objective or revelatory evaporates: religion can be studied as a form of behaviour and a phenomenon of human experience and before long this was done with great insight by William James in *The Variety of Religious Experience* (1901–2). Emerson had visited William James's family, apparently finding a copy of *The Dial* on the table and climbing the stairs to bless the baby William.

Emerson and Colonel Ingersoll were completely different

characters: Ingersoll declaimed where Emerson pondered, and saw himself riding a wave of reform and progress, while Emerson determined to be a solitary individual dedicated to eternal verities, Ingersoll tore fundamentalist religion apart with relentless logic, Emerson gently tugged at the carpet beneath the organized Churches.

Robert Ingersoll was born in Dresden in the state of New York. One Bible recorded the date of his birth as 11 August 1833 another 12 August 1833: 'So you will see that a contradiction was about the first thing I found in the Bible, and I have continued to find contradictions in the Sacred Volumes all my life.' His father was a severe and devout Presbyterian minister. He shared his wife's enthusiasm for the abolition of slavery, but not the tinges of scepticism which led her to read *The Age of Reason*. She died when Robert was only two and the father and five children became closer after her loss. He had a happy childhood, slowly extricating himself from his father's beliefs with tact and good nature. He claimed he could not recall a time at which he had not opposed the absurdities and cruelties of the Christian Church, but especially remembered a Baptist preacher's sermon on Hell which, at the age of seven, left 'a mark like a scar' on his mind. He and his brother Clark argued steadily with their father about his religion. Contrary to the more usual pattern of rebellion and rift, affection was retained and their father's views were modified, so that before he died he called for a reading from the *Death of Socrates*, not the Bible. 'Honest Bob', as he was known in his youth, had no trouble making friends although the family moved from community to community because of the unpopularity of his father's anti-slavery views. As a youth he published a poem in the Greenville *Journal* and attempted public recitation – a disastrous experience for he had a complete lapse of memory while trying to recite Thomas Hood's 'I remember, I remember'. He vowed never to recite again, learning that an orator must be 'someone who thinks on his feet, who has the pose of passion. . . .' He became an Illinois schoolteacher. According to one story he lost a post after telling a group of evangelists with whom he shared lodgings, 'With soap, baptism is a good thing.'

In Williamstown County, Illinois, he decided to follow his brother in the legal profession and in due course became a qualified attorney. His intellectual development was encouraged by Judge William Bowman, an outstanding rationalist and lawyer whose vast library became Ingersoll's university. The writers he devoured are a roll call of the sceptical tradition from Epicurus and Lucretius to Bruno, 'the bravest', Voltaire, 'who did more to free the human mind than any other of the sons of men', and Hume, Gibbon, d'Holbach, Mill, Huxley. He joined his brother in practice in Shawneetown, and at the age of twenty-three discovered his oratorical gifts. At a picnic on the outskirts of Shawneetown local folk were expecting an address from a clergyman. In his absence Ingersoll was persuaded to say a few words 'of devotional import'; he disturbed, but impressed, his audience with an extemporary speech in praise of Thomas Paine. As always he disarmed his potential critics by the charm and persuasiveness of his delivery.

He was now set upon a career in which his rhetorical skills were used in the service of both law and an anti-religious crusade in which for over forty years he attacked Christianity in almost every town in the USA. He met Eva Parker at the house of her parents, two noted infidels, and their marriage resulted in that domestic happiness which much impressed G. W. Foote and other English freethinkers who visited him. Only nine days after the wedding he departed to serve in the Illinois Cavalry Regiment in the Civil War. He became a colonel, was admired for his courage, and noted by the chaplain to be full of pity for the wounded. After capture he was honourably discharged and returned to the law.

His eminence as a lawyer grew. His freethought and legal interests combined in a blasphemy trial in 1886. An ex-clergyman freethinker, C. B. Reynolds, was lecturing in Boonstown in New Jersey, when his tent was wrecked by opponents. Reynolds brought an action against the town for damages. In riposte a charge of blasphemy was brought against him for distributing a pamphlet entitled *Blasphemy and the Bible* which contained passages taken from the infamous Christmas number of *The Freethinker*, itself the subject of a blasphemy prosecution in 1882 (see p. 166). Ingersoll's defence did not secure Reynolds from conviction, but it brought an eloquent defence of free speech: 'To deny what you believe to be true, to admit to be true what you believe to be a lie; that is blasphemy.'

Ingersoll became a candidate for the governorship of Illinois in 1868: he was a popular candidate but withdrew from the race after refusing to agree not to mention the topic of religion during the campaign. Although refusing office henceforth, he made a notable contribution to various campaigns by his political oratory.

The first public lecture in which he avowed his doubts about religion was given in 1860 and entitled 'Progress':

> Forward, oh sublime army of progress, forward until law is justice, forward while there is a spiritual or temporal throne, forward until superstition is a forgotten dream, forward until the world is free, forward until the human reason, clothed in the purple of authority, is king of kings.

His purple prose becomes as wearying as a perpetual drum-beat if read at length, but, judging by his popularity as a lecturer, his audiences were captivated. The principal arguments he wielded to make 'superstition a forgotten dream' were to attack the historicity and consistency of the Bible, to query the existence of a personal God or even a first cause, to delineate the development of different gods and religions as a cultural phenomenon, and to propose his alternative view of human happiness based on reform, reciprocity and reason.

His biblical criticism was staple fare for freethinkers and, if not original or subtle, was much prized amongst those wishing to confute evangelicals. A long essay 'Some Mistakes of Moses' was in the tradition of *The Age of Reason* and would not have alarmed Christians aware of the Higher Criticism. Nevertheless it is illumined by his own sense of wit and detail: in a section called 'Dampness' he considers the story of Noah and the Flood and asks: 'How were some portions of the ark heated for animals from the tropics, and others kept cool for the polar bears? How did animals get back to their respective countries? . . . Think of a couple of the slowest snails leaving a point opposite the ark and starting for the plains of Shinar, a distance of twelve thousand miles. . . . Volumes might be written upon the infinite absurdity of this most incredible, wicked and foolish of all fables contained in that repository of the impossible called the Bible.' They were. And if a sense of allegory or metaphor is lacking, so it was to those who proclaimed the literal truth of the Bible.

Two of his finest mature lectures were 'Why Am I An Agnostic?' (1896) and 'What is Religion?', delivered in 1899 the year of his death. He preferred the word 'agnostic' to 'atheist' because he felt there could be no certain answer to the question of the existence of God. But he saw no evidence for a personal God and no trace of a beneficent hand in the world: 'According to the theologians, God prepared this globe expressly for the habitation of his loved children, and yet he filled the forest with ferocious beasts; placed serpents in every path; stuffed the world with earthquakes, and adorned its surface with mountains of flame.' A clergyman contested his view of the imperfection of Creation and asked him to 'name even one improvement you would make, if you had the power'. He replied that he 'would make good health catching instead of disease'. He attacked the idea of a first cause by claiming that matter 'cannot be destroyed' and 'that the indestructible is the uncreatable'. Above all he attacked 'the egotism of a man who believes that an infinite being wants his praise!' Like Voltaire he found the anthropocentrism of belief in a deity that cares for man quite ridiculous and told how 'a colony of red ants lived at the foot of the Alps. It happened one day that an avalanche destroyed the hill; and one of the ants was heard to remark: "Who can have taken so much trouble to destroy our home?"'

Clergymen detested his negative depiction of religion as 'fear' which 'builds the altar and offers the sacrifice', which 'bends the knee and utters the prayer'. But he countered with the view that clearing the forest was valuable for new growth and proposed his own view of reciprocity and happiness. His own version of the Golden Mean rejected the idea of returning 'kindness for injury' (turning the other cheek) for the more realistic 'For benefits return benefits and for injuries return justice'. One of his most oft-quoted remarks came in his early lecture 'The Gods': 'Reason, Observation and Experience – the Holy Trinity of Science – have taught us that happiness is the only good; that the time to be happy is now, and the way to be happy is to make others so.'

He certainly achieved happiness in his own life with financial security, domestic comfort and a taste for food, whisky and tobacco. In 1896 he suffered a slight stroke. Angina was also diagnosed and, while reducing his programme, he continued to lecture. Three years later his heart gave way. The famous eulogist was eulogized. Amongst the tributes were words from Haeckel and Clarence Darrow. After the cremation his ashes were placed in an urn on which were inscribed the words:

L'urne garde
La poussière,
Le coeur
Le souvenir.

(The urn guards the dust, the heart holds the memories.)

In a career of dramatic success and failure, Mark Twain, one of the greatest of American novelists, never found the complete personal contentment which Ingersoll enjoyed. Late in his life, after experiencing spectacular financial disaster and the agonies of bereavement, he wrote: 'Every man is a moon and has a dark side which he never shows to anybody. . . .' Twain's dark side contained the view that life is ultimately meaningless, that man may be of no significance in the universe, and that progress and a sense of moral purpose are an illusion. This side was shown to few until his last decade, but throughout his career as a lecturer and writer he had hated sham and pretension and spoken with the voice of popular mistrust of creeds and institutions. He was a humorist and not a philosopher, but his voice is close to that scepticism which has probably always existed as an undercurrent of popular thought.

Samuel L. Clemens, for 'Mark Twain' was a pseudonym, was born in a small town in Monroe County, Missouri, in 1835. His childhood in the region of the Mississippi fed his imagination in all his best writings. His mother was pious and her piety dogged him all his life. His father was a store-keeper, house-builder and would-be frontier developer; where Emerson and Ingersoll's preacher fathers had promised heaven for the faithful, Clemens's father dreamed the American dream of prosperity and perfection on earth. It was a dream which his son felt deeply, but never quite without doubts.

After rudimentary schooling, Clemens joined his elder brother in a printing concern; the desire for fame from journalism and wealth from typesetting dominated his career. Setting forth to travel to South America, he reached New Orleans, where his money ran out and he became a Mississippi pilot at a time when the importance of river routes had not yet been diminished by the railway. ('Mark Twain' was a pilot's phrase for two fathoms of water.) After a brief period in the Confederate army, he rejoined his brother, and they took the stage-coach journey westwards. *Roughing It*, as he entitled the book which he wrote about his experiences out West, was an apt description of his life of drinking, mining, gambling and quarrelling. He began to realize that his tale-telling skills were a realizable asset and to write pieces for the numerous new regional papers. A 'villainous backwoods sketch' called *The Celebrated Jumping Frog of Calveras County* was widely published and was regarded as a comic masterpiece. He then wrote a successful travel piece after a trip to the Sandwich Islands.

At the age of thirty he had lived much and achieved little. He travelled to New York to conquer the Eastern intellectual establishment. He talked himself into a passage as a reporter on the Quaker City, a luxury tourist cruise-ship to Europe and the Holy Land, and gained material for his first book, *Innocents Abroad* (1869), which was an instant success. The voyagers were polite, prosperous, pious New Englanders. Twain wanted to impress them, but could not resist mocking them. This tension between his desire to puncture the pretensions of such people and to be accepted as one of them affected all his writing: it kept his criticism comic and good-humoured and prevented the publication of his darker thoughts for many years. On board he was pleased to be sharing a cabin with a man who was 'splendid, immoral, tobacco-smoking, wine-drinking, godless'. He detested Puritanism and complacency: he described a passenger, who asked the captain if the ship would halt for the Sabbath, as a candidate 'for a Vacancy in the Trinity' and later referred to the 'old familiar Plymouth Church self-complacency' as 'the way God looks when he has had a successful season'. He was not impressed with European aristocratic traditions and their plethora of superstitions and relics. His comment about the Sea of Galilee has entered the repertoire of after-dinner speakers (among whom Twain was a past-master): an Arab boat man offering to take the travellers across the Sea of Galilee wanted to charge eight dollars – 'Do you wonder now that Jesus walked?'

The occasional denunciation from the pulpit and newspaper criticism of his lectures on the voyage as 'foul with sacrilegious allusions, impotent humour, and malignant distortions' could not dent his enormous popularity as an author and lecturer. His power over an audience was remarkable: 'He succeeded in doing what we have seen Emerson and other literary magnates fail in attempting. He interested and amused a large and promiscuous [*sic*] audience' (*Missouri Republican*). The shift from the educational lecture to entertainment was part of the rise of the leisure industry and the mass audience. The money and time which many people, for the first time in history, possessed for leisure and entertainment made religion seem irrelevant to their lives. Where religion had provided the commonest form of entertainment, instruction and social activity, its influence was inescapable; once these activities were secularized the pervasive influence of religion was bound to diminish. In the 1870s, perhaps sensing a rival force, the moralist Dr Josiah Holland denounced the new breed of Lyceum lecturers and claimed that these jesters 'ought not to be tolerated by any man of common sense interested in the elevation and purification of public taste'. Twain quickly wrote a counterblast in which Dr Holland was depicted as moving 'through the lecture field as remorseless as cholera', 'a perambulating sack of chloroform'.

Twain's scathing comments on religion were checked by his marriage in 1870 to Olivia Langdon. She was beautiful and very pious; her father, a wealthy manufacturer, took some persuading to relinquish his daughter to a story-telling, hard-drinking devotee of tobacco and billiards. 'Lyvy' at first persuaded him to observe the outward forms of religion, but his was the more persistent view and eventually, to her bitter regret, doubts overtook her. She has been criticized for censoring the livelier and more irreverent aspects of Twain's writing: but it is fair to say that his yearning to be accepted by the New England establishment, his fear of losing his public audience, and his own ideal of the pure – as embodied in his wife and daughters – made him a willing victim. The family lived for over twenty years in Hartford, Connecticut, where the money to pay for Twain's extravagant tastes had to be acquired by perpetual lectures and journalism.

During this period, apart from memoirs and travel books, he produced his best-known novels, *Tom Sawyer* and *Huckleberry Finn*. The latter, acknowledged as a masterpiece, possesses irrepressible vernacular vitality and pokes fun at convention through the eyes of the roaming lad and his friend, an escaped negro slave. Before attaining the freedom of life on the Mississippi, Huck is adopted by the genteel and devout Miss Watson. Huck's reflections on his upbringing hover between innocence and profundity:

> Then Miss Watson she took me in the closet and prayed, but nothing come of it. She told me to pray every day, and whatever I asked for I would get it. But it wasn't so. I tried it. Once I got a fish-line, but no hook. It warn't any good to me without hooks. I tried for the hooks three or four times, but somehow I couldn't make it work. By-and-by, one day, I asked Miss Watson to try for me, but she said I was a fool. She never told me why, and I couldn't make it out no way.

His family censors dealt with minute details in his novels; conscious of the eyes of his critics he had changed 'They comb me to hell' to 'They comb me to thunder' in *Tom Sawyer*. So he was aghast when an engraver added a male sex organ to an illustration; thousands of copies of the plate had to be replaced. The reception of *Huckleberry Finn* was cautious, but sales were helped by the announcement of the Library Committee in Boston that the book was to be banned as unsuitable for children.

Hand in hand with Twain's success as an author went his entrepreneurial dreams. He was obsessed with the wealth he could achieve with a new mechanical typesetter. His hopes were illusory, better technology was to overtake him, and the combination of the economic depression of the 1890s and his enormous and ill-chosen investments ruined him. At the age of sixty he had to start again. He organized a world tour to recover his fortune, and, even though he had come to hate lecture tours, showed utter determination to rebuild his finances. After a two-years' tour taking in Vancouver, South Africa, India and Europe, he regained his solvency. He thought his happiness was ensured, but chance, which he came to believe was the bitter arbiter of human destiny, dealt him a second blow. His daughter Suzy died from meningitis in 1896, and he never totally recovered from his desolation.

He returned to New York and wrote journalism, invective, fragments. He was once again celebrated, fêted, secure. Beneath was the sadness of his wife's failing health, for which they travelled to Florence, where she died in 1904. Again he returned to New York and became a semi-retired man of letters, dictating his *Autobiography* and always happy to speak at a dinner or receive another honour.

During the last thirteen years of his life his journalism became harsher, his fragmentary writings bitter and sceptical, and his publications less cautious. The double blow of financial failure and bereavement encouraged this, but in part it was a surfacing of a side that had always been there. In the year of his marriage he had planned a six-hundred-page book on the cruise of Noah's Ark (no doubt with highly comic intentions) and written an article on *God, Ancient and Modern*:

> The sole solicitude of the God of the Bible was about a handful of truculent nomads. He worried and fretted over them in a peculiar and distractingly human way. One day he coaxed and petted them beyond their deserts. He sulked, he cursed, he raged, he grieved, according to his mood and the circumstances . . . when the fury was on him, he was blind to all reason – he not only slaughters the offender, but even his harmless little children and his cattle.

The article was not published. Such biblical debunking was enjoyed by freethinkers like Ingersoll, as was the kind of comment which Twain made on Theodore Roosevelt's attempt to remove the words 'In God We Trust' from coins because it 'carried the name of God into improper places'. Twain praised the motto: 'It is simple, direct, gracefully phrased; it always sounds well – In God We Trust. I don't believe it would sound any better if it were true.'

How far Twain believed in God is arguable. A theistic creed written fairly early in his life was found in his papers untouched, but it can be doubted how firmly he would have held to the first sentence in later life:

> I believe in God the Almighty.
>
> I do not believe He has ever sent a message to anybody, or delivered one to him by word of mouth, or made Himself visible to mortal eyes at any time in any place.
>
> I believe that the Old and New Testament were imagined and written by man, and that no line in them was authorized by God, much less written by Him.
>
> I think the goodness, the justice, and the mercy of God are manifested in His works. . .
>
> I do not believe in special providences . . .
>
> I cannot see how eternal punishment hereafter could accomplish any good end, therefore I am not able to believe in it . . .
>
> There may be a hereafter and there may *not* be. I am wholly indifferent about it . . .
>
> I believe that the world's moral laws are the outcome of the world's experience . . .
>
> If I break all the moral laws I cannot see how I injure God by it, for He is beyond the reach of injury from me – I could as easily injure a planet by throwing mud at it . . .

He may have retained belief in an impersonal creative force, but certainly abandoned any idea of the goodness, mercy and justice of God. Some of his tales, many published posthumously, display withering contempt for the idea of a benevolent God. In *Little Bessie* a child describes how an adult friend had told her 'there isn't a bird or fish or reptile or any other animal that hasn't got an enemy that Providence has sent to bite it and chase it and discipline it and make it good and religious.'

In 1905 Twain published *What Is Man?*, an idiosyncratic exposition of his views of man and his place in the universe. He had been working on the draft for many years and only the death of his wife enabled him to feel free to publish it. He sees man as a machine controlled by external forces, whose conduct is conditioned by a ceaseless desire for self-satisfaction and self-approval, and whose temperament is determined by heredity and cannot be changed. In this picture there is no room for Emerson's moral intuition, nor Ingersoll's hopes of reform and progress. And religion has no significance, for it cannot change human behaviour and is culturally determined. History shows:

> a thousand wild and tame religions, every kind of government that can be thought of, from tiger to house-cat, each nation *knowing* it has the only true religion and the only sane system of government, each despising all the others, each an ass and not suspecting it, each proud of its fancied supremacy, each perfectly sure it is the pet of God, each with undoubting confidence summoning Him to take command in time of war, each surprised when He goes over to the enemy, but by habit able to excuse it and resume compliments – in a word, the whole human race content, persistently content, indestructibly content, happy, thankful, proud, *no matter what its religion is, nor whether its master be tiger or house-cat.*

In this bleak picture he did allow a little hope. The book is in the form of a dialogue between an Older Man and a Younger Man, and the former admonishes the latter: 'Diligently train your ideals *upward* and *still upward* toward a summit which, while contenting you, will be sure to confer benefits upon your neighbour and the community'. This is the common denominator of all religions and of non-religious ethical systems and Twain came close to being too nihilistic even to concern himself with such upward-looking at all.

His late stories show an obsession with perspective; with man as a microbe, with man travelling across oceans while transmuted into a speck of water under a microscope (*The Great Dark*). In an entertainment published in instalments in 1907 and 1908, but written as early as 1868, *Captain Stormfield's Visit to Heaven*, he shows a human being arriving in Heaven only to find that earth is in one of the least known tiny corners of the universe. (The whole concept of Heaven is debunked: it too must contain a proportion of pain and pleasure, like life, because 'happiness isn't a thing in itself – it's only a contrast with something that isn't pleasant'.) The import of these shifting perspectives, as is indicated in the title *The Great Dark*, is that 'you come from a small and insignificant world'. Beneath the corn-cob humorist, Twain had affinities with Nietzsche's *Angst* at the death of God and the nihilist, Stavrogin, in Dostoevsky's novel *The Devils* (originally conceived with the title *Atheism*). He foreshadowed the alienation and existentialism of the twentieth century which has led thinkers to stress the necessity for human beings to create their own significance and purpose in an insignificant and purposeless world.

A month before his death Twain recalled in a letter that Halley's comet had appeared in the year of his birth. In 1910 the comet had approached again and he wryly imagined it as a sign of his death with God saying: 'Here are these unaccountable freaks. They came in together, they must go out together.' If Twain had had a God, he would have had to have a sense of humour, but if God is merely a spectator of 'unaccountable freaks' what need for him at all?

15
Bertrand Russell: A passionate rationalist

Bertrand Russell (1872–1970) was, literally, heir to the nineteenth-century liberal tradition: his grandfather, Lord John Russell, had been Prime Minister and his godfather was John Stuart Mill. He was sufficiently of the Establishment to have once referred, in his early life, to the government as 'We', but the long standing tradition of dissent in his family stretched back to William Russell, who, when sentenced to execution for alleged complicity in the Rye House Plot (1683), ordered his chaplain to write a life of Julian the Apostate to argue that resistance against authority may be justified. His grandmother's grandfather had been 'cut by the County for saying that the world must have been created before 4004 B.C. because there is so much lava on the slopes of Etna' (*Autobiography*). Bertrand Russell's dissent and doubt were to extend much further. He inherited a fearless individualism, and the texts which his grandmother inscribed in the fly-leaf of his Bible affected him profoundly: 'Thou shalt not follow a multitude to do evil' was precisely observed and 'Be strong, and of good courage; be not afraid, neither be thou dismayed, for the Lord Thy God is with Thee wheresoever thou goest' was followed in what Russell saw as the cause of humanity rather than the Lord.

In his long life spanning the nineteenth and twentieth centuries he became a renowned and controversial philosopher, atheist, publicist and political reformer. He is, perhaps, the most famous and most passionate rationalist of the century, like Voltaire a polymath whose gifts lay in lucid and witty exposition and dramatic publicity for diverse causes – conscientious objection, education, rational morality, world peace – as much as any single piece of original work. He wrote at the opening of his *Autobiography*:

> Three passions, simple but overwhelmingly strong, have governed

> my life: the longing for love, the search for knowledge, and unbearable pity for the suffering of mankind. These passions, like great winds, have blown me hither and thither, in a wayward course, over a deep ocean of anguish, reaching to the very verge of despair.

Russell's parents, Lord Amberley and Kate Stanley, were acquainted with Mill and his circle and involved in radical politics. Lord Amberley's brief foray into Parliament was discontinued because of his controversial support for birth control. He embarked on a laborious study of world religions, from which he extracted a universal religion published as *An Analysis of Religious Belief* (1877). His detailed examination of scriptures from all over the world led him to conclusions which echo the views of eighteenth-century deists such as Shaftesbury:

> No man can truly oppose their religion [the adherents of universal religion] for he who seems hostile to it is himself but one of the notes struck by the Unknowable Cause, which so plays upon the vast instrument of humanity as to bring harmony out of jangling sounds, and to bring the universal chords of truth from the individual discords of error. Scientific discoveries and philosophic inquiries, so fatal to other creeds, touch not the universal religion.

Lady Amberley also held radical views, especially on the position of women. Her mother, Lady Stanley, was 'an eighteenth-century type, rationalistic and unimaginative, and contemptuous of Victorian goody-goody priggery' (*Autobiography*). She was one of the founders of Girton College and declared that 'so long as I live there shall be no chapel at Girton'. Russell recalls noisy arguments in her house at Sunday luncheon between her sons who variously espoused Catholicism, Unitarianism, freethought, positivism and Mohammedanism: 'A favourite trick of my Uncle Lyulph at Sunday luncheon was to ask: "Who is there here who believes in the literal story of Adam and Eve?" His object in asking the question was to compel the Mohammedan and the priest to agree with each other, which they hated doing.'

Russell's mother died from diphtheria when he was only two and two years later his heartbroken father died from bronchitis and lack of will to live. Russell moved to Pembroke Lodge in Richmond Park, where the former Prime Minister, Lord John Russell, lived in retirement. He died soon after Bertrand's arrival and Lady Russell was the dominant influence on his upbringing. He was not sent to school since his elder brother Frank had in Lady Russell's view fallen under bad influence at public school. A sombre puritanical regime and a succession of tutors provided a lonely and gloomy childhood. His self-education was assisted by the range of his grandfather's library. He learnt much of Shelley's poetry by heart.

In his teens he kept a diary written in Greek characters for secrecy. At the time of his sixteenth birthday it recorded his sorrow that he did not share the religious belief of others:

> I should like to believe my people's religion, which was just what I could wish, but alas, it is impossible. I have really no religion, for my God, being a spirit shown merely by reason to exist, his properties utterly unknown, is no help to my life. I have not the parson's comfortable doctrine that every good action has its reward, and every sin is forgiven. My whole religion is this: do every duty, and expect no reward for it, either here or hereafter.

Soon even the First Cause was to vanish when he was convinced by a sentence in J. S. Mill's *Autobiography* '"Who made me?" cannot be answered, since it immediately suggests the further question "Who made God?".' He read Gibbon, and Milman's *History of Christianity*, and *Gulliver's Travels* unexpurgated. 'The account of the Yahoos had a profound effect upon me, and I began to see human beings in that light.'

Two consolations for the loss of faith and the yahoodom of humanity were his realization that he was very clever and his passion for pure mathematics. He overheard an uncle referring to his progress and 'realizing that I was intelligent, I determined to achieve something of intellectual importance if it should be at all possible'. The appeal of mathematics lay partly in his 'delight in the power of deductive reasoning' and partly in the appeal of a universe which 'operates according to mathematical laws' and a hope 'that human actions, like planetary motions, could be calculated if we had sufficient skill.' (He could not calculate the stormy emotions of his own life.) An impersonal universe attracted him: 'I like mathematics because it is *not* human & has nothing in particular to do with this planet or with the whole accidental universe – because, like Spinoza's God, it won't love us in return.'

The horizons of Pembroke Lodge were enlarged for him at seventeen with his study at a crammer's in Southgate for a Cambridge scholarship and with his visits to his uncle in Hindhead, Surrey, and friendship with the neighbouring Pearsall Smith family. The crammer brought him merciless teasing from English 'gentlemen' and a scholarship at Trinity College. The Pearsall Smith acquaintanceship introduced him to progressives such as Shaw, Frederic Harrison and the Webbs, and to Alys Pearsall Smith with whom he fell deeply in love.

At Cambridge Russell's life was lit with the friendship and intellectual stimulus which had been absent from Pembroke Lodge. Alfred North Whitehead, who had recommended his scholarship, was his teacher, colleague and in due course collaborator. His many friends included the Trevelyan brothers and G. E. Moore, whose philosophy was eventually to influence him profoundly. The elite debating club, the Apostles, elected him into their company. Here it was that he heard Moore read a paper which began, 'In the beginning was matter, and matter begat the devil, and the devil begat God'. 'The paper ended with the death first of God and then of the devil, leaving matter alone as in the beginning' (*Autobiography*).

Russell's interest in the logical basis of mathematics led him to a fascination with philosophy. After gaining his mathematics degree, he decided to study Moral Sciences for a year. After completing the Moral Sciences Tripos, he turned to the foundation of geometry for a fellowship thesis and the basis of ethics for a paper to be read to the Apostles. Meanwhile, at the age of twenty-one he had inherited sufficient means to ensure financial independence and persuaded Alys Pearsall Smith, whom he had courted for three years, to marry him. Alys came from a rich American Quaker family of temperance campaigners. Lady Russell vehemently opposed the marriage, but Russell, after agreeing to spend three months in Paris in the diplomatic service, proved that no opposition could cool his ardour. They were married in 1894 at a Quaker Meeting House in London. 'Don't imagine that I really mind a religious ceremony,' he wrote in a letter to his *fiancée*, 'any ceremony is disgusting & the mere fact of having to advertise the most intimate thing a little more or less doesn't make much odds'.

Russell's marriages, extra-marital affairs and his book *Marriage and Morals* became notorious and were attacked by those who wished to couple atheism and immorality. His marriage with Alys which lasted nearly thirty years, although with complete separation for nearly half of it, was deeply unhappy and sexually unsatisfactory; both parties were by turn patient, bitter and despairing. In middle age Russell found years of repressed sexuality and loneliness were unleashed, and his quest for fulfilment and companionship might be seen as a response to the loneliness and puritanism of his childhood. His affairs with Ottoline Morrell and with the actress Constance

Malleson each resulted in a life-long correspondence and friendship. His marriage to Dora Black brought intellectual and idealistic partnership and longed-for children; his marriage to Patricia Spence brought assistance with his work and faithful support at a difficult time; his final marriage to Edith Finch brought profound contentment, though the cynic might wonder whether its stability was due to the waning energy of old age.

In their early years of marriage Russell and Alys much enjoyed travel, for pleasure and study. They visited Berlin in 1895 and Russell set about a study of the German Social Democratic Party. He recalled a moment one spring morning in the Tiergarten when he planned to 'write a series of books in the philosophy of sciences, growing gradually more concrete as I passed from mathematics to biology; I thought I would also write a series of books on social and political questions, growing gradually more abstract'. His plan to write the most technical (and abstruse) books and the most popular journalism was fully achieved. His first published work, *German Social Democracy* (1896), arose from a series of lectures he gave at the London School of Economics and placed German socialism in the tradition of Saint-Simon and Robert Owen, while also suggesting a debt to Kant and Hegel which turned it from a political party into a 'self-contained philosophy of the world and of human development', making it 'a religion and an ethic'. Russell was later to characterize forms of socialism and Marxism as religious and strongly to oppose their doctrinaire nature and tendency to produce fanaticism.

Having been awarded a six-year fellowship at Trinity College for his work on the foundation of geometry, Russell pondered his first major original work *The Principles of Mathematics* (1903). A preliminary in the seven years' work was his liberation from Hegelian idealism which felt, he wrote, 'as if I had escaped from a hot-house onto a wind-swept headland'. The work was given further stimulus when he attended the International Congress of Philosophy, Logic and the History of Science in Paris in 1900.

Russell related changes in his philosophical outlook to moments of personal insight about his feelings for others. He recalled that a consciousness of his love for Mrs Whitehead made him consider 'loneliness in general, & how only love bridges the chasm – how force is the evil thing, & strife is the root of all evil & gentleness the only balm'. He became 'infinitely gentle' for a time and 'turned against the S. African war & imperialism'. He pinpointed a similar moment of crisis when smitten with despair and anguish at his realization that he did not love Alys. In the initial stage of emotional turmoil he completed *The Principles of Mathematics* 'because the oppression of it grew unendurable'. After nearly a year of depression, they travelled to Italy to stay with Aly's sister, who was married to the art critic Bernard Berenson. Now, in Fiesole on the hills surrounding Florence, he tried to come to terms with his unhappiness by writing out his philosophy of life in the essay *A Free Man's Worship*. It is written in passionate, lyrical prose untypical of Russell's usual lucidity. He finds humanity placed in a purposeless, impersonal universe – a position which much twentieth-century thought has been forced to accept, relish or deny. He writes of a world 'purposeless' and 'void of meaning', 'which Science presents for our belief' and proposes:

> That Man is the product of causes which had not prevision of the end they were achieving; are but the outcome of accidental collocation of atoms; that no fire, no heroism, no intensity of thought and feeling, can preserve an individual life beyond the grave; that all the labours of the age, all the devotion, all the inspiration, all the noonday brightness of human genius, are destined to extinction in the vast death of the solar system, and that the whole temple of Man's achievement must inevitably be buried beneath the debris of a universe in ruins – all these things, if not quite beyond dispute, are yet so nearly certain, that no philosophy which rejects them can hope to stand.

Russell describes how Man, feeling 'the oppression of his impotence before the powers of Nature', has created gods to worship which were at first savage forces and then a God 'all-powerful and all-good'. The world is not good, yet we wish to worship either force or goodness: 'Shall we worship Force or Goodness? Shall our God exist and be evil, or shall he be recognized as the creation of our own consciences?' Russell rejects the worship of force 'to which Carlyle and Nietzsche and the creed of Militarism have accustomed us' and proclaims that 'man's true freedom' lies in his 'determination to worship only the God created by our own love of the good, to respect only the heaven which inspires the insight of our best moments'.

Russell argues that happiness and wisdom, given our unachievable desires, are only reached by renunciation and resignation – values which he recognizes have been found in religions. He concludes with an affirmative picture of Man 'proudly defiant of the irresistible forces that tolerate, for a moment, his knowledge and his condemnation, to sustain alone, a weary but unyielding Atlas, the world that his own ideals have fashioned despite the trampling march of unconscious power'. The essay is not entirely typical of Russell – indeed, he came to be cynical of this approach 'because no gospel will stand the test of life'. But it expresses a powerful strand of thought of man not so much 'Against the Faith' as 'without a faith'.

Writing *A Free Man's Worship* did not purge Russell of his unhappiness, and intermittent despair was countered by walking tours and work. His *magnum opus*, written in collaboration with A. N. Whitehead, was *Principia Mathematica*, which contained an attempt to find a logical foundation for mathematics and was published in 1910–1913. The authors were only able to resist the publisher's attempt to shorten it by subsidizing the publication themselves, thus earning, as Russell put it, 'minus £50 each by ten years' work'.

It was not until the 1920s that he expressed most strongly his feeling that religious belief was pernicious. For some years he attempted to understand the religious feelings of his lover Ottoline Morrell. He defined, in a more generous way than in his later essays, the difference between himself and the religious believer in a letter to her:

> What you call God is very much what I call infinity. I do feel something in common in all the great things – something which I should not think of quite as you do, tho' it is very mysterious & I really don't know what to think of it – but I feel it is the most important thing in the world & really the one thing that matters profoundly. It is to me as yet a mystery – I don't understand it. I think it has many manifestations – love is the one that seems to me the deepest & that I feel most when I am very deeply moved. But truth is the one I have mainly served, & truth is the only one I *always* feel the divinity of . . .

He continued:

> I think Christ was right to put love of God before love of my neighbour. Only I don't think God *exists* ready-made. I think he is an idea we can conceive & can do something to create, tho' he will never exist *fully*. That is why human actions are important – *because* God does not exist already. There is of course *one* great difference between your beliefs and mine. I do not think any spiritual force outside human beings actually helps us – there may be such a force, but if so it is only as incarnated in human beings that it helps us. Therefore I cannot pray or lean on God. What strength I need I must get from myself or those whom I advise. And this view does seem to me nobler, sterner, braver

> than the view which looks for help from without, besides seeming to me truer.

His ideas on religion were further expounded in the paper 'Mysticism and Logic' which became one of his best-known essays and in which he dealt more harshly with religious belief.

Another influence of Ottoline upon his writings was the stimulus to explain philosophical problems to the non-specialist reader. When he was first asked to write a shilling volume for the Home University Library to present *The Problems of Philosophy* to the masses, he rejected the idea, but he in fact produced a small masterpiece, refined by his constant clarification of the text in conversation with Ottoline. He came to feel the value of philosophy to the 'man in the street': it keeps alive 'that speculative interest in the universe which is apt to be killed by confining ourselves to definitely ascertainable knowledge', but above all it enlarges man's interests beyond 'the circle of his private interests' and 'in such a life there is something feverish and confined, in comparison with which the philosophical life is calm and free'.

Russell, to whom philosophy never seemed to bring great serenity, entered a period of hectic public activity on the outbreak of the First World War. His opposition to the war and defence of the rights of conscientious objectors transformed him from a well-known academic into a figure of national renown. His initiation into politics had taken place in 1907 when he stood as a candidate for Parliament for the National Union of Women's Suffrage Societies in the Wimbledon constituency in South London. He was never at ease in the political world of compromise and deals, but was grateful that 'ten days of standing for Parliament brought me more relations with concrete realities than a life-time of thought'. The concrete realities included a rat released to disturb a public meeting and an egg which gave Alys a black eye as she accompanied him on the hustings. Henceforth, his political activities were limited. He stood as a parliamentary candidate for Chelsea in the 1920s and became entitled to a seat in the House of Lords on the death of his elder brother in 1931, but his activities were essentially extra-parliamentary and single issue campaigns.

From his opposition to the First World War in his forties to the campaign against the use of nuclear weapons in his eighties and nineties, he was powered by the emotion expressed in his despondent observation of the enthusiastic jingoism in the months following August 1914: 'Hardly anyone seems to remember common humanity – that war is mad horror & that deliberately to cause the deaths of thousands of men like ourselves is so ghastly that hardly anything can justify it.' His quarrel was with particular wars (at the outset of the First World War he thought at first that a neutral Britain and America could impose peace on a warring Europe) and particular forms of warfare (he saw no justification for the genocide that atomic warfare would create) rather than a consistent, logical pacifist crusade. Although he was deeply attached to the landscape of England, he disliked nationalism which he saw as a kind of religion from which humanity must progress:

> Men have learned gradually to free their God from the savagery with which the primitive Israelites endowed him; few now believe that it is his pleasure to torture most of the human race in an eternity of hell-fire. But they have not learned to free their national ideals from the ancient taint. Devotion to the nation is perhaps the deepest and most widespread religion of the present age. Like the ancient religions, it demands its persecutions, its holocausts, its lurid, heroic cruelties; like them, it is noble, primitive, brutal and mad.

As a pacifist he lost his lectureship at Trinity College, Cambridge, and achieved the half-sought martyrdom of six months' imprisonment. He discovered his ability to influence large audiences and found that exhaustive campaigning brought a sense of fulfilment: 'Quite lately I have somehow found myself – I have poise and sanity. I no longer have the feeling of powers unrealized within me, which used to be perpetual torture.'

His encounter with war and pacific resisters made him conscious of 'the volcanic side of human nature', of the violence of feelings amongst patriots and pacifists. An anti-war meeting in the Brotherhood Church, Southgate, was broken up by violence. He had earlier written to Ottoline: 'What is wrong with men's opposition to war is that it is negative. One must find other outlets for people's wildness, and not try to produce people who have no wildness.' Nor did Russell underestimate the passionate aspect of human nature, writing from prison to Constance Malleson:

> I must, I *must*, before I die, find *some* way to say the essential thing that is in me, that I have never said yet, a thing that is not love or hate or pity or scorn, but the very breath of life, fierce and coming from far away, bringing into human life the fearful passionless force of non-human things . . . I want to stand for life and thought – thought as

> adventure, clear thought because of the intrinsic delight of it, along with the other delights of life. Against worldliness, which consists in doing everything for the sake of something else, like marrying for money instead of love. The essence of life is doing things for their own sakes . . . I want to stand at the rim of the world, and peer into the darkness beyond, and see a little more than others have seen of the strange shapes of mystery that inhabit that unknown night . . . I want to bring back into the world of men some little bit of new wisdom. There is a little wisdom in the world; Heraclitus, Spinoza, and a saying here and there. I want to add to it, even if only ever so little.

In the subsequent inter-war decades Russell added to the sum of ideas and books more than a little with numerous popular books which were undertaken as journalistic tasks to support himself. Like Thomas Paine, he had the gift of expressing himself with great force and clarity directly to the common reader. One of his most controversial books was *The Practice and Theory of Bolshevism*, written after a visit to Russia in 1920. He had welcomed the Bolshevik revolution in 1917, but the reality quickly disillusioned him and he found himself 'infinitely unhappy in this atmosphere – stifled by its utilitarianism, its indifference to love and beauty and the life of impulse'. Like Diderot, he was given the opportunity to talk to a Russian leader, but Lenin did not have the time to listen to his ideas that Catherine the Great had found to give ear to the French *philosophe*. Russell was impressed with Lenin's strength, which 'comes, I imagine, from his honesty, courage, & unwavering faith – religious faith in Marxian orthodoxy, which takes the place of the Xtian martyr's hope of paradise, except that it is less egotistical. He has as little love of liberty as the men who suffered under Diocletian & retaliated (on heretical Xtians) when they acquired power.'

A year later he visited China, where he was invited to give a course of lectures at the university in Peking. He thought China was 'what Europe would have become if the 18th century had gone on till now without industrialism or the French revolution' and was delighted to observe that 'people seem to be rational hedonists, knowing very well how to obtain happiness'. He became so ill with pneumonia that a report of his death was published in a Japanese paper and he had the rare pleasure of reading in his own obituary in a missionary paper that 'missionaries may be pardoned for heaving a sigh of relief at the news of Mr Bertrand Russell's death'. He wrote in his *Autobiography*: 'I was told that the Chinese said that they would bury me by the Western Lake and build a shrine to my memory. I have some slight regret that this did not happen, as I might have become a god, which would have been very *chic* for an atheist.'

He shared with his second wife, Dora Black, an interest in progressive education – an interest that was given practical impetus as they brought up their own children. They started a school at Beacon Hill in Sussex with the intention, in Dora's words, of 'providing a really modern education which, instead of training young children to maintain every prejudice of traditional society, or teaching them new dogmas, should try to help them to think and work for themselves, and so fit them for meeting the problems of the changing world they will have to face when they grow up'. Dora and Bertrand, like Owen and Carlile, saw education as a tool for enlightenment and social change. The school was notorious. An apocryphal story told how the local vicar was greeted at the door by a young child with no clothes on; to his exclamation, 'Oh, my God!', the child replied, 'There is no God'. In fact, the local rector was quite friendly with the children.

To support the school Russell continued to write prolifically and to accept opportunities of lucrative American tours. Among his popular books were *Marriage and Morals* (1929) and *The Conquest of Happiness* (1930). It was not a conquest which he found easy and the then controversial view that divorce ought to be made easier was reached from personal experience. He separated from Dora and the school in 1935 and married Patricia Spence in the following year. His hand-to-mouth free-lance existence gave him insufficient opportunity for philosophical study and he was pleased to return to this when he gave a course of lectures on Language and Fact at Oxford in 1938. Despite his doubts about breaking away from England at a time when war loomed, he accepted a post as visiting professor of philosophy at Chicago in 1938–9. He moved from there to California University, where friction with the President led him to resign on the expectation of a position at the College of the City of New York in 1940. The refusal to confirm the appointment, because of the pressure of religious groups led by Bishop Manning, became a *cause célèbre*. Both his book *Marriage and Morals* and his personal life led to the oldest of charges against the unbeliever – immorality. Despite opposition the New York Board of Education appointed him; but the appointment was challenged in the State Supreme Court by a student's parents on the grounds that he was an alien who had not passed a competitive exam for the post and who advocated sexual immorality. Russell was amused, not to say flattered, by the brief of the lawyer opposing him, with its accusation that he was 'lecherous, libidinous, lustful, venerous, erotomaniac, aphrodisiac, irreverent, narrow-minded, untruthful, and bereft of moral fibre'. He concluded that his only predecessors were Apuleius and Othello. The case was tried by a Roman Catholic, Justice McGeehan, whose biased judgement contained the memorable indictment that the appointment would establish 'a chair of indecency'. Russell lost the case and the American academics belatedly rallied to defend freedom of speech. On the title page of a later book, Russell included amongst a list of his distinctions – 'Judicially pronounced unworthy to be Professor at the College of the City of New York (1940)'.

Russell, supporting his children in American higher education, went through considerable hardship during the Second World War. His earning capacity as a lecturer was at first much reduced by the notoriety arising from the New York College case. He was saved by an invitation to deliver the William James lectures at Yale, and then by the patronage of a wealthy American, Dr Abbott Barnes, who contracted him to lecture for five years on the history of philosophy. The William James Lectures developed into his last important philosophical work, *An Inquiry Into Meaning and Truth*. The lectures for the Barnes foundation, although not completed because of quarrels with Dr Barnes, led him to write his *History of Western Philosophy*, which eventually became such a world-wide best-seller that he enjoyed financial security for the remainder of his life.

Russell had not opposed the Second World War. In 1940 he sent his views to Kingsley Martin for publication in the *New Statesman*: 'I am still a pacifist in the sense that I think peace the most important thing in the world. But I do not think there can be any peace in the world while Hitler prospers, so I am compelled to feel that his defeat, if at all possible, is a necessary prelude to anything good; I should have felt as I do if I had lived in the time of Genghis Khan.' He agonized over whether to return to England and accepted an invitation to return to Trinity College, Cambridge in 1944 with relief.

During the post-war era, Russell, in his seventies, experienced a brief halcyon period as a figure of fame, almost returning to the Establishment. He was awarded the OM and the Nobel Prize for literature, invited to lecture all round the world and given the chance to become a pundit on the expanding media of radio and television. His undiminished vigour while on a lecture tour in Norway enabled him to swim to safety when his plane came down in Trondheim Fjord. The remainder of his life was dominated by his detestation of war and his crusade against nuclear weapons. The zeal of his conviction and the various tactics which he was prepared to adopt soon removed him from his pedestal and put him back in the controvesial zones of opposition where he had spent most of his life. He said in his speech accepting the Nobel Prize for literature:

> The atom bomb and the bacterial bomb, wielded by the wicked communist or the wicked capitalist as the case may be, make Washington and the Kremlin tremble, and drive men further and further along the road to the abyss. If matters are to improve, the first and essential step is to find a way of diminishing fear. The world at present is obsessed by the conflict of rival ideologies, and one of the apparent causes of conflict is the desire for the victory of our own ideology and the defeat of the other.

He found peace himself in his last marriage to Edith Finch and in his rural home in Wales. In his nineties, there were numerous rumours that, with the approach of death, he had returned to religion. He thanked the American Humanist Association 'for bringing to my attention these continuing rumours of my imminent conversion to Christianity' and commented: 'Evidently there is a lie factory at work on behalf of the after-life. How often must I continue to deny that I have become religious. There is no basis whatsoever for these rumours. My views on religion remain those which I acquired at the age of sixteen. I consider all forms of religion not only false but harmful. My published works record my views.' He claimed, perhaps mischievously, that he had contemplated compiling an illustrated joke-book about the Bible, but had dropped the idea since it would cause offence.

Russell had no need to compile such a book to consolidate his reputation as an anti-religious atheist. He had become the best-known media rationalist, expounding on the radio discussion programme The Brains Trust, broadcasting a talk on 'What I believe' and participating in an extended radio debate with the distinguished Jesuit Father Copleston on 'The Existence of God'.

One of the most clear-cut expressions of his beliefs had been given in a lecture entitled 'Why I Am Not a Christian' delivered for the National Secular Society in Battersea Town Hall in 1927. After consideration of the first cause argument, the natural law argument, the argument from design, the moral arguments for deity and the argument for remedying injustice, he concluded that no argument in favour of the existence of the deity could convince him. In his debate with Copleston, he considered the arguments with more philosophical subtlety and accepted the appellation 'agnostic' on the ground that he could not prove the non-existence of God. (An argument frequently used by believers to force unbelievers to soften their terms by accepting their opponents' definition; 'Atheist' means without a concept of God that is logically convincing, not with proof that God does not exist.) Elsewhere he was frequently happy to refer to himself as an atheist. For all the complexity of the debate, he adjudged that 'What really moves people to believe in God is not any intellectual argument at all. Most people believe in God because they have been taught from early infancy to do it, and that is the main reason.'

In an essay on 'What I believe', published in 1925, Russell had made his doubts about immortality clear: 'All the evidence goes to show what we regard as our mental life is bound up with brain structure and organized bodily energy. Therefore it is rational to suppose that mental life ceases when bodily life ceases. The argument is only one of probability, but it is as strong as those upon which most scientific conclusions are based.'

The same essay betrayed an over-confident faith in science: 'Physical science is thus approaching the stage where it will be complete, and therefore uninteresting . . .' – the kind of overstatement which has produced something of a reaction against science in recent years. But it was central to Russell, as to all the figures in this book, that 'It is not by prayer aand humility that you cause things to go as you wish, but by acquiring a knowledge of natural laws' (*Autobiography*).

Russell could be acerbic in his attitude to Christianity, never more so than in 'Why I am not a Christian'. He thought Christ made some good points such as 'Judge not lest ye be judged' and 'If thou wilt be perfect, go and sell all that thou hast, and give to the poor', but he thought that most Christians did not take much notice of them. He observed that 'historically it is quite doubtful whether Christ ever existed at all', but thought that Christ as presented in the Gospels had many defects, including his teaching about a Second Coming and Hell, and his exhortation to 'take no thought for the morrow'. The history of Christianity he depicted as a lamentable story and commented that 'you find this curious fact, that the more intense has been the religion of any period and the more profound has been the dogmatic belief, the greater has been the cruelty and the worse has been the state of affairs'. Somewhat sweepingly (and perhaps for the benefit of his audience of secularists) he remarked: 'You find as you look around the world that every single bit of progress in humane feeling, every improvement in the criminal law, every step towards the diminution of war, every step towards better treatment of the coloured races, every moral progress that there has been in the world, has been consistently opposed by the organized Churches of the world. I say quite deliberately that the Christian religion, as organized in its Churches, has been and still is the principal enemy of moral progress in the world.' Elsewhere he wrote: 'My own view of religion is that of Lucretius. I regard it as a disease born of fear and as a source of untold misery to the human race. I cannot, however, deny that it has made some contributions to civilization. It helped in early days to fix the calendar, and it caused Egyptian priests to chronicle eclipses with such care that in time they became able to predict them. These two services I am prepared to acknowledge, but I do not know of any others' ('Has Religion Made Useful Contributions to Civilization?').

Personal fraility came to Russell in his last few years. But he was well cared for by his wife and enjoyed family life, observing the countryside, reading and writing letters. He knew that his body was giving way and observed: 'I do so hate to leave the world.' On 2 February 1970, aged ninety-seven, he died. A simple gathering commemorated, his departure at Colwyn Bay crematorium.

In contrast to the deists and sceptics of the early eighteenth century, Russell was able to publish and publicize his views on religion without fear of imprisonment and without too much vilification of his personality. He was passionately concerned with the future of a world in which it was impossible to be as optimistic about human nature or the beneficence of the natural world as the Enlightenment *philosophes* had been. Looking back on his life at the end of his *Autobiography* he commented on the ferocity of twentieth-century wars and twentieth-century ideologies: 'Communists, Fascists, and Nazis have successfully challenged all that I thought good, and in defeating them much of what their opponents have sought to preserve is being lost. Freedom has come to be thought weakness, and tolerance has been compelled to wear the garb of treachery. Old ideals are judged irrelevant, and no doctrine free from harshness commands respect.' Most of those individuals represented in these pages would be forced to agree with his admission that 'I may have thought the road to a world of free and happy human beings shorter than it is proving to be . . .' Nevertheless, many of those *Against the Faith*, including myself, still share his 'pursuit of a vision, both personal and social. Personal: to care for what is noble, for what is beautiful, for what is gentle: to allow moments of insight to give wisdom at more mundane times. Social: to see in imagination the society that is to be created, where individuals grow freely, and where hate and greed and envy die because there is nothing to nourish them.'

Epilogue

Two years before the First World War the popular novelist, Marie Corelli, dedicated her novel *The Mighty Atom*:

> [To] those self-styled 'Progressivists' who by precept and example assist the infamous cause of education without religion and who, by promoting the idea, borrowed from French atheism, of denying to the children in board-schools and elsewhere, the knowledge and love of God, as the true foundation of noble living, are guilty of a worse crime than murder.

There could hardly be a stronger indication of the fear which the atheist-sceptical tradition has inspired. The dedication is a back-handed compliment to the impact of humanist ideas and a warning of the tenacity with which they have been resisted. The myth that the French Revolution produced the disintegration to which society was prone once its religion had been challenged was long-standing. It was a pivotal point half-way between the sceptics and deists with whom we began and Russell with whom we concluded. Bridging the Enlightenment *philosophes* and the populist freethinkers was Thomas Paine, so old-fashioned and devout a deist for his day, yet so demotic and democratic a radical. Paine wrote *The Age of Reason* during the French Revolution and he, like so many of those about whom I have written, looked to the future with optimism: but the second half of the twentieth century is clearly not an age of reason or of optimism.

Not long after what had been dubbed 'the war to end war', Sir James Frazer wrote in 1922 an essay entitled 'Condorcet on Human Progress'. He praised a man who 'believed that the progress of civilization, as manifested in the formation of large social groups, the invention of the arts, and the growth of morality, resulted from the natural development of human faculties and not from a primitive revelation, communicated by a deity to the ancestors of the race and handed down by tradition to their descendants'.

Anatole France (a figure whom I should have liked to include) wrote that 'Man is indebted to Sir James Frazer for a glimpse at least of how he passed from barbarism to civilization'.* Unfortunately, the twentieth century has shown how easy it is for man to pass from civilization to barbarism. The eclipse of James Frazer, once a dominant figure on the intellectual landscape, is partly due to the loss of belief in linear progress from magical religion to scientific thought, from the primitive to the modern. His attempt to create an explanation of all myth and religion as arising from the deification of kings who become sacrificial victims is no longer taken seriously. The metamorphosis of *The Golden Bough* into *The Waste Land* by T. S. Eliot involved a transformation from the golden optimism of the nineteenth century to the pessimistic ashes of the twentieth century.

Frazer, an imaginative writer more than a scientific field worker, was accused by Wittgenstein of a failure of imagination: he 'cannot imagine a priest who is not basically an English parson of our times with all his stupidity and feebleness.'† Could a similar failure of imagination be levelled at all those *philosophes* and radicals who analysed religion critically? I think not. The attempt to empathize with other religions or to explore, as did William James, the varieties of religious experience, does not preclude the possibility of exposing the absurdities of religious theory and the anti-social practices of religious institutions.

Arguments about religion have moved on to a different plane since the great rationalist historians, Lecky, Bury, J. M. Robertson, compiled their documentation of how the mysterious, the magical, the dogmatic gave way to the reasonable, the scientific, the individualistic. Sociologists such as Durkheim proposed that religion should be examined in terms of its function as a cohesive social force and as a tool with which to face ultimate questions. Although the functional approach is non-theological in its concern about the truth of religion, it makes rationalist criticism of biblical contradictions or arguments about the illogicality of a beneficent, omnipotent creator

*Preface by Anatole France to Sir James Frazer's *The Gorgon's Head and other Literary pieces*. Macmillan, 1927.

†Quoted in 'Judgments on James Frazer' in Mary Douglas: *In the Active Voice*. RKP, 1982.

irrelevant to the value of religion: it can be untrue and still possess powers of social cohesion and emotional satisfaction.

However, some sociologists have gone so far as to regard all that is socially cohesive as a kind of religion. A sociological study of American baseball as a form of religion is often cited, but more seriously Marxism, nationalism and fascism have been looked at as functioning in ways comparable to religion. Russell was disposed to see Marxism and nationalism as religions, and pernicious ones at that. In Eastern Europe religion can act as a focus for dissidence in a way that unbelief acted in opposition to society in Europe at an earlier period. I remember being impressed on a visit to Moscow in the 1960s by how churches were treated as historical museums, while Lenin's tomb was indubitably a shrine. D'Holbach, who has been much studied by Marxists, would have shared their philosophic materialism, but no doubt his temperament would have made him a prolific *samizdat* pamphleteer – and would he have been able to guard his anonymity so successfully as under the *ancien régime*?

The idea that religion can be illuminated by understanding the workings of the unconscious mind would have surprised most of the figures in this book, though Diderot in *D'Alembert's Dream* used the dream as a vehicle to display taboo thoughts. Freud's attitude to religion is indicated by the title of the book in which he wrote most directly about the subject: *The Future of an Illusion*. Although he thought it extraordinary that religion survived despite 'the impossibility of proving the truth of religious doctrine', he did not underestimate the 'fresh psychological problem': 'We must ask where the inner force of those doctrines lies and to what it is that they owe their efficacy, independent as it is of recognition by reason.' The concept of unconscious forces of anger, greed and sexual desire can be accepted without the full mythical structure of Freudianism and still provide a valuable, if ultimately reductive, way of looking at religious behaviour. Freud's speculation that attitudes to an imagined deity may be influenced by an internalized parental figure has had enormous influence in the twentieth century. Russell sent an insulting letter which he had received from a bishop to Freud's chief English disciple, Ernest Jones, as a case study. He was highly amused at the reply, which gave him 'the pleasure of seeing myself as a formidable father-figure inspiring terror in the Anglican hierarchy'. An understanding of the emotional importance of forgiveness, self-esteem and feelings of inadequacy helps to explain the persistence of religious rituals, but I doubt if the priest is best replaced by the analyst. Freud wrote in a letter: 'I want to trust analysis to a profession that does not yet exist, a profession of secular ministers of souls who don't have to be physicians and must not be priests.'* I would prefer to see neighbours and friends taking this role and education for self-autonomy and self-realization to reduce its necessity: but is that an illusion with no future?

Apprehension of the psychological value of religion may cut no ice with fundamentalists, but has been of enormous value to liberal Christians eager to equate God with 'the ground of our being' or that 'goodness' which is within us. One can imagine a delightful symposium between, say, Hume, Mill and John Robinson (author of the headline-catching *Honest to God*) or an evening's drinking with Paine, Ingersoll and Harry Williams, but how much meeting of minds would occur? Perhaps what might most have astonished Paine or Ingersoll is the adaptability of Christianity, its ability to incorporate almost any fresh historical or scientific insights as part of the unfurling of God's world; just as deists saw nature as the pattern of a deity, so modern Christians can see life on Earth as God in process (though the unbeliever who watched David Attenborough's superb *Life on Earth* television series can be forgiven for wondering whether God would want to be associated with some of the bizarre life therein).

Even the historical demolition of the Bible as the word of God has been undertaken with enthusiasm by twentieth century theologians. No theologian would be alarmed by freethinking discussion of whether the ark could have been made large enough to include all the species. Now that the Old and New Testaments' historical accuracy and consistency have been analysed about as thoroughly as is possible, an a-historical approach has appeared, which implies that such criticism is redundant. Edmund Leach, in the Huxley Lecture for 1980, said: 'I agree with Huxley that the Bible is not true as history, but for the millions of individuals who consider the Bible to be a sacred tale it is certainly true as myth'.† He then proceeds to offer the a-historical tool of structuralism to analyse the meaning of the Bible as myth. From Gibbon to Huxley writers have removed

*Freud, in a letter to Oscar Pfister. Quoted in review of *Freud and Man's Soul* by Bettelheim in *New Statesman*, 19 August 1983.

†Edmund Leach & D. Alan Aycock: *Structuralist Interpretations of Biblical Myth*. CUP, 1983.

God from the tale of history. Is history now to be removed from the story of God?

Although God has disappeared from the study of nature, science and religion are not seen to be the opponents that some thought them in Darwin's day. Although a few scientists may be religious, religion is not relevant to scientific research.* Nevertheless the confident trinity of progress, science and unbelief are slightly less comfortable allies than Carlile or Bradlaugh would have supposed them. 'Scientism' is a neologism created to describe the exaggerated belief that science can solve all problems: and the potential catastrophes from world pollution or use of nuclear weapons have dented the image of science in the popular mind. The picture of the cosmos which scientists bequeath to us is highly relevant to our beliefs. The phrase 'the Uncertainty Principle' has been wrested from Heisenberg by those wishing to attack science for claiming a certainty which it never assumed. More important has been the picture of a vast random cosmos without underlying purpose and with human beings as miniscule and irrelevant specks within it. The phrase 'Chance and Necessity' which Jacques Monod used as a title for his book on genetics, serves as a description of our place in a random universe operating according to predictable laws.

The human inability to accept chance as a cause of the events with which they collide is a prime motive for the invention of religion. Much twentieth-century thought – whether nihilistic, existentialist or humanistic – tries to find meaning, to create meaning or live without meaning in a universe which may have no purpose which we do not forge for ourselves. The tradition of thought which expresses anguish at man's unbelief and strives to give meaning to our existence, is somewhat apart from those in this book who, with the exception of Mark Twain, do not appear to have found permanent difficulty in abandoning conventional religion and yet retaining a belief in straightforward human purposes such as the attainment of happiness, removal of poverty, injustice and tyranny. Sartre, in his fascinating essay *Existentialism and Humanism* (1946), shows how twentieth century atheism need be neither a combat against religion nor a pessimistic acceptance of life without meaning. He concludes his essay:

*A scientist like Alister Hardy who has attempted to classify and analyse religious experience in a scientific way is quite untypical. See Alister Hardy: *The Spiritual Nature of Man*, Oxford. 1979.

> Existentialism is not atheist in the sense that it would exhaust itself in the demonstration of the non-existence of God. It declares, rather, that even if God existed that would make no difference from its point of view. Not that we believe God does exist, but we think that the real problem is not that of His existence; what man needs is to find himself again and to understand that nothing can save him from himself, not even a valid proof of the existence of God. In this sense existentialism is optimistic, it is a doctrine of action, and it is only by self-deception, by confusing their own despair with ours that Christians can describe us as without hope.

Paradoxically, although we may be more conscious of the random cosmos than were people living in previous cultures, we are also more aware of our ability to control and give direction to our lives: we are less at the mercy of disease and accidents than were earlier generations. In that sense antibiotics and drains and insurance policies, all of which reduce our likelihood of sudden extinction or collapse of fortune, mean that, within limits, we can shape our lives with more confidence than ever before. Death looms less perilously for us if we have a reasonable prospect of living out our three score years and ten. Insurance in heaven is less important when it is available at Lloyd's.

There has been much written about the secularization of the modern world,* that process by which religious thinking, practice and institutions have lost their social influence in Western Europe. As causes of this, people have pointed to urbanization and the diversity of views offered by the expansion of the press followed by the media of radio and television. It must be the case that not many of people's religious or anti-religious attitudes are reached by a thorough examination of the arguments of famous deists, sceptics and atheists. I have not presumed to say whether those whom I have written about are a consequence or a cause of changing ideas and changes in society. But the exemplar of other lives, whether famous or humble, apart from the intrinsic fascination of other people, is of as great value to people as ritual or myth in helping to arrive at a satisfying approach to life. Humanists would turn to a hagiography of the great and inspiring not as a route to God but as a path to human strength and human delight.

*For instance, from a historical and Christian perspective, Owen Chadwick: *The Secularization of the European Mind*, or from a sociological and humanist perspective, Bryan Wilson: *Religion in Secular Society*. C. A. Watts & Co., 1966.

The major buildings, the central works of art, the objectives of those in power have not in the twentieth century been constructed with reference to the transcendent. In that sense secularization in Western Europe is complete, though some may still campaign for an end to blasphemy law, a more complete separation of church and state, an inculcation of morality without religion. These are areas in which humanist and rationalist organizations have continued to campaign as pressure groups. In Britain alone, the Rationalist Press Association by its publications, the National Secular Society by its continuation of *The Freethinker* and its public campaigns on blasphemy law and religion in schools, the British Humanist Association as a focus for humanistic ideas, the South Place Ethical Society as a continuation of the ethical tradition – all have in a small way contributed to perpetuating some of the traditions of enlightenment scepticism and individualistic reform.

I looked at the current situation with regard to a campaign on which Bradlaugh's whole career turned: the right to affirm rather than take the oath of allegiance on entry to Parliament. I tried to obtain figures for the number of MPs who had affirmed at the opening of the 1983 Parliament: no figures are available, they are not recorded – which is a measure of the public interest in the issue. There is a record of the form of allegiance made by those who enter Parliament after a by-election: out of the thirty MPs elected between 1974 and 1979 only two affirmed rather than subscribed to the oath. Clearly the question of social convention and social stigma is as important as belief. The European Parliament has no such ceremony.

What do most people actually believe and how does this compare with other periods? If religious belief has declined, as is often said, that must be from a height: was the height of Victorian piety a rather unusual period of history, an illusion polished by Victorian divines? In pre-industrial village communities some form of religious adherence was more or less obligatory, with the very strong sanction of custom and conformity, apart from the legal obligations.* How far can we tell what those who, perhaps unthinkingly, followed religious routines believed? Engels wrote in 1845: 'All the writers of the bourgeoisie are unanimous on this point, that the workers are not religious, and do not attend church.' He may be thought a biased witness, but the census of 1851, which was the only one ever to ask

*See Peter Laslett: *The World We Have Lost*. Methuden, 1965

questions about religious belief, confirmed his observation. The official report said that 'it must be apparent that a sadly formidable portion of the English people are habitual neglectors of the public ordinances of religion . . .'* In many towns fewer than one in ten regularly attended any place of worship. The report shocked people, and strenuous efforts were made to counteract this godlessness: nevertheless a clergyman in 1896 was able to write: 'It is not that the church of God has lost the great towns; it has never had them . . .' Church of England attendance in England in 1983 showed a usual Sunday attendance average of 2.7% of the population as a whole, while at Easter, a peak event in the Christian calendar, communicants were 4.7% of the adult population.

A recent survey by the European Value Systems Study Group† published preliminary results in 1982. They found that taking Europe as a whole 75% of people believed in God. No details are given of what kind of God (or what kind of belief) this is – whether the belief is in a life force, a personal deity, in idealized good – but the fact that only 25% believe in the Devil, 23% in Hell, 40% in Heaven, and 21% in re-incarnation indicates that a large number of those who believe in God do not believe in a conventional Christian God. Another part of the same survey showed that only 5% of people in Europe and 1% of people in the USA were prepared to identify themselves as 'convinced atheists'. The fact that 53% believe that 'there is no *one* true religion but there are basic truths and meaning to be found in all the great religions of the world' and that 60% believe 'there can never be clear and absolute guidelines about what is good and evil, what is good and evil depends entirely upon the circumstances of the time' suggests that the ideas of deistic religion and relatavist morality have made enormous impact.

A form of superstitious deism may always have been the mainstream religion. Aldous Huxley's amalgamation of 'basic truths' from all religions into a 'perennial philosophy' might have intrigued Toland or Emerson, but his inclusion of transcendental and mystical elements would not have appealed to many in the atheist-sceptical tradition. Julian Huxley's attempt to promote evolutionary humanism is closer to the tradition of his grandfather and of Mill and George Eliot. He gave a broadcast talk in 1960, 'The Faith of a Humanist', in which he said:

* See K. S. Inglis: *Churches and the Working Classes in Victorian England*. Routledge, 1963.

† Figures kindly supplied by Gallup.

> . . . we have faith in the capacities and possibilities of man: most immediately in his capacity to accumulate his experience, and in the resultant possibilities of increasing his knowledge and understanding. We have seen their results in science and medicine; we have faith in their possibilities for psychology and politics, for conservation and eugenics. But we must think of man's other capacities, too. His capacity for disinterested curiosity and wonder leads him both to seek and to enjoy knowledge. His capacity for enjoying beauty pushes him to create, to preserve, and to contemplate it. His capacity to feel guilt impels him towards morality, his sense of incompleteness leads him to seek greater wholeness. He is endowed with a sense of justice which slowly but steadily brings about the remedying of injustice. He has a capacity for compassion which leads him to care for the sick, the aged, and the persecuted, and a capacity for love which could (and sometimes does) override his capacity for hate.*

The title of a book by Toland, *Christianity Not Mysterious*, encapsulates a theme of my book – the removal of mystery from Christianity. What is Christianity without mystery? Its adaptability and flexibility over two thousand years suggest that the slip of the tongue of the radio broadcaster who said, 'First of all he was a Christian and didn't believe in anything'† may be taken more seriously than was intended. But can many live without mystery? Bayle thought not, and wrote that people 'like much better a doctrine that is mysterious, incomprehensible and above religion. They are more likely to admit what they do not comprehend . . . all the ends of religion are much better to be found in incomprehensible things.'

The expansion of knowledge and ideas in the two hundred and fifty years since Bayle wrote those words has brought new insight and new problems. The Encyclopedists, who perhaps conceived knowledge as a fixed entity, thought it would be entirely illuminated if torches were shone far enough; they forgot that the further you shine a torch the more you realize what you cannot see. If those 'Against the Faith' had encountered a modern theologian's statement 'I did not invent the faith therefore I do not have to defend it. I can only swear to you that it is true . . .'‡ would they have felt all their arguments had been sidestepped, like a boxer punching a shadow? Or would they have realized that they were proposing an alternative to

* Quoted in Margaret Knight: *Humanist Anthology*. RPA, 1961.
† Out Takes. *The Listener*, 25 August 1983.
‡ Attributed to Karl Barth.

faith? If so, I think E. M. Forster put it very well in his essay 'What I Believe' (1938):

> I do not believe in Belief. But this is an Age of Faith, and there are so many militant creeds that, in self-defence, one has to formulate a creed of one's own. Tolerance, good temper and sympathy are no longer enough in a world which is rent by religious and racial persecution, in a world where ignorance rules, and Science, who ought to have ruled, plays the subservient pimp. Tolerance, good temper and sympathy – they are what matter really, and if the human race is not to collapse they must come to the front before long. But for the moment they are not enough, their action is no stronger than a flower, battered beneath a military jackboot. They want stiffening, even if the process coarsens them. Faith, to my mind, is a stiffening process, a sort of mental starch, which ought to be applied as sparingly as possible. I dislike the stuff. I do not believe in it, for its own sake, at all. Herein I probably differ from most people, who believe in Belief, and are only sorry they cannot swallow even more than they do. My law-givers are Erasmus and Montaigne, not Moses and St Paul. My temple stands not upon Mount Moriah but in that Elysian Field where even the immoral are admitted. My motto is: 'Lord, I disbelieve – help thou my unbelief.'

Forster's gentle, ironic scepticism seems to me admirable and it is as an admirer of such an outlook that I have presented this gallery of those who have criticized and combated conventional religious belief.

Selected Bibliography

Introduction

DON CAMERON ALLEN, *Doubt's Boundless Sea: Skepticism and Faith in the Renaissance* (Johns Hopkins Press, Baltimore, 1964).
GEORGE T. BUCKLEY, *Atheism in the English Renaissance* (Russell & Russell, New York, 1965 reissue).
PETER BURKE, *Montaigne* (Oxford University Press, 1981).
E. R. DODDS, *The Greeks and the Irrational* (University of California Press, Berkeley, 1951).
E. R. DODDS, *The Ancient Concept of Progress and other Essays in Greek Literature and Belief* (Oxford University Press, 1973).
W. E. H. LECKY, *History of the Rise and Influence of the Spirit of Rationalism in Europe* (1865).
J. M. ROBERTSON, *A History of Freethought: Ancient and Modern to the Period of the French Revolution* (Watts & Co, 1936).
JAMES THROWER, *A Short History of Western Atheism* (Pemberton Books, 1971).
JAMES THROWER, *The Alternative Tradition: A Study of Unbelief in the Ancient World* (Mouton Publishers, The Hague, 1980).

1. Pierre Bayle and Jean Meslier

HOWARD ROBINSON, *Bayle, The Sceptic* (Columbia University Press, 1931).
JEAN DEPRISS, ROLAND DESNÉ, AND ALBERT SOBOL, Eds, *Oeuvres de Jean Meslier*, 3 Vols (Editions Anthropos, Paris, 1970–1972).

2. The English Deists

THOMAS FOWLER, *Shaftesbury and Hutcheson* (1882).
BASIL WILLEY, *The Eighteenth Century Background* (Chatto & Windus, 1940).
DAVID BERMAN, 'Anthony Collins and the Question of Atheism in the Early Part of the Eighteenth Century' (Proceedings of the Royal Irish Academy, 1975).
JOHN REDWOOD, *Reason, Ridicule and Religion: the Age of Enlightenment in England* (Thames & Hudson, 1976).

3. Voltaire

THEODORE BESTERMAN, *Voltaire* (Blackwell, 1969).
HAYDN MASON, *Voltaire: A Biography* (Granada, 1981).

4. Diderot and the Encyclopedists

ARTHUR M. WILSON, , *Diderot* (Oxford University Press, 1972).
RICHARD N. SCHWAB AND WALTER E. REX, *Preliminary Discourse to the Encyclopaedia of Diderot* (The Bobbs-Merrill Company, New York, 1963).
DIDEROT: *Thoughts on Religion*, Tr. by Nicolas Walter (New Humanist, Winter 1982).

5. D'Holbach

PIERRE NAVILLE, *D'Holbach et la Philosophie Scientifique au xviiie siècle* (Gallimard, 1967).
W. H. WICKWAR, *Baron D'Holbach: A Prelude to the French Revolution* (Allen & Unwin, 1935).

6. David Hume

E. C. MOSSNER, *Life of David Hume* (Nelson, 1954).
A. J. AYER, *Hume* (Oxford University Press, 1980).
NORMAN KEMP SMITH, Ed., *Dialogues Concerning Natural Religion* (1947).

7. Gibbon

D. M. LOW, *Edward Gibbon* (Chatto & Windus, 1937).
G. M. YOUNG, *Gibbon* (Peter Davis, 1932).
EDWARD GIBBON, *Autobiography* (1796).

8. Thomas Paine

MONCURE D. CONWAY. *The Life of Thomas Paine* (G. P. Putnam's Sons, 1892).
AUDREY WILLIAMSON, *Thomas Paine: His Life, Work and Times* (Allen & Unwin, 1973).
PHILIP J. FONER, *The Age of Reason with a Biographical Introduction* (Citadel Press, New Jersey, 1974).

9. Heine and Büchner

JEFFREY L. SAMMONS, *Heinrich Heine: a modern biography* (Princeton University Press, 1979).
JULIAN HILTON, *Georg Büchner* (Macmillan Press, 1982).
A. H. J. KNIGHT, *Georg Büchner* (Blackwell, 1951).

10. Shelley and Carlile

RICHARD HOLMES, *Shelley the Pursuit* (Weidenfeld & Nicolson, 1974).
JOEL H. WIENER, *Radicalism and Freethought in Nineteenth Century Britain: The Life of Richard Carlile* (Greenwood Press, 1984).
EDWARD ROYLE, Ed., *The Infidel Tradition from Paine to Bradlaugh* (Macmillan, 1975).
EDWARD ROYLE, *Victorian Infidels: The Origins of the British Secular Movement, 1791–1866* (Manchester University Press, 1974).

11. Bradlaugh and Secularism

LEE E. GRUGEL, *George Jacob Holyoake: A Study in the Evolution of a Victorian Radical* (Porcupine Press, Philadelphia, 1976).
G. J. HOLYOAKE, *Sixty Years of an Agitator's Life* (T. Fisher Unwin, 1892).
DAVID TRIBE, *President Charles Bradlaugh, MP* (Elek Books, 1971).
EDWARD ROYLE, *Secularists and Republicans: Popular Freethought in Britain, 1866–1915* (Manchester University Press, 1980).
JIM HERRICK, *Vision and Realism: A History of 'The Freethinker', 1881–1981* (G. W. Foote, 1982).

12. John Stuart Mill and George Eliot

MICHAEL ST JOHN PACKE, *The Life of John Stuart Mill* (Secker & Warburg, 1954).
JOHN STUART MILL, *Autobiography* (1873).
GERTRUDE HIMMELFARB, Ed. and Intro, *John Stuart Mill: On Liberty* (Pelican, 1974).
JOHN STUART MILL, *Three Essays on Religion: Nature, the Utility of Religion and Theism* (1874)).
GORDON S. HAIGHT, *George Eliot* (Oxford University Press, 1968).

13. Thomas Huxley

CYRIL BIBBY, *Scientist Extraordinary: Life and Scientific Work of T. H. Huxley* (Pergamon, 1972).
RONALD CLARK, *The Huxleys* (Heineman, 1968).
LEONARD HUXLEY, Ed., *Life and Letters of T. H. Huxley*, 2 Vols (Macmillan, 1900).
WILLIAM BÖLSCHE, *Haeckel, His Life and Work*, Tr. by Joseph McCabe (T. Fisher Unwin, n.d. *c.* 1906).

14. Emerson, Ingersoll, Twain

RALPH L. RUSK, *The Life of Ralph Waldo Emerson* (Charles Scribner's Sons, New York, 1949).

HERMAN E. KITTREDGE, *Ingersoll: A Biographical Appreciation* (Watts & Co., 1911).
EVA INGERSOLL WAKEFIELD, Ed., *Life and Letters of R. G. Ingersoll*, UK edition ed. by Royston Pike (Watts & Co., 1952).
JUSTIN KAPLAN, *Mr Clemens and Mark Twain* (Jonathan Cape, 1967).
MARK TWAIN, *What is Man?*, Intro. by S. K. Ratcliffe (Watts & Co., 1936).

15. Bertrand Russell

BERTRAND RUSSELL, *Autobiography*, Vols 1, 2, 3 (Allen & Unwin, 1967, 1968, 1969).
BERTRAND RUSSELL, *Why I am Not a Christian* and *The Faith of a Rationalist* (Rationalist Press Association and National Secular Society, 1983).
RONALD CLARK, *The Life of Bertrand Russell* (Cape and Weidenfeld & Nicolson, 1975).

Index